Chicken Soup for the Soul®

Divorce and Recovery

Chicken Soup for the Soul®:
Divorce and Recovery; 101 Stories about Surviving and Thriving after Divorce
by Jack Canfield, Mark Victor Hansen & Patty Hansen

Published by Chicken Soup for the Soul Publishing, LLC   www.chickensoup.com

The publisher gratefully acknowledges the many publishers and individuals who granted Chicken Soup for the Soul permission to reprint the cited material.

Cover photos courtesy of iStockPhoto.com/suemac and Photos.com

Cover and Interior Design & Layout by Pneuma Books, LLC
For more info on Pneuma Books, visit www.pneumabooks.com

Distributed to the booktrade by Simon & Schuster. SAN: 200-2442

Publisher's Cataloging-in-Publication Data
(Prepared by The Donohue Group)

Chicken soup for the soul : divorce and recovery : 101 stories about surviving and thriving after divorce / [compiled by] Jack Canfield, Mark Victor Hansen [and]Patty Hansen.

    p. ; cm.

  ISBN-13: 978-1-935096-21-4
  ISBN-10: 1-935096-21-4

1. Divorced people--Literary collections. 2. Divorced people--Conduct of life--Anecdotes. 3. Divorce--Anecdotes. I. Canfield, Jack, 1944- II. Hansen, Mark Victor. III. Hansen, Patty. IV. Title: Divorce and recovery

PN6071.D585 C485 2008
810.8/0352653   2008934199

PRINTED IN THE UNITED STATES OF AMERICA
on acid∞free paper
16 15 14 13 12 10 09 08   01 02 03 04 05 06 07 08

Chicken Soup for the Soul®

Divorce and Recovery

101 Stories about
Surviving and Thriving
after Divorce

Jack Canfield
Mark Victor Hansen
Patty Hansen

Chicken Soup for the Soul Publishing, LLC
Cos Cob, CT

Chicken Soup for the Soul

Dedication

To all of the hearts that have been broken:
may you find help and hope within this book—
maybe even some laughter—
to help you heal again.

Chicken Soup for the Soul

Contents

❶

~Is This the End... or the Beginning?~

❷

~Forgiving and Letting Go~

❸

~It's Over... and We're Still Friends~

❹

~A Broken Family but Not Broken Hearts~

❺

~Special Moments and Everyday Miracles~

❻

~Life on the Front Burner—Now, It's All About Me!~

❼

~New Fish in the Dating Pond~

❽

~You and Me... and Kids, Too?~

❾
~New Insights and Ageless Wisdom~

Chicken Soup for the Soul

Foreword

*T*he big "D." Divorce. The legal breakup of a marriage. Despite the fact that almost one out of every two marriages in the United States ends up in divorce court, no one enters a marriage thinking they may end up as part of that statistic. Yet, it happens. In most cases, lines are drawn, sides are chosen, and a new dance begins—one in which the partners spar, dodge, and throw punches as the final date of dissolution approaches. The effects of uncoupling reach far beyond the two people involved—it touches friends, siblings, parents, grandparents, and certainly the children. It is not only the couple who may be considering a divorce, or those who are in the process or the aftermath of it—each and every person who knows you and loves you will be affected by the outcome in one way or another.

It is a phenomenon that can be the worst or best experience of your life—the worst while it is happening, and the best (hopefully) after the dust has settled and you have moved on. While you are actively involved in the process, it can be difficult to view your situation from the "big picture" perspective. The person who you thought you would spend the rest of your life with disappears—emotionally for sure, usually physically as well. Life, as you knew it, turns upside-down. The words "forever," "eternally," and "everlasting love" are dropped from your vocabulary and are replaced with words like "depressed," "coping," "stressed," and "major change." Finances, jobs, daily schedules and living arrangements are affected. The divorce, in and of itself, can be a financial hurdle.

You may start to question your physical attributes, lovability, self-worth, and level of attractiveness—at some point, you will most certainly question your sanity. You will no longer be creating memories with your partner—instead you will be practicing how to forgive (with a little luck), forget, let go, and put the past behind you. Some people lose weight (known as the "Divorce Diet" to the ex-generation) and go shopping for a whole new wardrobe. Others may gain weight from nights of sitting in front of the television eating every comfort food known to the human race—ice cream, macaroni and cheese, tapioca (warm, preferably), chips and salsa (maybe with a margarita thrown in) popcorn, and chocolate—not necessarily in that order.

This snapshot we just took you through? It's true only if you are lucky enough to go through a "good" divorce!

We know. Each of us has had our own divorces; Jack and Patty count two each, and Mark has been through one. We can relate to these stories from our own experiences, which is why we created this book—to provide the kind of Chicken Soup for the Soul support that can help you get through your own divorce. Shared insights, personal introspection, hints of wisdom, thoughts on forgiveness and healing, hope for the future, and even slices of humor are tucked into the pages of the book you are holding. You will see that some couples have chosen to approach their divorce with integrity and dignity, honor for each other's feelings and welfare, a wish to continue as friends, and a common desire to complete their Big D without a lot of drama (with a capital D!).

If you are at the point where you are just considering ending your marriage or are already deep in the process—even if you are already an active, official member of the ex-generation—take this book and keep it by your bedside. When you have one of those down moments and you need to know that you are not alone in this mess—reach out and read someone else's story. You will see that others have gone through the D experience and have come out on the other side, better because of it. Most have been able to find themselves, learn their strengths, discover the joy of a new freedom, and realize their own potential. There is light at the end of the tunnel.

~Jack Canfield, Mark Victor Hansen, and Patty Hansen

Divorce *and* Recovery

Is This the End...
or the Beginning?

*Perhaps our eyes need to be washed by our tears once in a while,
so that we can see life with a clearer view again.*
~Alex Tan

A Little Clump of Dirt

To carry his load without resting, not to be bothered by heat or cold and always be content: these three things we can learn from a donkey.
~Indian Proverb

I was convinced no one in the world had ever hurt as badly as I was hurting. The pain was constant and deep. I was hysterical, inconsolable, and completely devastated. I wanted to find something—anything—that would make the pain stop. Sadly, I even understood the despair that could lead to suicide. Not that I gave it serious thought, but I understood it.

I was so clueless. How could I have been so blind? How did he turn away without my realizing what was happening? Was I that stupid or just naive? Maybe. Maybe not. I trusted him. Completely. And after fifteen years of marriage, one which everyone had thought was perfect, including me, it all fell apart in a blinding flash. They say the wife is the last to know. That was certainly true in my case.

Oh sure, it had been coming for a few months, in his mind—but for me, it was a shock. I lost thirty-five pounds in six weeks because I couldn't keep food down. I couldn't sit still long enough to even watch a television commercial, much less a thirty minute show. Many times I dressed for work, got halfway there, and realized I had on clothes or shoes that didn't match. I cried so much I could have filled a lake with my tears.

How did I get through it? I tried every possible thing everyone or anyone suggested. I let myself cry as much and as often as I needed to. I got a journal and wrote my thoughts, page after page after page—late into the night, early in the morning, anytime I had something to say. I found new music that consoled me and comforted me. I tried a new hobby that had no connection to my marriage. I went through all the motions with friends and family even though I felt empty inside and alone. I talked and talked and talked about it, to anyone who would listen. My friends and family were probably sick of me and my tears, but they were steadfast and true and stuck by me.

I read everything I could get my hands on about marriage, divorce, mid-life crises, how to survive, how to heal my broken heart. I ended up with enough books to fill a library. Obviously I was in the company of thousands of other people who suffer this kind of hurt every day. But I was still convinced my pain was worse than anyone else had ever experienced.

Friends sent me every possible uplifting e-mail story. The computer became my lifeline. I read them all—many times over. A few of them really stuck with me. There was one story about a little donkey that fell into a deep well. The farmer couldn't figure out how to get the poor donkey out of the well, so he decided just to bury him by throwing in shovel after shovel of dirt. The donkey, however, would shake off each shovel-full of dirt and stomp his feet to tamp down the dirt. Little by little, as each shovel-full of dirt landed on the little donkey, the level of the ground rose until he was able just to walk out of that deep hole. I thought about that donkey a lot, and I decided to try to be like him and get out of the deep hole I was in.

Story after story, tear after tear, step by step, day after day, I began to finally get better. I remember thinking I could go ten minutes without crying. Then thirty minutes. Then a whole hour! I was improving. Baby steps. But they were steps in the right direction. Oh sure, there were still times I fell apart. But those times became fewer and further apart. I felt it was a huge improvement when I finally went through one whole day without crying. That took a long time. The pain was still there, but I was improving. I knew deep down that I could survive this. I kept thinking about that little donkey.

And I did survive it—with determination, the unwavering support of my family and true friends, and a new understanding of my faith and the strength you gain from it. Maybe more of us should be like that poor little donkey. Shake off that dirt and stomp it down until you can simply walk out of that deep dark hole into the sunshine.

~Mary Mason

"I want to talk with you, Henry, about you and me,
formerly known as 'us'."

Revelation

*I*t was looking grim. I had tried talking, talking, talking — writing letters to him which he refused to read — and counseling. My last resort was a trial separation. I'd made arrangements to move in with my sister over Thanksgiving weekend. Only one detail remained — to tell my husband.

I planned to talk to him on a Saturday morning in late October. I rehearsed and fretted. Would he be shocked, surprised, hurt? Profess his love for me and beg me to stay? Would this make him agree to go to counseling with me? My mind raced through several scenarios, all of which ended in my not really having to move out.

That Saturday morning was October perfection — sunny, Indian-summer-warm; the maple trees aglow in fiery reds, oranges, and yellows. After stalling over my coffee, I asked, "Can we talk?"

"If you want."

"Let's go out on the porch."

"Fine."

We settled in on our newly-purchased, comfy porch chairs. I fidgeted with the cushion as I realized my rehearsed words had escaped me.

"So... what's up?" he asked.

"Well, I... I don't think it's any secret this marriage isn't working."

"I'd agree with that."

"We exist as separate entities under one roof. We don't talk, we don't know anything about each other's lives. I guess you don't need me to tell you about all the things we don't do together."

"I can't argue with anything you've said."

"It's for those reasons that I'm going to be moving out."

"When?"

"Thanksgiving weekend."

"Well, before you move out, do you want to... (Here my heart was aflutter; I was waiting for the words that would mean I wouldn't have to move out!)... buy new tires for the Camry?"

I looked at him for a few seconds, expressionless. Then, I nearly fell out of my chair guffawing, belly laughs, full body laughs. When I was able, I croaked out, "I imagined a hundred scenarios. That wasn't one of them. Thanks for the comic relief."

Finally, I knew. It was really over.

~Melinda Stiles

The Little Pink House

Every house where love abides
And friendship is a guest,
Is surely home, and home sweet home
For there the heart can rest.
~Henry Van Dyke

After years of struggling in a marriage that was no longer working, a friend of mine, Denise, finally decided to walk away. It wasn't an easy decision, especially since she had two young daughters and would be facing life as a single mom in her forties. I would later tell her, "Sometimes it takes more love to leave than to stay—love for yourself, your children, and even your estranged spouse. Sometimes leaving is the only true way to move forward."

By leaving her marriage, Denise was also giving up her beautiful large home in town, with its long, wrap-around driveway, sprawling front porch and back deck, and endless yard. A simpler life started to call her. She decided to move out to the country into the little pink house where her late grandmother had lived her entire life. Her grandmother had only passed away the year before, and the house was still filled with her belongings—overflowing with them, actually.

On moving day, when Denise arrived at the pink house with her daughters and the family dog, the task before her seemed overwhelming. Inside the house there was hardly even a place to sit. Like many in her generation, Denise's grandmother never threw anything away. The upstairs bedrooms were clogged with hundreds of vinyl records and books, furniture, and trinkets collected over nearly a century of living. The bedrooms had ceased serving their intended purpose and were now a glorified attic. Denise's grandmother, a tough and feisty former preacher woman, had slept downstairs on the couch, foregoing a traditional bedroom. The downstairs too, was cluttered with knickknacks and hundreds more books, especially the classics and many titles long since forgotten. Grandmother's years of smoking had yellowed the ceilings and walls throughout.

Starting over seemed like an impossibly cruel feat. There wasn't even an adequate bedroom for her or her daughters to sleep in, for heaven's sake. Perhaps she hadn't made the right choice, Denise worried.

That's when the brigade arrived. Denise's parents, brothers, cousins, friends, and new neighbors, as well as her older son from a first marriage and that first ex, began pulling into the small dirt-laden driveway. Eventually, the driveway and old country road leading to the house were lined with the cars and trucks that carried special guardian angels to Denise's aid.

Denise was no longer standing alone before the daunting task. It became a team effort forged from love and friendship, a unified goal to help a friend to move ahead — not backward.

A chain of workers wound through the back door and up the stairs, handing off books and records and other items to one another until they were removed from the house. Denise's mother began scrubbing the kitchen to make the smoke stains disappear. Denise and some cousins cleared the musty living room, opening the windows to let in the fresh country air while they started applying a fresh coat of white paint to the walls. Denise's son and his father began to restructure the bathroom and later transformed a storage area off the side of the house into a cozy family room. Denise's daughters ran errands, getting water for the workers and carrying old boxes and scrap wood outside to a roaring fire. And the family dog, Duchess, raced around, becoming acquainted with the new sights and smells.

By the end of the exhausting weekend, the little pink house had a clean, charming front porch, downstairs rooms that smelled of pine and lemon, and an upstairs that was now inviting, as two freshly painted bedrooms, one in green and one in yellow, awaited Denise and her daughters' first nights in residence. Later, Denise's son would create a back patio with bricks recycled from beneath the front yard, and cheerful plants and flowers would surround the house.

The little pink house was once more a home—Denise's new home. Thoughts of the large house and her former life in town were now miles away behind her. She soon realized that deep within her, she possessed the strength and courage and feisty nature of her grandmother, whom we all knew would be thrilled to see her house reinvigorated and enjoyed in this special way.

Best of all, in those forty-eight hours, Denise realized that the new journey she had embarked on was not one she would have to travel alone. Her new life would be filled with the warmth and security of unconditional love and friendship, gifts she believed would render no future endeavor impossible. Especially in her little pink house.

~John E. Schlimm II

The Gut Speaks

Let us learn to appreciate there will be times when the trees will be bare,
and look forward to the time when we may pick the fruit.
~Anton Chekhov

The thought of divorce meant entering a dark place, one I was determined never to know. Raised as a Roman Catholic, with parents married for thirty-seven years, and two brothers married with children, the thought of disappointing my family frightened me. I didn't want to be the one who failed; the first in our immediate family to be divorced. When the time came to actually confront the possibility, I steered away from the thought and instead drowned myself in shame.

I knew that the relationship was toxic before we even married, but I ignored the silent alarms, believing that my imagination concocted them. I entered marriage foolishly, thinking that the bond would bring me eternal happiness. I was naïve, yes. I believed, like many others, that I could change someone. I questioned the flaws I saw, mistaking my gut feelings for commitment issues. I was determined to overcome any concerns on my own. I liked the challenge, which gave me a sense of importance. I was twenty-three and this was my chance to settle down and start a family, so I plunged forward ignoring all of the red flags that were waving wildly.

A few months into the marriage, I became conscious of the warnings I had chosen to ignore. Rather than pursuing the divorce route, I felt I deserved to suffer the consequences of my mistake. Two years into the marriage, I had become a shadow of my former self. I was trapped in a town, a house, and a marriage that were no longer familiar. I couldn't look in the mirror without crying. I lost my positive drive, no longer had dreams of my own. I cared less about my job and more about his, working for him during my spare time. I focused tremendously on my appearance, exercised more, bought new clothes, always nervous about how I looked and behaved in his presence. The screaming matches over his deceit became a daily occurrence. The sleepless nights began to affect my career, my appearance, my mind. Couples counseling and church offered no relief; nothing would improve while I was the sole person in the relationship working to fix the problems.

By our third year together, I was miserable, yet fearful of leaving. I waited it out, feeling sad and alone. I started to believe the countless times my husband reiterated that my insecurities were the cause of our problems.

Finally, my fears of divorce couldn't hold me back. The thought of disappointing people could not supersede my own chance for happiness and good health. I packed my belongings and left, knowing that I couldn't live that life anymore. For the first time, I was doing what was best for me. I finally acknowledged that I deserved more.

I feared the stigma attached to a divorced woman. I felt branded, no longer pure. I behaved as if I had done something wrong. I was afraid to reveal to others that I was divorced. I considered myself damaged goods. I was afraid to date, believing a man wouldn't want a divorced woman. With the support of my family and friends the stereotype that consumed me began to slowly dissipate.

Through counseling and journaling, I overcame the negative feelings and realized that I get one chance at life. I could spend it bottled up and cut off from the rest of the world or I could live each day as a gift. I was given a chance to start over. I took the plunge, opening myself up to new experiences. I ended up meeting a man who reestablished my faith in men and in relationships. One who shares my likes, my sense of adventure, and accepts my flaws without making me feel less of a woman. He pushes me to achieve my goals, even ones that seem far out of reach. Naturally I was a bit shy to reveal that I was going through a divorce, but to my surprise he didn't flinch. He stood by my side giving me nothing but support. He too had suffered a difficult relationship and because of this we both had learned the importance of appreciation.

We moved to Italy for a year to discover Europe together. There we lived in a little hamlet, enjoying every aspect of the Italian culture, from working in a vineyard to picking olives; the happy memories we created washed away our negative experiences.

As humans, we are always worried about disappointing others and keep from doing what we really believe is right. We question ourselves, when really, we should question the very people causing us to doubt who we know best. Had I listened to my gut in the first place and acknowledged the red flags waving boldly, I would have saved myself from emotional devastation. The experience was painful, but had I not lived it, I wouldn't appreciate life or the people in it as I do now. For that reason I am thankful to have gone through what I did. The stigma fades and the bitter feelings subside, as long as you let them. Love will manage to squirm its way back into your life, whether you're looking or not.

~Angela Chiaro

The Toolbox

"So, how was your day?" Chuck, my ex-husband, asked on this, his third call of the day. It was Friday night, I'd had a long week and I had to report to my second job, waitressing at a pancake house early the next morning. Usually, I screened his calls, but that night I was wondering what the heck I was doing with my life. We had been married for eighteen years. We had a son in his senior year of high school and college-bound. I was sleeping on a mattress on the floor because Chuck had taken the waterbed when we divorced. Was I really better off?

Chuck went on, "I'm really missing you... and Alex of course. I've learned a lot, and I think we should talk about getting back together. When are you going to get over this so I can come back home?" We had separated four months earlier—which included the three during which we were formally divorced. I had started the divorce proceedings in March, moved out of our master bedroom to the guest room, and got a second job to help soften the blow of losing his income.

In late March, I took a trip and drove to my sister's house in California, partly just to get out of the house, but also to give myself time alone to think. Was I abandoning my marriage vows? Was I going against my religious beliefs? I trusted my sister, and during one late night talk at her kitchen table, I talked to her about my fears.

Her answer: "Chuck has never lived up to his vows as a husband. He never worked in the marriage and has not taken care of you or Alex, physically or emotionally. You've had to shoulder the role of wife, husband, mother, and father for too many years. No wonder you're burned out." Her words helped me to focus my doubts about getting a divorce and made me realize I had been unhappy for many years.

Now Chuck's call came at a time of weakness. Had I wanted too much? Was life just about this—living with someone who you have memories with and can finish your stories—or, is there more out there? Someone to love who can love me back? I went to bed on my mattress and slept poorly, thoughts and doubts running through my head, as I wondered whether I should give him a second chance.

The next morning, before I went to my waitressing job, I realized the light bulb on the back porch needed replacing. I felt insecure with the light being out, right next to my sliding glass window. I went for the toolbox that Chuck had made up for me before we parted.

Before he moved out, as I was packing up the kitchen, I made sure he got his fair half of everything, including anything his parents had given us. When he packed the garage, he asked, "What do you want out of my tools?" I had purchased tools for him every birthday and Christmas, hoping he'd find a hobby to fill all his free time.

"Just make me up a toolbox so I can repair little things around the house," I'd replied. And, as I helped him move out that July day, I noticed a small toolbox set aside for my use. It was a busy day and I never did go over to check on what he had left for me in the tool-box—until that October morning.

I pulled out the toolbox to find one flat head screwdriver, one Phillips-head screwdriver, an old rusty set of pliers, and a broken hammer. This, after I gave him half of the kitchen stuff and he doesn't even cook! While I made use of the old and broken tools to replace the light bulb, using every cuss word I knew directed at Chuck, I realized that this thoughtlessness was the real reason we had divorced. He had never thought of my well-being at all—and the toolbox was my physical proof that kept me from making the big mistake of taking him back, just because I was lonely.

I'm happy to say it was the right decision. After dating some total losers during my first year of singlehood, I found a gem seven years later.

I threw away the old toolbox and tools without a second thought.

~Mia Gardner

Reprinted by permission of Dan Rosanndich.
©2000 Dan Rosanndich.

6

A Win-Win Situation

You have to accept whatever comes and the only important thing is that you
meet it with courage and with the best that you have to give.
~Eleanor Roosevelt

ruth be told, I never really had a husband or a marriage. We were separated more than we were together, and when we were together we constantly fought and argued. I wasn't happy with him, and I wasn't happy without him.

My husband had been such a major part of my life. I met him when I was sixteen, we married when I was nineteen. Now, I was forty. For all of those years, it was an up-down, on-off, love-hate, roller coaster relationship—a ride filled with apprehension, tears, shattered hopes and dreams. He was the operator, and I was his passenger.

Our daughter was now grown, and I was so tired of accepting short-term love affairs with my own husband, and waiting for things to change. I lost all needs, desires, and hopes that previously kept me hanging on. It was time to get off the roller coaster and stay off. But how?

I started to put things into motion strategically. I faced reality, built up my self-esteem, learned to love myself, put the past behind me, read self-help books, started thinking positive thoughts about my future, walked, exercised, prayed, and took as much me-time as I needed to heal. Then I put a wall around my heart, and topped it off with barbed wire for some extra assurance. I promised myself to never love, trust, or marry again. When I was strong enough and ready in every aspect, I filed for divorce.

The day finally came; I walked into the courthouse a changed, independent, strong, determined woman. While waiting for our case to be called, I stole glances down the hall at him and our eyes would momentarily lock. He wanted to say something; I wanted to respond; I felt myself getting weak; I still loved him; I wanted to go to him and say "maybe...." I heard our names being called.

Inside the courtroom, everything was settled in an hour. Twenty-three years of whatever we had together was over. We entered the same elevator, standing worlds apart as it descended to the main floor. We walked out into the street and did what we'd always done: we went in opposite directions. I don't know if he looked back, because I didn't.

When I returned home, I hadn't been in the house for ten minutes before the phone rang. I picked it up; I heard his voice, a whisper, saying my name. He started to say something, but stopped and cleared his throat. There was silence. I knew he was searching for words. I had already given him too much of my time; I had already waited too long. Without saying a word, I gently laid the receiver back on its cradle.

I sat at the kitchen table feeling lost, lonely, and angry; thinking, wondering, and reminiscing. I cried, letting the tears cleanse away years of hurt and pain. I was sent an invitation to a pity party, but I turned it down.

After awhile, I started feeling light, a weight had been lifted. I was free, he was free, no more roller coaster rides—it was legally over, over in the sight of God and man—but was it really over in our hearts?

When I received a copy of our divorce decree, my ex had not signed it. I never asked him why, I already knew the answer. I had seen it in his eyes, heard it in his voice, and in that still silence.

That was almost fourteen years ago. Since then, I have moved several states away, built a new home, retired, and met someone that has torn down the wall that I had built around my heart. I voluntarily removed the barbed wire. He is absolutely everything that I want in a companion. A short time ago, I was diagnosed with breast cancer; during those critical times, he never once left my side and even shaved his hair off when I lost mine. We travel, we laugh and have fun, we communicate, and we give and receive each other's love and respect. I've grown to trust again. I have found true love, peace and contentment. After seven years of being together, we recently decided to get married.

I rarely see my ex, but when I do, we are very cordial to each other; through the years, we have silently formed a truce. I no longer feel anger or bitterness towards him, there's no room in my heart or my life for such negative emotions. Our common bond is our daughter and four beautiful grandchildren.

~Beanie Baldwin

7

Home Is Where Your Heart Lives

She sits upon the sand, looking out across the waters wide
Holding back the tears she's spent years trying to hide.
Wishing for adventure—instead of bills, babies, and rain.
Loneliness creeps into her soul with every tear of pain.

For ten long years she'd been married, but often lived alone.
He never paid attention, ignored her feelings, was never ever home.
He looked past her like she was a painting hanging on the wall;
Broken bits of glass, colors washed away, waiting there to fall.

Then one day she came home and found that he was gone.
Babies crying, supper burning, no letter left—no call.
She looked around the empty house and started to just cry.
For everything she ever believed in had just gone and died.

She picked herself up off the floor and took a breath of air.
The pieces of her shattered life floated around her everywhere.
She realized life wasn't over, that she wasn't alone.
She packed her bags, took the kids, and headed back for home.

She traveled for three long days and nights on the open road.
Reaching the town she grew up in, with her broken heart in tow.
She pulled into the driveway, as her mama stepped outside.

She took one look at her baby girl, and held her arms open wide.

She ran into her mama's arms, and hugged her really tight.
Told her everything that happened, how she'd driven
     through the night.
When she was finished with her story, her mama smiled wide.
"Don't worry darlin', grab your babies and bring yourself inside."

The house that she'd grown up in hadn't really changed.
Same furniture, old and broken. Nothing much rearranged.
Her daddy walked up to her. He kissed her tears away.
Wrapped his strong arms around her and then she heard him say,

"Home is where your heart lives; it's the one place you can go
Where all your dreams are safe and forgiveness you will know.
The people you love will help you; they'll pick you up
     when you fall.
Home is where your heart lives; it's the one place you can call."

Days later she realized she was going to be just fine.
She was a true survivor, and that healing may take time.
No matter where you are in life, you can look back at what you had.
To everything you used to know and not feel quite so bad.

In the arms of people who love you, you will never feel alone.
No matter where life may take you, you will always have your home.
People you love will help you; pick you up when you might fall.
Home is where your heart lives—so go ahead and call.

~J. P. Shaw

Disconnecting

Resolve, and thou art free.
~Henry Wadsworth Longfellow

He called the night of our middle son's fourth birthday. His voice strained to be cheerful.

"So, can I talk to the birthday boy?" I walked casually out of the room where three little boys were waiting for bedtime stories. They were so calm, and I couldn't bear to have that disrupted.

"Well," I peered out the window into the darkness, "have you had your drug test?"

I knew he hadn't. I used the same calm tone I do with the boys when they ask a question they already know the answer to.

"You mean I actually can't talk to my son on his birthday? Why not?" His voice was shaking, and I closed my eyes and pondered his question.

When he left, the boys were six, three, and four months old. Shocked by our breakup, people would ask, "But he's seeing the kids, right?"

"Oh, yes," I would answer, and together we'd nod. "That's good."

There is a belief that contact with a father is by definition a gift. People seem to picture a reservoir inside the souls of children, labeled "Daddy Love." Any drop added to the reservoir is good, and can be stored up against drought.

The reality between a father and a child is far more complex. It is messy and organic. Between my sons and their dad ran a network of emotional connections. Through this bond flowed all he had to give as a man—the elements that I cannot provide, because they come from the heart of a father.

Then, for whatever reason, he left. Within a short period of time he broke off all contact, severing the many connections between him and his children. The pain and longing that poured out of them was massive, and there were days I could not imagine that they would survive.

If the days were interminable, the nights were worse. One of the boys always seemed to need me. The baby was hungry, or the six-year-old had a nightmare, or the three-year-old thrashed and moaned with night terrors that wouldn't relent.

One night I woke up in the rocking chair next to the crib, frightened because the baby wasn't in my arms. I searched for him on the floor for a few panicked minutes before I found him sleeping safely in his crib. I stumbled back to my bed, grateful but deeply shaken.

As I lay there, I whispered to myself a verse I'd been using as a sleep aid. Rather than allow my mind the freedom to roam over the thoughts about my life, I repeated, "I waited patiently for the Lord, and He inclined to me and heard my cry. He brought me up out of the pit of destruction, out of the miry clay, and set my feet upon a rock, making my footsteps firm." I murmured it to myself until I could go mercifully to sleep.

We did survive. Weeks went on, and life calmed down. The ache in all of us ebbed. Then one day in the midst of our calm... his call: "I want to see the boys."

I gathered them up and delivered them to him. They spent a few hours together. He called a few days later to say he couldn't come the next time he was supposed to. Unavoidable, but they would do something special on the following weekend instead. Then he was gone. No phone calls and he didn't show up for that "something special." And again I held my wounded sons as they screamed, had nightmares, bit, and did all the things children do when they are hemorrhaging pain.

That cycle didn't have to repeat itself too many times before the mother in me rose up and bared her fangs.

I hunted down a lawyer and pressed my legal advantage. I would have disappeared in the night if necessary, but all I had to do was stand tall in court. To face him and accuse him of the sins we both knew he was guilty of. All I had to do was tell the truth I had kept silent about to save him from shame.

Now I am armed with a court order for drug tests. Until he can pass random drug tests, he may not have any contact with his children. It has been over three years, and he hasn't even tried.

One night I dreamed I was him. In my dream, the blackness that envelops him flowed into me and I awoke, gasping for air. In the moments before reality returned and the pain receded, I would have done anything to escape. I lay there in the dark, weeping. I understood his choices for the first time.

And then I thought of the kids, and imagined them reconnecting with him, mainlining that despair.

"No." I was unwavering. "You can't talk to the birthday boy." There was a long silence while he searched his arsenal of replies.

"A father should be able to talk to his son on his birthday." His voice was low, anger battling with self-pity.

"You're right." I replied. "That's very sad."

And then I hung up. I turned back to my children, and in my head I heard the echo of a promise fulfilled.

"I waited patiently for the Lord, and He inclined to me and heard my cry. He brought me up out of the pit of destruction, out of the miry clay, and set my feet upon a rock, making my footsteps firm."

~Vera Jacobs

The Heart Knows Best

The D-word. It's most people's worst fear, but, in a bittersweet way, it was my greatest joy. In divorce, you gain something and you lose something. There is no way around it, and in the end, it is best for everyone, whether they know it at the time or not.

I'm thirteen years old, and I know what it feels like when parents split up, because mine did last fall.

My parents had been unhappy for years. When my father started cheating on my mom, things went downhill. I thought they would divorce instantly. I tried to picture my life after my parents split up—living at my mom's house during the week, and my father's house on the weekend. I was scared. But my mom decided to be the bigger person and try to stick it out, so that my siblings and I would know what it was like to have a family. Things didn't get better though.

I would always strain to hear the quiet arguments they didn't want me to hear. They weren't getting along and they weren't happy. But I could tell that they didn't know what they would do if they broke up. They took comfort in just coming home to someone, no matter what they had done. They were both scared, even if they didn't admit it. They would face their problems, together or apart, and know that when things got bad—they had each other. People don't like change and they don't want to find out what could happen. Most people don't want to take a chance because there is a fifty percent chance the result could come out good or a fifty percent chance that it won't. I learned though, that you dictate your own future and when someone is pulling you down, you can change their impact on you and that is just what I did.

My father had never really been there for me. He was there physically but not emotionally. He yelled a lot and never really showed any interest in going to my piano recitals or watching my dance performances. Everything we asked him to do, he had another excuse—a lie. We just sort of ignored it and went on with our lives like nothing was the matter.

Then last summer, there was real trouble in paradise. My siblings and I went out to Los Angeles to pursue acting and while we were out there, my father cheated on my mom again, and this time my brother, sister, and I all found out. He was going to make us move back to Florida and leave L.A. forever. L.A. was the best thing that had ever happened to me, my brother, my sister, and my mom. We were finally all happy. We decided to stay in L.A. and leave my father in Florida.

Our actions resulted in divorce. We didn't know if we were making the right decision or not. My mom went back and forth. She wanted what was best for her children. She confronted me and asked me if I thought we should go back to Florida or stay in Los Angeles. I replied, "There is nothing in Florida for us anymore. Out here in L.A., we have so many dreams that can come true. We shouldn't let him abuse us anymore. Finally, we are free."

My brother, sister, mom, and I finally were able to start over and let our happiness rise to new levels. We were allowed to become whoever we wanted to be and let our dreams soar to the sky. We weren't overshadowed by my dad anymore, and he couldn't hold his reputation and actions above our heads. Sometimes I still wonder what life would be like if my parents had not divorced, and I become deeply upset about what I have lost. But the gain was far greater.

The divorce was the best thing that had ever happened to me and the rest of my family. I don't regret anything about it. I now know that taking chances is the best thing to do. Even though I was scared at first and had my doubts about the divorce, I was glad it happened because now I could start my life over. The bond between my mom and me grew to great heights.

I will always remember what my mom said to me every time I would become upset over everything that had happened. "We are going to rise above." And we did. I gained my life back from the divorce and now I am the happiest I have been in my whole life.

Everyone thought my life before was perfect. The trophy mom, the successful father, a cute brother, a wonderful actress as a sister, and then me. I was the perfect child that every parent wanted. The girl who received all A plusses on her report card, cared about the world, excelled in piano, an elegant dancer—I appeared to be the happiest girl in the world.

But I wasn't—and neither was my life, so I never will regret the divorce and no one else should either. People who divorce take a chance to make their lives better.

Finally, I accept that love doesn't always last. If, in your heart you can feel something is not right, then follow your heart. In the end it's going to be your only true guide. To have and to hold. For richer or poorer. Your heart will never let you down.

~Kiera Peltz

10

Repossession

ear Mother-In-Law:

I am writing to you to inform you that I am returning your son for a voluntary repossession. I am returning the deed to our marriage and the keys to my heart tomorrow morning. If your son refuses to come along (he is good at stalling) you may have to come and tow him. You'll find him in the doghouse. If you choose not to come and collect him, I may have to have him towed; if this is the case, I will send you the towing bill.

Several years ago I entered a contract with him in good faith. The first few years he did fine, but since then it became more and more obvious that I have purchased a lemon. I am not a good cook, so making lemonade out of lemons is not one of my strong points.

When you tried to sell your son to me, you conveniently forgot to mention a few kinks. Sometimes I wonder if you didn't mention them on purpose—you probably couldn't wait to get him out of your house. I should have known better than to marry a man who still lived with his mother at the age of thirty-something.

I understand that a repossession may look bad on my credit history. However, after weighing the pros and cons, I have come to the conclusion that the repo on my credit is, by far, less threatening to my leading a happy life than keeping your son and putting up with him would be. He's causing severe damage to my emotional well-being, and that damage is much harder to fix than a divorce showing on my relationship history. Eventually, I'll be able to fix myself up so I won't be damaged goods to another man.

I may just decide to stay single. If I go that route, there will be no one but myself to be angry at if the house is messy and the laundry piles up to the ceiling. My house will not smell like stale cigarette smoke after I come home from the store. I will not have to listen to how hard his day was, and then be left with silence when I would like to describe my day. I will not have to rub someone's back and then be left with a snoring piece of wood when I want my back rubbed.

Here are some details of my complaint:

1. **The heater does not work.**

    I have to turn the waterbed on high even in the summer as his affection index has been below the lukewarm level for the past few years. Last week he told me, "You are just not attractive anymore." Disregarding the fact the he is the one who increased his pant size from a 30-inch waist to 38, while I only went from an anorexic 118 pounds to a healthy 135.

2. **The blinkers do not work.**

    I never know whether he will be in a right-wing or left-wing mood from one minute to the next.

3. **The starter is fine, but there is a problem with stalling.**

    He gets up and goes to work, and he has many good ideas for projects. However, he stalls more than I can handle. When he took three weeks off work four years ago to build me a beautiful porch, he left me with a moat (four-foot hole for a new foundation) and a plank (a piece of plywood across the moat, so we could get to the driveway) for two years. His carpentry-skilled cousin came over and, after two weekends, I had a floor, walls and a roof. Of course, the gaping holes where the window and the sliding door are supposed to go have been an open invitation for rain and snow to enter for the past two years, and now the floor needs to be redone as it is beginning to rot.

4. **He is a gas guzzler, the likes of which I have never seen.**

As an example, five years ago our town was hit by a tornado. We really lucked out because our house was still standing. The only damage was that the siding was dented and part of the roof was caved in. The insurance company gave us a nice settlement. Five years later, we still have the caved-in roof and the dented siding. I have no clue where the money is. I can only suspect that it went down the river on your son's fishing trip. (Of course, his old boat wouldn't do, and he had to buy a new one for the trip—the boat that has now been sitting in expensive storage for several years.)

He still has a job, so you can send him off to work for quite a few hours each week. Just be prepared not to ask for any monetary compensation for his stay with you, as he has a tendency to lose most of his paycheck on the way home on paydays, thus, I might add that his gas tank may have a leak.

5. **Your son's bluebook value may be difficult to estimate.**

However, once you have calculated it, please deduct $39,000. That is the amount of money I saved him for the quality childcare that I provided for the past five years. After all, I wanted to get my tubes tied, and he wanted a son instead. I ended up working long and stressful hours for peanuts in a childcare setting so I could take our son to work with me.

6. *He definitely needs an oil change. He is not as smooth as he used to be.*

As you can see, a repossession has become much less of a concern to me than the option of keeping up with this life.

I am sorry I have to do this to you, but look at the bright side: I am keeping your grandson.

Sincerely,

Your soon-to-be ex-daughter-in-law

P.S. His last ex-wife and I are planning on writing a letter to the Better Business Bureau to make sure he will be prevented from causing further heartbreaks.

~Annemarie Wagner

11

An End Is Also a New Beginning

There will come a time when you believe everything is finished.
That will be the beginning.
~Louis L'Amour

One day, almost by accident, I revisited the apartment I moved into after my husband and I separated seventeen years earlier. I was checking out a new store in the neighborhood and found myself driving down the familiar roads of the funky, low-rent section of Takoma Park. When I had first come there so long ago, I was looking for a short-term lease because I was still hoping we would reconcile. I lived there seven years.

In the ten years since I moved out and into a new home with a new husband, I had driven by two or three times just to look, wondering who was living there now and appreciating the distance I had traveled. I would linger a few minutes, smile to myself and drive on.

This time, as I turned onto Sligo Creek Parkway, I felt an odd tightening in my chest. The lush serenity of the park had always seemed a cruel counterpoint to the turmoil during that time of my life. I forced a deep breath to quiet my sudden anxiety.

I rounded the turn and pulled into the neighboring parking lot, where I could look directly up at the second floor windows of my old apartment. An "Apartment Available" sign was posted on the building, and I idly wondered what the rent was now. Minor cosmetic improvements had been made to the outside—landscaping, trash enclosure, entrance awnings.

I started to leave, as I had every time before, but for some reason, I shut off the engine and got out of the car. I didn't know what more I would see by walking up to the entrance, but I felt guided to do so. Like a curious observer, I watched myself walk from entrance to entrance and back again, trying to see into ground-floor windows and knocking on the resident manager's door. What was I doing? Why didn't I just leave?

Finally, the manager answered my knock. She was a large, homely woman dressed in a caftan, shuffling her feet as if every movement were an effort. I told her I wanted to see the apartment.

"The one-bedroom?" she asked.

"Yes." Really, I didn't care how many bedrooms it had. I just wanted to see what had been done to the inside, and any apartment would do.

The woman lumbered back into the recesses of her apartment and returned with a handful of keys on a ring. I had anticipated that she would accompany me, but instead she handed me the whole set and instructed me on the security system. She pointed to the other entrance and said, "Number 202."

My heart stopped. "202?" I barely managed to get out.

"Yes. 202."

That had been my apartment. I couldn't believe that of all the apartments, it would be the vacant one, and I would happen by on this particular day.

I opened the outside door and climbed the (now) carpeted stairs to the second floor. Putting the key in the lock, I struggled to turn the latch, and as I pushed the door open, I felt like Alice in Wonderland.

The apartment was hardly changed from the way it had looked when I'd seen it for the first time seventeen years before—a young woman newly separated, seeking temporary refuge which instead became a crucible for the woman who stood there now. Tears stung my eyes, and I could not seem to catch my breath.

I walked through the four rooms, noticing the few changes, remembering where each piece of my furniture had stood, dressing the empty rooms with my memories. Here in the living room, I had sat on the bare wood floor eating pizza with the dear friend who had helped me move my boxes into the apartment early. And there, on moving day, I had sat in my rocker, crying quietly; I could hear the grunts of my dad and another friend carrying my heavy furniture up the stairs as I wondered what I was doing here and whether I had the courage to tell them to take it all back to the truck. Rocking, rocking—back and forth between two lives.

There was the picture window where I had placed my first Christmas tree, purchased at the last minute on December 23rd because I hadn't thought I wanted to acknowledge the holiday at all that year, and then when I did, I bought the biggest tree I could find because it was all mine.

Each room was crowded with images as suddenly alive as if they had happened but a moment ago.

And finally, I opened the door to the walk-in closet which was New Beginnings' first "office." It was such a tiny space, barely big enough for a narrow bookshelf and a small table to hold my old IBM typewriter. I stood very still, reaching back through the years, to hear the tap-tap-tapping of the keys. With the phone on a long cord stretching from its outlet in the kitchen, I had eagerly spoken to each new person who called, breaking through my own isolation by responding to theirs. "I hear you have a group," the hesitant voice would say. The echoes of all those conversations whispered like ghosts in my ears. "My husband left me...." "My wife took the kids...." "She won't talk to me...." I blinked. It was really just an empty closet, and this was sixteen years later.

My eyes swept the apartment one last time, taking pictures in my mind that I would pull out and muse on, one by one, quietly, later on. This visit, I knew, was a gift from the universe, a warp in time, and I would not be back. Nor would I need to return. I closed the door, returned the keys, and got in my car to leave. As I drove away from that place, that time, I was overcome by great gulping sobs, surging up from some deep hidden place, long forgotten or pushed aside. The terrible pain of that horrific time, when everything was so intense, engulfed me like a surprise wave that pounds you to the sea floor and leaves you gasping for air.

Out of that time, New Beginnings was born. The ripples from my personal journey have touched the lives of many other pilgrims, whose own journeys have in turn profoundly enriched my life. The chance to stand again where I stood so many years ago was a powerful reminder that by sharing our common humanity, wherever we are along the way, we broadcast a message of hope: You are not alone. I understand your pain.

An end is also a new beginning.

~Carol Randolph

EDITOR'S NOTE: Established in 1979, New Beginnings is a non-profit organization that helps people in the Washington D.C. metro area cope with separation and divorce.

Divorce *and* Recovery

Forgiving and Letting Go

*The fairest action of our human life
Is scorning to revenge an injury;
For who forgives without a further strife,
His adversary's heart to him doth tie:
And 'tis a firmer conquest, truly said,
To win the heart than overthrow the head.*
~Lady Elizabeth Carew

Forgiveness Is a Choice

To forgive is the highest, most beautiful form of love.
In return, you will receive untold peace and happiness.
~Robert Muller

In February, when my father passed away after a long illness, I felt called to give his eulogy. In the months that preceded his death, I sifted though my memories of him and pondered what I would write.

Dad had several qualities that were adorable, but none stood out like his ability to forgive people for being fallible. I was always amazed that no matter what a person did, he always found it in his heart to forgive. Part of my tribute to him had to be to point this out to the world. But, I was faced with a serious dilemma.

How could I tell people that he had taught me to forgive the seemingly unforgivable — while not having forgiveness in my own heart?

You see, my world was shattered when my marriage ended. My childhood best friend and my soon to be ex-husband moved in together, leaving me with two small children, a broken-down car, and no health insurance.

I was angry, blaming, and bitter.

Even simple procedures like exchanging the children drained me with hatred. Eventually, the boys stopped going to their dad's and I was relieved to not have to deal with it anymore.

It was a cold day in January when I called my ex-husband to tell him Daddy was dying. He promptly planned a visit with Dad to say his goodbyes and Dad graciously welcomed him.

Still, there was one more thing to do. I called my former childhood friend and asked her to meet me at the hospital. At first, she was concerned about the other members of my family and how they would react if they saw her there.

I asked for some time alone with Dad that night. As I sat with him, I was nervous. I began to realize that I wanted my friend's forgiveness as well. I hadn't exactly been an angel to her since the divorce.

Around eight o'clock, she showed up at the hospital. When Daddy woke up and found us both there, he looked surprised. For once, he was at a loss for words. We laughed when he opened his mouth and nothing came out. He finally managed to say, "Well, my lord…."

I regret I never asked him later what he was thinking, but knowing my dad, I'm sure he was proud and happy that I was able to put all the anger and bitterness behind me at last.

Daddy died a few weeks later and I gave his eulogy as my last gift to him. Yet, his last gift to me had been priceless.

Today, my friend and I have resumed talking and going to lunch or dinner occasionally. We have forgiven the hurt, and focus on old times and good times to come.

We are always accompanied by her little girl, who looks and acts remarkably like my oldest son. I enjoy being in her life and we have forged a special bond. In a way, I feel like I have a little girl of my own.

I have learned through all of this that forgiveness is a choice we can all make, if we are willing to set aside pride and hurt feelings. On the other side of forgiveness lies immeasurable peace.

~Katherine Van Hook

Fixing Things According to Sadie

All God's angels come to us disguised.
~James Russell Lowell

Listening to Sadie talk for hours was easy. My favorite stories were about when she was growing up. Sadie always talked about her practical parents: her mother would wash aluminum foil after she cooked with it; her father was happier mending old shoes than buying new ones. Her parents' marriage was good; their dreams were focused, Sadie would say proudly.

My dear friend, Sadie, lived barely a wave away from my home. With my eyes closed, I can see Sadie and her husband now: Ed in trousers, T-shirt and a Detroit baseball cap. I see Sadie in a light blue oversized housedress pushing the lawn mower with one hand and a dish towel in the other.

Sadie and Ed came from the time when you fixed things yourself: a curtain rod, the kitchen radio, a screen door, the toaster, the hem of a dress. It was a way of life. Sadie admits that on occasion it made her crazy—all the re-fixing, eating all the leftovers in the refrigerator. "I wanted just once to be naughty and wasteful," Sadie would joke. But waste meant affluence. Throwing something away meant you knew there'd always be more, or new to buy.

After twenty-one years of marriage, the judge split all the assets but he couldn't split the emotionally bound soul. A phenomenon happens when we humans marry and create a family. With each minute of sharing, even the sharing of mundane events, our emotions, spirits, and souls braid together with our spouse's. On paper, things can be divided—but it's not so easy for the spirit. There is no way to prevent that invisible bleeding that results from the canyon-sized incision created by a splitting couple. It's that simple. As I walked out of the courtroom I was struck with the pain of learning that sometimes there isn't any "more." Sometimes what we care about most gets all used up, or quits and goes away—never to return.

About a month after my divorce, on a star-filled summer night, in a cold white hospital room, my friend Sadie died. She had been a wonderful, insightful woman.

A couple of days before she died, Sadie gave me angelic advice. I don't know what else to call it. Her thoughts were like prevailing winds for a homesick sailor. My dear friend knew I was devastated and she was concerned that I would harden my heart towards my ex and others. Sadie feared that instead of fixing my heart, I would grow to ignore blushes of color, walks in the rain, and the warmth of sunbeams. Sadie spoke to me about how short life really is. She talked about how the thing that makes life euphoric is how we live—not how we die. Sadie said, "Love what you hold now, not later. Be tender, and mend what needs to be mended without hesitation." Sadie understood and accepted that in life things do break. She knew it was important to love, and make well, those precious items we adored. Sadie talked about giving care. Mostly Sadie talked about free will. "Don't give free will the opportunity to destroy anything that is precious. This includes a marriage, an old car, a best friend, memories of good times or a heart that wants to love and be loved."

I'm blessed that Sadie's words held fast to me and aided me in my path through my divorce to a new life, a different life with a different light. I made the choice to fix my heart with prayer and the love I cherish for my children.

Unlike a car or a mower, a new heart cannot be purchased. It needs to be fixed—or it does harden. I made a choice to forgive my ex, and enjoy the memories of our wonderful times. I wanted to remember how good it had been.

And if Sadie were here... she would adore my new love, just as I do.

~Laurence Mitchell

Baking Away Bitterness

Cooking is like love... It should be entered into with abandon or not at all.
~Harriet Van Horne

Today is the first anniversary of my ex-husband's death. My mind is flooded with memories of Harry; my heart is filled with a jumble of emotions.

We spent sixteen years together, building a number of small businesses with various degrees of success. He was in charge of sales and I took care of production. We made a dynamic team—but we were better in business than we were on a personal level. So we kept our focus on work.

We founded a company that turned into my dream venture. I loved everything about it. I went to work each day with eager anticipation. It was my pride and joy.

After the third year, my husband became bored with the company. But I did not want to leave the job I had grown so fond of. So we decided to split our directions. He would start something new, while I continued with the already established business. However, without each other's abilities, neither of us was able to succeed.

I soon realized that without a business venture we could share, there was nothing keeping us together. We began attacking each other—not physically—but as many people know, mental scars can be the hardest to heal.

By the time our divorce was finalized, my bitterness toward Harry was overwhelming. I never wanted to hear his voice, see his face, or even hear his name again.

I remarried, and my new husband and I enjoyed our life together with our baby daughter. After a long absence, happiness was finally a part of my life again. A few more years passed, and we added two more children to our happy family. The bitterness was finally melting away from my heart.

One year, we invited our neighbors to celebrate Thanksgiving with us. I decided to make a carrot cake for dessert, mainly because my son had requested it. I pulled out my old recipe, and the stained 3x5 card immediately brought back memories of my ex-husband. I had often made this particular dessert for Harry's birthday and on other special occasions. It was his favorite. After a moment of hesitation, I went ahead and started to make the carrot cake.

As I assembled the ingredients for the cake, the phone rang. It was my neighbor, Herb. He was calling from the hospital where he had taken his wife, Nancy, because of a complication from a broken arm. Apparently, Harry was also in the hospital. The doctors didn't expect him to get out. Cancer had taken over his body. Because Herb was a long-time friend of Harry's, he had called to tell me that Nancy, he, and Harry would be having Thanksgiving dinner together at the hospital.

As I hung up the phone and stared at the carrot cake ingredients sitting on the counter, I felt a strange urge to send my ex-husband a large piece of the cake. For me, it would symbolize forgiveness. I knew, deep in my soul, that God was telling me I needed to do this—for Harry and for myself.

As I made that carrot cake, memories of good times with Harry crossed the barriers I had built up in my mind. I hadn't allowed myself to think anything but negative thoughts about him for so long, it seemed strange to not be angry anymore. I still didn't want to talk to him. I simply didn't have the words. I hoped the cake would let him know that I no longer held any hard feelings for what had happened between us.

I asked Herb to pick up my ex's piece of cake on his way to the hospital on Thanksgiving morning. That afternoon, he called. "When Harry found out the cake was from you," he said, his voice cracking,

"I saw tears come to his eyes. And he refused to share a single bite with anyone, even me."

Harry died the next day.

Now, a year later, I'm thankful I was able to express my forgiveness to Harry before it was too late. I hope he understood it for what it was. I believe God made sure he did.

~Linda Fitzjarrell

Thank You for Leaving

ear Mom,

I can hardly believe that thirty years have passed since the day you told me that you were leaving Dad. I was twelve years old, and silence had already become my habitual response to emotional situations, so I don't think I said much at the time. But I want to make sure you know what I felt then, and feel even more strongly today.

Thank you. Thank you so much for leaving. Thank you for changing your life, and mine.

Mom, did you ever know how scared I got when you and Dad fought? I'd be in my room playing with the cool Barbie camper you got me for Chanukah, the one that had the orange and yellow psychedelic flowers on the plastic roll-up sides. My favorite game was to pretend that Barbie and Ken had just gotten married and were going on their honeymoon. I'd be humming along as I helped Barbie pack for her trip, until suddenly I'd notice noise coming from downstairs. Dad was yelling, his big voice rushing up the stairs like a train rumbling up from underground. I'd freeze like a frightened rabbit, my ears quivering as I strained to hear what he was yelling about. But I never could hear the words, only the booming noise of the explosion. I'd get quiet, so quiet. Because maybe the quieter I got, the quieter Dad would get. But then I'd hear your voice, your voice that was crying and shouting all at the same time.

That's when I would start feeling really really bad, like if it didn't stop, if you and Dad didn't stop, I would break into a million trillion little pieces and nobody would ever find me. To make it stop, I'd creep over to my bed, the twin bed where you slept with me when you weren't sleeping with Dad, the bed that used to be all mine—the bed I hated sharing with you, because if you were there, it meant that you and Dad were fighting. I'd creep over and pull my pillow over my ears and my covers over my head, and curl up tight, rocking and humming in my salt-stained cocoon. I'd stay there as long as it took, holding myself together, humming and rocking.

After a while... fifteen minutes... an hour... forever?... I'd uncover one of my ears, like a scope on a submarine, to check the surrounding territory. If the battle seemed over and the air seemed still, I'd creep silently as a spy back to my dolls. I'd comb Barbie's hair, my nose runny and my eyes burning.

When I would come downstairs later, I'd pretend not to notice your red eyes and shaking hands, Dad's broken mug or his empty chair. I ate the dinner you'd prepared, my stomach jumping in time with my pulse, while the air vibrated with the force of words flung like sloppily targeted missiles, striking not just their intended victim but anyone in their vicinity. The food stuck like shrapnel in my throat, but I ate.

Did you know that this is how it was for me, Mom? Is that why you left, after twenty-five years of staying? Or was I just lucky enough to be a passenger on your journey away from a house that had not been a home for so many years, from a marriage that was a war zone with ever-increasing battles where the rules of conduct had long been discarded?

When you told me the two of you were getting divorced, I began to breathe again. I know you were worried that I'd be angry at you for leaving. I know that many people told you that you should stay for your children's sake or that it was wrong to break up a marriage. But the truth is that I wish, both then and now, that you'd left years sooner. Even though you were taking me with you from New York to Florida, and I was leaving the only home I had ever known, even though I didn't yet know any other kids whose parents were divorced,

I wasn't mad or even scared. For the first time in a long time, I felt some relief, some hope that I could live in a place where the walls weren't permeated with bitter words and tearstained pleas. That I could do my homework at night in clean, blessed silence. For the first time in a long time, I felt hope.

Things weren't exactly easy for us, Mom, when you and I moved away from everyone we knew and loved. But, it was worth it. It was the first time in my life that I experienced a peaceful household. I blossomed in school, I made friends, and my nightly nightmares and daily stomachaches stopped. I no longer had to keep a pillow handy to block out the sounds from the war zone.

The quiet didn't survive our side-by-side entry into our respective hormonal rites of passage: puberty for me, menopause for you. Our voices had become the ones raised in anger, and I could tolerate this no better than I could tolerate hearing you and Dad fight. Like a tethered wild horse escaping into the open land, I ran off to college as soon as I could, and I knew I would never return. Just as you needed to leave Dad, I had to leave you. I know that, in time, you came to understand.

Life is so very mysterious, Mom. When you and Dad split up, you had nothing good to say about each other. During the decade after the divorce, the two of you couldn't be in the same room without raising the ambient temperature, as he insulted you and you criticized him. And yet, it was you who flew to New York to stand at Dad's hospital bed when he had emergency heart surgery. It was Dad who flew to Florida to take care of you when you grew ill and all your children were grown and gone.

It was at your funeral that my siblings and I, for the first time in our lives, saw our seventy-seven-year-old father cry. Neither of you ever remarried, and at the end you traveled full circle to fulfill those long-ago vows: in sickness and in health, until death do you part.

Dad never did get over your death, and his own heart stopped beating five years later. I like to picture the two of you hanging out together at the shore of some celestial lake, doing a little fishing. You're standing next to each other quietly, ankle-deep in cool clear water, at peace in a way that you were just beginning to approach at your lives' end. So thank you, Mom, for finally leaving a bad marriage, for your sake and mine. For letting Dad come back when you needed him and he needed you. Thank you for showing me that there is a right time to leave—and a right time to return. That there is always the possibility of finding a path to forgiveness, and a path that leads us home.

~ Joyce Zymeck

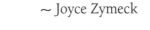

"... and they got a divorce and
lived happily ever after."

Thoughts on Love and Forgiveness

Forgiveness is the key that can unshackle us
from a past that will not rest in the grave of things over and done with.
~Lewis B. Smedes

In May of 2001, I received one of those dreaded phone calls no one wants to receive. My brother, Mike, called to tell me our dad was seriously ill and not expected to live. I was quite surprised by my feelings, because my dad and I hadn't exactly had the ideal father-daughter relationship. In fact, we hadn't kept in touch for years for various reasons, mostly because he had divorced my mother when I was around ten years old. He moved to another state and didn't seem to have much time for my brother and me. He missed our graduations, forgot birthdays and broke promises.

One Christmas, when I was about twelve years old, I truly believed he was going to "come to his senses" and come home to us. I sat for hours in our living room, facing the front door, listening to Bing Crosby croon "I'll Be Home for Christmas." I played that record so many times, I almost wore it out. I just knew that he would burst through the door any minute, loaded down with gifts for all of us, and ask for forgiveness. It was a scene I played repeatedly in my wistful daydreams. I made sure the porch light was on, so Dad could find our house. Of course, it never happened.

Even after becoming an adult, I still held onto some deep-seated sadness. I guess the little girl's pain inside me would never go completely away. But, I realized divorce is never just one person's fault and I began to feel differently about my dad. I wanted to have him in my life again.

I'll never forget watching a movie on TV entitled, *Max Dugan Returns*. It was about a grown woman's father returning to her life after years of separation, bringing outrageously expensive gifts, trying to make up for everything. The film had a profound effect on me. I wrote to my dad shortly after seeing it and it was the beginning of a slow road back to getting to know each other. Our letters, phone calls, and occasional visits were few and far between and usually only initiated by me.

As the years went by, I told myself I had forgiven him for everything, but I came to realize I hadn't completely done so. That happened after the time I went to Iowa to see him while he was in the ICU.

As he lay in the hospital bed, I held his hand and marveled at the softness of his skin. His hand was not the firm, muscular one I remembered grasping as a young girl. I felt tears roll down my cheeks as the emotions welled up inside me. I began to feel a love for him I hadn't allowed myself to feel in many years. It was at that point I thought to myself that no matter what, he still was—and always would be—my dad. I began to pray for his recovery and I asked God to give us more time together. He was seventy-six years old and I barely knew him. I wasn't finished with him yet.

As he began to recover, I realized I could laugh at his know-it-all ways and excuse his flirting with the young nurses. He had been married four times, yet here he was, a lonely old man.

After he was released from the hospital, we talked on the phone and e-mailed fairly often. He told me things that amazed me about those years he was away. He truly didn't know the hurt he caused us. He was so consumed with his own wants and desires, he really didn't understand the heartbreaking effect of his selfishness. It was very hard for me to understand why he chose to live his life the way he did, but my new-found forgiveness let me know I didn't have to understand it. I simply accepted it. I decided I wouldn't let the past stop me from trying to be the daughter my dad wanted and needed now. I wished he didn't live so far away, because I wanted to help take care of him, but it just wasn't possible.

Dad died the following year, a few days after Thanksgiving. I was saddened by his death, but also extremely thankful we had found each other and had reconnected.

When he and my mother divorced, she was so hurt, angry, resentful and embarrassed, that she scattered her emotions over and through our lives until my brother and I were as miserable as she was. Mother died years before Dad did, so she never knew I had come to terms with everything. I even forgave her for her self-pity during those years and for her lack of desire to see joy in everyday life. I never told her any of those feelings though, because she really wouldn't have understood.

A very wise friend once told me she believes part of our journey here on earth is to forgive our parents, whether they were wonderful, horrifying or somewhere in-between. I believe I have accomplished that. Being the joyful person I have become, I think my children won't feel the need to forgive me for any damaging emotional wounds. That would certainly be one of my proudest achievements.

~Becky Povich

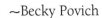

17

Much Too Loved

*T*he bitter and acrimonious divorce was more durable than the marriage. My ex-husband's mother, Mai, had urged us to get married and then, soon, wanted our divorce. When her second wish was granted, I was an unprepared teen-aged mother.

I came to hate this woman, who I blamed for many of our marital problems. She was too bossy... never let her boy grow up. When had I exhausted my list of accusations, I created new allegations.

The years passed, my son grew up, graduated from high school and became an outstanding young man. My life was going well. I accepted resentment as an inevitable state of living.

That would change.

In time, I joined a spiritual group that recommended I search my heart and review troubled relationships in a different light. I should ask myself: Where was I at fault? What problems did I bring to a relationship?

The judgments I had made about my former mother-in-law rose to the surface of my mind. To my unpleasant surprise, memories of my own actions surfaced: refusing to help prepare meals, arguing harshly with my husband in front of her, my sharp tongue cutting her spirit. I tried to stomp out these memories. But she pestered me mentally. I added that pestering to the reasons I didn't like her. While I was struggling with my pride, a tragedy occurred. Gerald, my ex-husband and Mai's son, died from a lingering illness.

My anger was cut short. Who could wish that kind of pain on

anyone? Unbidden, my heart softened. I felt extremely sorry for her. I saw my earlier actions towards her in a new light. I could no longer live with my regret. Not wanting to cause her more pain, I waited to call until several weeks after Gerald's funeral. I was uneasily surprised when she agreed that I could come and visit her.

When she answered her door, I was shocked. The frail woman, stooped and wrinkled, was far different from the strong matriarch of my memories.

She greeted me warmly and seated herself carefully in her wool-lined chair. I made tea for us, stumbled over small talk. This fragile woman confused me.

Over tea, she asked about her grandson. In return, I asked how she was holding up. She was worried about Gerald's grave. She couldn't afford a stone, and his grave was marked solely by a small metal marker. Her wrinkled eyes filled with tears as she discussed her son's death.

Enough procrastination, I chided myself. This woman has had enough pain. I cleared my throat. "Mai, I've needed to talk to you for some time."

She averted her gaze, something across the room suddenly summoning her attention. Then, she surprised me by nodding. Had she been expecting this conversation?

I continued. "I have carried hard feelings, much anger towards you for many years...." I paused. This is harder than I had expected, I thought. Maybe I can stop, run away. I'm good at running. She met my eyes. She was sitting very straight in her chair. Maybe I wasn't the only one harboring negative thoughts. I fearfully looked back at her. Well, nothing to do but finish this and leave.

"I'm here to ask your forgiveness. I've been rude to you and you watched me treat your son in hurtful ways. I am so sorry. Can you forgive me?" I felt small, vulnerable.

Now her gaze held mine. She arched her back. I realized she was in pain, maybe constantly. She probably wanted me to get out, stop bringing up sad memories. I started to rise, reach for my purse. I had no right to bring up painful memories to this grieving mother. I sure could mess things up sometimes.

A gnarled, overly-veined hand reached out and touched me gently, indicating I should sit back down. The room was very still. I could hear a fan blowing in the next room. Songbirds chittered outside. I felt cold, even though the room was warm.

"Jeannie... please, stay?" her voice was soft, her request a question. I had to strain to hear her. I sat back in my chair. I could be such a fool. I looked up and met her gaze. She had the kindest look on her face. She was showing me love. I tilted my head, querying her next move.

"Honey, (was my hearing failing me?) I not only forgive you..." She fumbled as she reached for her walker, slowly bringing her weakened body upright. She stepped toward me and placed her hands on my head. "...but I bless you as well." These last words were spoken strongly. They rang out like bells from a chapel on Sunday morning. A thrill, starting at the base of my neck went skittering down to my tailbone. I felt blessed. Something momentous was occurring. I sat speechless.

She continued, "I forgave you long ago, dear. But I am pleased to bless you. Also, no matter what you think, my son loved you very much. He spoke of you on his deathbed."

I bent over and covered my face with both hands. These unexpected and powerful words were too much for me to bear. I had longed for her forgiveness. I did not expect to receive it. But I had received that and much more. I could not stop my tears.

The remaining years of her life were few. But she was a tremendous source of love. When she died, I received a handwritten note telling me again how much she loved me and how much I meant to her. This letter is one of my most prized possessions.

Several months after my last conversation with her, I was able to purchase a tall, black, mother-of-pearl engraved headstone for her Gerald — my son's father. She believed her son's soul would rest easier with this monument to his too-short life.

I hope so.

The words on his stone are: "Much too Loved to Ever Be Forgotten."

~HJ Eggers

18

Close Encounter of the Healing Kind

Love is a thing that can never go wrong.
~Dorothy Parker

When I answered the phone and said, "Hello," I heard nothing except for a slight intake of breath. My first instinct was to hang up, thinking I'd received a nuisance call. For some reason, I remained on the line and repeated, "Hello?" The response was one word, my name, uttered in a hesitant voice: "Jenny?"

I hadn't heard that voice for eighteen years, but I recognized it immediately. It belonged to my first husband, Michael.

I couldn't believe it. We hadn't parted on good terms. There had been neither an "other man" nor an "other woman." I had merely realized after almost five years of marriage, we weren't seeking the same things in life.

Sadly, that realization was mine alone, and Michael felt betrayed by my disaffection. During the first year we were divorced, he called from time to time, hoping, I believe, that I would "come to my senses" and return to him, although I did nothing to encourage his optimism.

I then met the man who would become my second husband—the man who I remained married to for almost twenty-five years. I relocated to another state to begin life afresh with my new partner.

It wasn't long after I moved that I began receiving letters from Michael—letters filled with animosity. I was devastated. His words destroyed a belief about the nature of love that I had had up until then. I had always felt that individuals who have shared genuine love at one time would always remain connected on some level. How could people who have wholly revealed themselves to one another ever totally forget such intimacy? That was the reason I had been willing to continue a relationship of sorts with Michael, even though the marriage had ended.

However, after receiving his letters brimming with condemnation and reproach, I severed contact with him completely. I hadn't heard from him for eighteen years.

Until now.

"Why now?" I asked, too shocked to manage anything more.

Michael told me that he and his family, which now included a wife and three children, were going back to the country where he had been born.

"I need to see you before I go. It would mean a great deal to me. Please."

It was a convincing plea, and, although I hadn't forgotten the letters, I admit that both curiosity and a resurrected desire for closure made me say, "Yes."

The day finally came. Michael was traveling from another city. I arrived at our designated meeting place early. As I waited, I worried. What if this meeting turned into another episode of recrimination? Feeling eyes upon me, I looked up. Except for a thicker waist and thinner head of hair, Michael looked the same.

He recognized me instantly.

"You're thinner," he noted. I wasn't, but didn't argue. I didn't want to introduce even the slightest hint of aggression.

Directly after ordering drinks, Michael began to unload parcels from a bag he'd been carrying. He plunked the packages down in front of me. "For you," he said.

Among an assortment of trinkets was a cassette that included a song entitled, "Jenny." It wasn't in English, but I knew it. It was an apologetic love ballad. Even before I had a chance to say thank you, Michael said, "Let's talk about your family and mine. But first, I want to tell you that hardly a day has passed in eighteen years that I haven't thought about you."

I wasn't prepared for this sort of emotional bombshell and I was speechless. "It's not what you're thinking. I'm very happy with my wife and my kids. It's just that I've thought about how much in love we once were. I've been sorry that with such a bright beginning, we finished up so miserably. I couldn't leave the country without at least trying to end the bitterness between us."

I took his hand and smiled while I wept cleansing, healing tears.

As if on cue, our drinks arrived, giving us a chance to toast both days gone by and those yet to come.

As Michael had predicted, we spent most of our meeting talking about our respective families. We parted as loving friends. That meeting took place ten years ago. We haven't exchanged a word since.

That reunion had a profound effect on me. It verified my deeply-held belief that love has a life of its own and can sometimes survive a relationship that has died. Until I'd seen Michael again, the memory of his caustic letters had prevented me from remembering some of the sweet moments we had shared. For me, our belated encounter cleared a path to recollection, giving me back a memory of a love I can now reflect upon without regret.

~Jenna Romano

19

Flower Power

My garden of flowers is also my garden of thoughts and dreams.
The thoughts grow as freely as the flowers, and the dreams are as beautiful.
~Abram L. Urban

"I hate you!" she screamed. "I hate Dad too! Why couldn't you and Dad just get along?" She threw her school books on the floor, ran to her room, and slammed the door.

It was that way the entire first year after my divorce from her father. The littlest thing could set her off. The doctor called it "childhood stress." He said it was a force that parents in today's world must face. No respecter of persons, stress can affect the most sheltered, protected and loved child, confusing a youngster with overwhelming emotions. Children may have to deal with moving, changing friends, difficult school years, death of family members, or losing a sibling to marriage. For my daughter and me, it was the divorce and the move from the family home that so deeply affected us. She bitterly resented having to go to a different school and make new friends, and of course, because I was the parent who was near at hand, I received the bulk of her wrath.

My daughter didn't want to go to counseling, even though she had nightmares and sobbed in her sleep. But as the periods of frustration grew longer and occurred more often, I decided that one of us needed to seek professional advice—even if that someone was me. The therapist explained that sometimes a child may grapple with feelings of failure for reasons the parent is completely unaware of. I wasn't alone, he told me. Many single moms and dads face problems like mine. The parent wants to help, but the child tends to shut everyone out, refusing to talk or even to listen.

I was hopeful that this trained and educated counselor would offer some wonderful words of wisdom that would turn things around for us. Instead, the advice the therapist offered was simply this: plant flowers.

At first, I thought it ludicrous to expect anything so simple to effect a change in our coping abilities, but I tried it. Indeed, there was something relaxing and fulfilling about digging in the dirt—something about watching flowers take shape and raise their little heads proudly in bloom. In fact, I realized that planting and tending flowers was probably just what my daughter and I needed as a reminder to nurture one another.

One day, I had a wheelbarrow-full of well-fertilized topsoil too heavy to manage by myself. Teetering as I tried to steady the load, I called to my ten-year-old daughter for help. She came on the run, tipping over the wheelbarrow—and her mother—in her haste. We both fell into the manure mixture, laughing at our clumsiness. It was our first gut-level, I'm-not-thinking-about-anything-else good time since the divorce. After that, she was hooked on gardening. We spent the spring and summer planting, fertilizing, cutting, and just generally "tending" the flowers.

Now she is a teenager, happy and busy with a life full of activities—too busy to help me in the garden much anymore. But we often eat on the patio and linger after the meal to look at the flowers. She may see a rose and ask if she can cut it and take it to her room. She likes to put them in one particular crystal vase we own. It makes me nervous to think that it might break if she knocked it off her dresser with her backpack. But then I weigh it out—shattered vase? Shattered child? Take the vase, honey.

~Elaine Ernst Schneider

20

Taking the Plunge

racey was barely out of high school when she married Rick. She looked forward to motherhood despite the warnings about divorce rates and the almost unbearable pressure that can befall young parents. "What do they know?" she laughed, snuggling against her new husband and delighting in the feel of their baby's first kick inside her. She counted fingers and toes when the newborn arrived, and rocked and sang to her daughter, night after sleepless night.

In the beginning, it was hard, but Rick helped. They were struggling, but so was everyone else they knew.

When their second baby arrived four years later, most of their friends were already either divorced or separated. Tracey had thought about that a lot, too: taking some time apart. Instead, she got pregnant. This time she walked the floors alone because Rick was either at his second job or somewhere else. Somewhere else is where she wished she could be, too.

The last straw came for her on Thanksgiving. Tracey was trying to make a perfect holiday dinner. It would only be the four of them: Tracey, Rick, and the girls, now six and two. She made pies from scratch the day before, and their sweet aroma still hung in the tiny kitchen. Yams were baking and the turkey was browning.

"Rick? Can you run to the store for butter? I ran out and we're going to need it for the corn."

He stepped into the steamy kitchen. "Can it wait? I promised to stop by Jeff's house for a few minutes." Tracey felt the perspiration on her neck as she pushed a straggling curl behind her ear. Suddenly, she felt like a mess. A knot hardened in her stomach.

"It can wait. Remember the bird will be done at four."

Four o'clock came and went, and so did five and six. She fed the girls, but wasn't hungry herself. The knot in her stomach had grown and spread up into a lump in her throat. The girls were long asleep when Rick finally came home.

"I'm so sorry, honey. We got caught up in the game...."

Tracey set Rick's plate on the table. "You'll have to warm it up." Her voice showed no trace of hostility, or anger, or pain. She reached for her jacket and the car keys. "I still need that butter."

Rick quietly watched her back out of the driveway. She pulled up to the food store and paused. She didn't go inside. Instead, she kept driving — far away from the girls, far from Rick, out of town, out of state. She never planned it. It just happened.

When Emmalynn met Rick, he was up to his neck in fragrant cedar-water in the shallow part of the lake and laughing as his daughters romped alongside him, squealing as they each grabbed a leg and ducked him under. The three of them kicked sand her way by accident as they stumbled onto the nearby blanket.

"Whoops! Sorry." He had a crooked smile, and he was cute. Emmalynn saw his left hand was tanned all over, no wedding-ring line. Like hers. By the time she could say, "No problem," his two tow-haired daughters were already back at the lake's edge, chasing and splashing her own kids. They were all nearly the same age.

"Funny how they just dive right in there and get on with it, isn't it?" The handsome daddy bit his lip. It was a habit her son had, too.

"They're light on the baggage," Emmalynn laughed. "They haven't had time yet to over-think friendship."

The two little families clicked at the lakeside — and the day after that, and the day after that. Not more than a year later, back at the shoreline, four children gathered barefoot and in formal clothes — like their respective parents — witnessing the vows that made them all a family.

It wasn't always upbeat. Some days weren't even close. On her thirteenth birthday, Rick's older child spent most of the day in the hall closet on the phone with Tara, her best friend.

"She's going all-out for my party. Yeah. It's okay, I guess. But do you know this will make six birthdays since I heard from my mother? No cards, no nothing?"

Emmalynn didn't mean to overhear.

"I mean, Emmalynn's alright, and all. But she's not my mother, you know?"

After the party that night, Emmalynn sat cross-legged on their bed. "Nice party, honey." Rick kissed her and threw back the covers. "I was never any good at that woman's touch thing."

Emmalynn looked intently into her husband's eyes. "It's not just a woman's touch she needs. It's her mother."

Rick spent the first six months after Tracey left hoping she would change her mind and return. At first, he was certain there'd been foul play. The detective brought his world down soon enough. "Rick, it happens all the time. Married too young, too much pressure. Men leave, and women do it, too. We've followed every lead. I'm convinced that she left of her own free will."

The next six months were denial. How could she? Why would she? Rick was sorry, he was confused, but most of all angry. After a year had passed, his question was, How dare she?

It was about that time that Tracey called. She'd hit the interstate that first night, alone. There had been no affair, no clandestine plan. She'd been overwhelmed. She didn't know where she was going, but she knew she needed time. Time to breathe, time to think, time to grow up.

"I couldn't be a good mother, Rick. I was only pretending. I was so angry, so lonely. I'm sorry. I left before I did something I couldn't take back."

Rick watched the girls playing on the backyard swings through his kitchen window. It was the same window he'd looked out over and over again until he could no longer stay awake on that Thanksgiving night long ago.

"Yeah, well, I'm sorry too. The girls are finally just beginning to get along without you. Do me a favor, Tracey. Don't call back." She didn't, not even when the divorce papers were served and signed and it was over.

Emmalynn knew what Rick was thinking, but she continued. "It's time to put it to rest. It's time to find Tracey."

Rick shook his head. "Let it lie, Emmalynn. Life goes on. My kids aren't the only ones who don't see a parent after the divorce. It's sad. It's awful. But why dig the whole thing up again? Besides, if hearing from Tracey is really what the girls want, don't you think they would have said so?"

Months later, on a Saturday morning, Rick was the one hearing snippets of a phone conversation between Emmalynn, and someone else.

"She looks just like you, and she's really a good kid. I'll get the school picture in the mail Monday. You take care, too."

Rick looked out the old, familiar window onto a new day, as his wife hung up the phone. "It's time, isn't it?" he asked.

Emmalynn nodded. "Just dive right in," she smiled. "And get on with it."

~Bobbie Cheshire

Wedded Bliss

Time heals griefs and quarrels,
for we change and are no longer the same persons.
~Blaise Pascal

ore than twenty-five years ago we stood at the altar, two freshly-scrubbed kids wearing fancy clothes with the same fervor as children playing dress-up. Responding when spoken to and reciting the empty words the pastor prompted, we took our vows and left the church with absolutely no comprehension of the impact that evening would have on the rest of our lives.

I was running away—always running away—from something. This time it was childhood. It had been horrible, replete with the wrath of the hurtful hands and cold heart of a calculating, manipulative mother. I longed for nurturing, but received none. I wanted a life like the families I saw on TV. I wanted a mother who'd fix my hair in beautiful ringlets and ribbons, a mother waiting with cookies and hugs for me after school. I wanted a mother who would warmly greet my daddy at the end of his long day at work.

Instead, my mother was a tyrant, and I fled from her straight into the arms of a product of the same dysfunction I was escaping. Through no fault of his own, my groom was about as ill-equipped at dealing with married life as I was. His parents, although married for many years and still enduring one another's company, were alcoholics and lived in perpetual denial of their affliction. In his family, a good time was when everyone got to watch his father get drunk and pass out in a plate of beans.

Misery does indeed love company, and so we stayed with each other for quite some time—long enough, in fact, to have three children. If dysfunction breeds dysfunction, we contributed heavily to its cause. We had less business having children than we did marrying in the first place. I remain thankful for the merits of good counseling, which each of the three has received.

I don't know exactly when I knew it was over. It wasn't a specific day or hour or moment. In fact it was a blur of time when I felt my words weren't comprehended and my actions were misconstrued. I just knew when it was time to go—and I went. Tumult followed for many years. We endured each other's injuries and insults, and hurled daggers of retaliation. The children were innocent victims often caught in our crossfire.

But the ensuing years proved to be an amazing healing tool. The healing ointment of time is called perspective, and it is applied it in small subtle doses. It seeps gently under the skin and results in a calming and soothing of the heart and mind. This salve is a gift.

When we open gifts, we mentally put them in one of two piles—the first, things we love and plan to use; the second, after muttering polite thanks to the giver, remains unused, untouched, and is eventually forgotten.

My ex-husband and I used this gift of time and perspective. Each of us, in our own way, utilized the strength that had come boxed and wrapped. We threw away the paper wrappings and bows and with them, a great deal of unnecessary debris. What emerged was clean, purified. Images of a world filled with hate and bitterness were replaced with serenity and beauty. Words that once rolled off harsh tongues were squelched and from sweeter lips come words of praise and encouragement and thanksgiving.

Gifts such as these lead us down new paths. Our paths obviously veered in different directions, yet with the anchor of the children, somehow stayed close enough. The road I took led me to the heart and arms of a wonderful soul, my husband of nearly eleven years. The years with this saint of a man have taught me to trust, to love, and to give of myself without holding back. But I wouldn't have achieved this level of appreciation for these blessings had I not endured some hardship and pain. Our family has grown with the addition of two more children. We have been blessed.

Soon, my husband and I will attend a wedding ceremony in a local chapel. Undoubtedly, one of my sons will usher me and my husband to our seats. I think guests of the groom sit on the right. As the bride walks down the aisle, I'll remember what I learned so many years ago in another time, another state, another life. I'll smile as she meets her groom, and I'll pray that God grants them many happy years together. A chapter in my life will close, the one that has been read and re-read, and now is filed away under "lessons learned." A new chapter will begin for the father of three of my children. He begins this marriage older, wiser, and more aware of what it takes to nurture a relationship. And I'll wish him well—from a seat in a pew on the right.

~Maggie Kelly

Chapter 3

Divorce *and* Recovery

It's Over...
and We're Still Friends

We are not enemies, but friends. We must not be enemies.
Though passion may have strained, it must not break our bonds of
affection. The mystic cords of memory will swell when again touched as
surely they will be by the better angels of our nature.
~Abraham Lincoln

Doing Divorce

It is not difficult to be unconventional in the eyes of the world when your unconventionality is but the convention of your set.
~W. Somerset Maugham

"We don't do divorce the same way other people do," my son stated one day after school. Knowing what he meant, I nodded my head and asked if something had happened to bring him to that realization. He shrugged his shoulders. "I just know what some of my friends at school say about their parents' divorce."

My son made this comment four years ago. It has been nine years since his father and I divorced. At first, my ex and I waltzed awkwardly around each other in the entryway when he showed up on Friday evenings to pick up the kids, then again on Sundays when he brought them back home. Fairly quickly, we decided that we had to try to act in a way that would be in the best interest of our two children. So we developed a new dance, coming together in a promenade at school events and church.

After I remarried, my new husband graciously accepted my ex's presence at family events. My ex joins us at our home for holiday dinners so that our children will never have to choose between their parents on Thanksgiving, Christmas, or Easter. Whoever is first to arrive at school plays, sporting events, musical performances, or awards ceremonies, saves seats for the others. My husband and my ex have worked together to move furniture, replace a toilet in the children's bathroom, and to set up a schedule for picking the kids up from school. My husband has driven my ex home from the hospital following surgery, and my ex mowed our lawn when my husband was working too many hours to do it himself.

I know our arrangement is not typical. I have had to endure teasing from my sister, who jokingly refers to my "two husbands." I have seen people's quizzical looks at church when we all share a pew. But I really don't care if other people think it is strange for a divorced couple and a new husband to sit together at church. For me, it would be strange for us to not sit together with the children we all love.

Divorce is never easy and we are far from perfect. There are still occasions when we disagree and say or do the wrong things, but, still, we keep trying.

When my daughter was in kindergarten, she had an assignment which involved drawing a picture of something about her that was special. Tears formed in my eyes when the teacher showed me my daughter's drawing: a picture of two stick figure men with the words scrawled in crayon, "I am special because I have two daddies who love me." Whenever a problem comes up in our parenting, I try to remember that drawing and stay focused on what really matters.

Our family does not "do divorce" the same way other people do, but when I look into my children's eyes, I know that I wouldn't have it any other way.

~Nancy Madsen-Ostinato

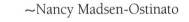

That's Life

© 2005, Mike Twohy.

cartoonistgroup.com

M2Ecomics@aol.com

"We're actually <u>not</u> back together again. We have an open divorce."

The Second Half
of Forever

Change always comes bearing gifts.
~Price Pritchett

I sat staring at the sleek, ten-button office telephone. I couldn't believe it was true. Today was my first day on the job, and just fourteen days earlier Dale and I had received our final divorce decree. We were both still numb with unforeseen pain.

The phone and the divorce demons were both glaring at me — the black monstrosity that was sure to ring at any moment and the stark reality of spending the rest of my life alone. I felt overwhelmed by the many challenges that lay ahead, and prayed I'd be able to get a handle on my life.

Our divorce was an agreeable parting; there just wasn't enough harmony or "glue" for staying together. We hadn't had any arguments or blow-ups to mark our distance from each other; it just seemed that one day the earth heaved, leaving a crevasse at my feet as deep and wide as the Grand Canyon, which then began filling up with pure pain.

We didn't want to be apart but we couldn't stand to be together — somehow that just didn't make any sense to me or to Dale. Together, we asked our marriage counselors, "Why?" Separately, and in individual sessions, we asked the same thing. One therapist waved his notepad in the air and said, "Ride it out, this will all blow over." Well, it didn't "blow over," but it did sweep through the marriage leaving emotional pangs of grief that were much like enduring the physical loss of a loved one.

Dale and I experienced what the marriage counselors, therapists, and anyone else who wanted to throw their opinion into the ring, called a classic case of "growing apart." It seemed like yesterday when we were high school sweethearts and later tying the knot as if we had the world on a string. After a four-year stint in the military, we spent the nickels we'd been rubbing together and bought our first home, which was a small fixer-upper on three acres of farmland in the Seattle suburbs. That's where we raised our two kids in what was close to a picture-perfect life, all the while tilling our huge garden every spring, pressing apple cider every fall, and refurbishing one room of the house every year.

We'd had a lot of good prosperous years together but our attempts to breathe new life into the relationship didn't work. The break-up had blind-sided us both. We were in such distress we couldn't talk about it to our children, friends or families; in fact we could only speak in short spurts with each other about the problems and the parting.

Twenty-five years had flown by. "What happened? What happened to us?" was our cry. The life we had together didn't just involve raising a family; it included growing old together, and enjoying our grandchildren on trips to Disneyland.

As these whirling thoughts were running through my head, a grapefruit-size lump was exploding in my throat and I felt my eyes welling with tears when the inevitable happened.

Ring... ring... ring.... I was quickly jarred back to the present.

I picked up the black contraption as though something was going to jump out and bite me on the lip, and with a voice laden with insecurity I said, "Computing Management Organization, this is Cynthia."

"Congratulations, Grandma!" A booming male voice blurted at me.

"Who is this?" I asked.

"It's me... Dale! I'm calling to let you know that you started a new job today as a grandmother!"

Finally changing gears, I asked. "How did you find me in this sea of people?"

"A stork flew past the delivery room door this morning and dropped off a healthy baby boy with your new work phone number pinned to his blanket," he said laughing.

"Well, congratulations to you too, Grandpa! With the birth of our first grandchild, it makes our divorce seem less final to me and I don't feel so alone. Maybe we can call this new phase of our life the second half of forever," I said.

I could feel him smiling. "I agree wholeheartedly; we had a terrific life. It—and we—just changed... but not together. This grandbaby has put some sweetness back into our lives. Have a good first day on the job, Grandma, and goodbye—only for now."

~Cynthia Briggs

I Have a Step-Wife

Life is mostly froth and bubble,
Two things stand like stone,
Kindness in another's trouble,
Courage in your own.
~Adam Lindsay Gordon

I simultaneously became and acquired a step-wife the day my ex-husband married again. Even though this event occurred over a decade after our own divorce, and quite some time after my own remarriage, we soon discovered its potential for disaster.

Ultimately, the best communication between my step-wife and me was no communication, except through the one person we had in common: my ex, her present husband. At times, I felt sure Jerry Springer or Dr. Phil would call and beg us to appear on their shows. Other days, I prayed eHarmony would consider developing dimensions of compatibility for step-wives and step-husbands.

For a few years, our unspoken agreement to remain politely civil at family occasions that required our mutual attendance served us well. For the sake of the children, we'd continue to maintain this acquired grace in one another's presence for as long as necessary—or until one of us moved to Mars.

I could not have predicted two uninvited, unyielding, and entirely unexpected females who would alter the course of our lives. Hurricanes Katrina and Rita not only changed physical landscapes, but relational ones as well.

My husband, Ken, my twenty-four-year-old daughter with Down syndrome, Sarah, and I left our home five days after Hurricane Katrina struck. Although our home was relatively undamaged, the business that employed my husband was barely recognizable. In the weeks that followed, my ex and my step-wife offered us financial help, rearranged their schedules so that they could help with Sarah, and blessed us with the assurance that they would take her for as long as it took us to resettle. During one of the times my step-wife and I were meeting for a Sarah drop-off, my step-wife slipped money into my hand, refusing to take it back. Her kindness humbled and overwhelmed me.

By September, we had decided to move to Lake Charles, three hours away from our former home. Because my husband was still roving to find jobs and I was living with friends, Sarah stayed in Texas with her father. The day I was to report to my new job, Ken and I woke to the news that Hurricane Rita was on her way.

Not only did we have to evacuate, so did the cities where my ex-husband, my step-wife, Sarah, my son and daughter-in-law, and my four-month-old granddaughter lived. At the time, it looked as though Rita was heading straight for them. Evacuations, now with heightened seriousness because of Katrina, meant that traffic clogged streets faster than cheesecake clogs arteries. A typical three-hour drive home — now ironically a safe place for us to go — ended almost seven hours later.

I was safe, but the rest of my family was not. In Texas, my son and his family spent three hours to reach my ex, his dad, who lived less than an hour away. They all had to reach safety, but how? During the long hours we were being pummeled by Katrina, I prayed and begged God to forgive my stupidity for having stayed. Before Rita made landfall, I once again begged God, but this time to protect my family in Texas who might not be able to find a way out.

Step-wife to the rescue. One of her clients sent his private plane to pick up my family and fly them to safety. My gratitude for her, once again, overwhelmed me. Even two years later, I feel my throat tighten when I recall how they were protected, as if God had sent angels to scoop them up.

Katrina and Rita were devastating forces whose aftermath is still evident today. For all their physical brutality, however, they destroyed an emotional wall that needed to be razed to the ground. I learned, from those two powerful females, that two other equally strong women could survive.

I learned that being and having a step-wife can result in miracles.

~Christa B. Allan

25

Full Circle

No love, no friendship, can cross the path of our destiny
without leaving some mark on it forever.
~Francois Mocuriac

When he said, "You only have one first love," I knew exactly what he meant. In fact, it was my first love who said it when we had lunch last week to celebrate his sixtieth birthday.

We had met in Sister Helen Marie's first grade class. Our paths hadn't crossed in kindergarten because he attended the morning session. I'd been an afternoon student. He lived two blocks from school and was a walker. I rode the big yellow bus.

Sister assigned our desks according to height. Being short, I was in front. He was tall and sat toward the back. We were both in the A reading group and he always chose the seat next to mine. One morning, he slid his arm across the back of my chair and kept it there. "I can hear those wedding bells now," Sister said, looking over the top of her wire-rimmed glasses. I blushed.

He and his buddies rode their bikes to my house and we played tag, kick the can, or hide-and-go-seek. When my girlfriends came over, they often dared me to call him on the telephone. Nice girls weren't supposed to phone boys, but we did it anyway. If a mother answered, we always hung up. Once, my Mom invited him to dinner. She set the table with the company plates and made chow mein—a dish he wasn't fond of, I found out years later. He'd eaten it to please my mother.

Between fifth and sixth grades, his family moved to a suburb too far away for him to ride his bike to my house. I knew he'd find another girl to sit close to in class at his new school.

The next year, my family moved to the opposite side of the city. I found a new sweetheart. But I never forgot my first love.

The summer between my junior and senior years of high school, a friend talked me into taking Latin II in summer school. A boy in the class knew my first love. I told him to say hello for me. Not long after that, our doorbell rang. "Someone's here to see you," my mother hollered down to the rec room.

He was standing inside the back door with a big grin on his face. He'd ridden all the way to my house on a motor scooter.

We eloped when we were college freshmen. We were too young to know what marriage entailed, but we longed to be together. Ours was an on-again-off-again kind of union. We loved each other, but weren't grown up enough to handle everything that went along with marriage. After twenty years, we found ourselves on opposite sides of the city once again. We barely spoke during the following twenty.

When I called to wish him happy sixtieth birthday and invite him to lunch, I was surprised—but pleased—that he said yes. It was a true reunion. We gabbed about old school friends, our sisters and brothers, our children and grandchildren, too. We talked about the people who loved us now, whom we loved in return. But as he said, you only have one first love.

And mine could always make me laugh. He could make me cry, too, and that's what he did last week. The sweet type of tears in your eyes when you realize the mean feelings you had for each other have passed, and you can move forward as friends. Not the pal you'd double date with at the drive-in, but the friend who shares the same grandchildren.

As we left the restaurant, he put his arm across my shoulder and said goodbye. I looked up at him and saw a glimmer of my first-grade classmate. My very first love.

~Andrea Langworthy

26

Graduating with My Three Husbands

A college graduation has its challenges for the multi-wed-ded. Eternal optimist that I am, I've been married three times and my daughter, Eden, has had a loving relation-ship with each of her father figures. So naturally, I expected them to all show up at the graduation dinner James and I were hosting. What a good sport he was about including my two ex-husbands.

A June night found me at a restaurant talking to Tim, ex-hus-band No. 1 (and Eden's biological father) who came with his mother, Winnie. It had been twenty-three years since our divorce, and now Tim was considering another go at love. Sharing a picture of his girl-friend, he said, "We're talking about getting married."

"Wow. Congratulations!" I said.

Keith, ex-husband No. 2, arrived with his girlfriend, Dina. I noted how his red flannel shirt and jeans contrasted with our dressy evening apparel. He is, and always has been, the rebellious criminal lawyer.

Keith tapped my shoulder and I turned, startled. "Hey, you made it!"

"Of course.... You remember Dina?"

Nicely attired, Dina radiated a classy friendliness. We embraced like old friends.When Eden walked in, her eyes widened in joy and she grabbed us all in a group hug, "I'm so happy you're all here!"

Chic in a black cocktail dress, Eden's open back artfully centered her Capricorn tattoo. Red rhinestone pins clipped back her dark wavy hair. Vampy.

Brandon, her boyfriend, looked brave. Consider the poor twenty-one-year-old consort meeting three dads and Eden's mother for the first time. Could you blame him for saying, "Gin and tonic, please?"

My three marriages were flying discreetly under the radar until Grandma Winnie insisted on snapping photos in front of the entire restaurant. How many combinations can you come up with?

Tim, Eden, and Winnie

Keith and Eden

Dina, Keith, and Eden

Tim and Eden

James and Eden

James, Eden, and me

Then Winnie said, "Now I want a picture of the original family."

Clenching my grin, I posed with Tim and Eden. This led to Keith's request for one of himself, Eden and me.

Honestly, how does Elizabeth Taylor do it? It's exhausting.

Ordering food was good for fifteen minutes of animation.

"I hear the swordfish is great!"

"Ooh, they have lamb."

"I can't eat prawns."

At the other end of the table, James talked about science. Bio-dad Tim probed Brandon's ambitions, while Eden nodded encouragement to her champion. Winnie peppered the air with non sequiturs.

Once dinner orders were taken, quiet ensued.

Keith suddenly directed his attention to Brandon. "So... where did you say you're from?"

"Flint, Michigan."

Keith said, "Well, a lot of people don't know where that is, but I do."

"Yeah, it's way out there," admitted Brandon.

Dina stepped in, "So, Eden says you like music."

"Yeah."

"What kind of instrument do you play?"

"All kinds. I can play anything."

"Really! What's your favorite instrument?"

"No favorite, I like them all. I can play them all."

"The piano?"

"Well, no. Not the piano."

Silence.

"Toasts! Toasts!" screamed Winnie.

Regrouping, Keith said, "I propose a toast to Eden. Congratulations on your graduation. We are proud of you. A job well done."

Cheers and clinks.

Tim raised his glass. "Eden, I love you with all my heart and we are so proud of your achievement."

Eden looked radiant with the fanfare.

Then Grandma gushed, "Mamma! Now it's Mamma's turn!"

I had memorized my toast a year ago. Dramatic pause.

"Your degree does not define you. What we all want for you will not define you. How you handle the challenges that will come to you will tell us who you are. And if history is any indicator, you will never disappoint."

Approving murmurs.

The food arrived amid lively camaraderie. We heard about the latest in the law from Keith, and what was new in the world of viruses from James. Asia was a hotbed of new architecture, according to Dina, and Eden fended off all attempts to share memories of her childhood with Brandon.

During dessert, James offered his toast, "Eden, we see you now, and you are beautiful. You've always made us proud. And a special toast to Brandon, because it took a lot of guts for him to come here tonight and deal with all of us."

We laughed at our bond. Weathered warriors, we knew what lay beyond the door for our little girl: the real world. School had been her cocoon and soon she would fly free.

Suddenly, our butterfly took us by surprise. Eden's red fingernails held her Merlot up high.

"Now... I want to make a toast. Thank you to my mom and James, for hosting this dinner. And thank you all for coming. This evening is very, very special to me. My entire family is here, and it means so much to have you all together at one table."

Eden's voice cracked. "I love you all and I know what it took for all of you to be here today. I will always remember this night."

James's eyes went shiny. Tears rolled down my face. Dina sniffled. Tim smiled and Winnie blurted out, "Honest to goodness, you're just like me!"

We collectively sighed. Never before had this group assembled in the same room. Chances were against a repeat performance, but for Eden, we had put aside our pride, our fears and our versions of what happened when. This night was our own milestone in moving forward.

Yes... it was our graduation, too.

~Zoe Alvarez

27

End of the Marriage, not "The End"

It's not only children who grow. Parents do too.
~Joyce Maynard

No sooner had the dust finally settled from our stormy divorce than Ben arrived in Texas from Washington, unannounced, for his first visit with the kids.

I was furious that he hadn't asked if it was a good time, even though it was July—an important time for him and for the kids. In the past, Ben, Grandmom McRae, and our middle child, Sallie, all had celebrated their shared birthday on July 18th as a family.

But this year, it was a really bad time for an unplanned visit.

Still weak following a year of recuperating from emergency surgery, I held down a much-needed job and kept the house running with the children's help. Our oldest daughter and the youngest were out for the day. It was Saturday—the only day Sallie had to prepare for her own unexpected trip.

Our schedule was already nearly impossible. Now this!

I would try to be civil.

Only days before his station wagon appeared unannounced in our driveway, we had found out that Sallie had been offered a full scholarship to a local private preparatory school. An unexpected bonus was a special "bonding" event held every July for all incoming freshmen: She was to leave that Monday for an Outward Bound hiking and camping trip.

When Ben arrived, our home filled with uneasy tension and mixed feelings. I spent the first hour explaining to him why Sallie must leave on Monday, the day after tomorrow, and miss their traditional birthday celebration.

Ben watched her run back and forth between the laundry room and bedroom while I fixed some late lunch. Sallie was holding her wet denim overalls in one hand while checking the list the school had provided to her in the other, when she stopped dead-still and let out a blood-curdling scream.

"Oh no! I've missed the bus!"

Somehow, a page from the previous year's schedule had been added to her trip information packet. The paper in Sallie's hand revealed the correct departure date: not July 12th, but Saturday, July 10th. Today!

At 1:00 P.M. Departing from Greenhill, forty-five minutes away! It was already 1:15.

When we called the school, a contrite and very upset headmaster confirmed that the buses had already left and the drivers weren't scheduled to call in until their arrival at their destination, more than eight hours away! Their first stop would be for supper somewhere in Abilene, 150 miles west.

Ben and I exchanged knowing looks. Without a word, we were a team once more. The only dialogue necessary was to calm our daughter, and let her know what we were about to do. But Sallie was inconsolable, rejecting every assurance that she could still go on the trip, still attend Greenhill, and that we would set this entire matter right for her.

Acutely aware of each other's faults after all those years of marriage, we also knew each other's strengths. Ben, an excellent, responsible driver, would safely deliver our daughter to that bus before it left Abilene—or drive all the way to New Mexico if he had to.

Ben knew I am a resolute, tenacious—okay, stubborn—mother hen. I would get word to the bus driver.

In a daze, Sallie kissed me goodbye. Watching her daddy toss her duffle bag into the back of the car, she shook her wet overalls in the air.

"So, what do I do with these?"

Ben laughed, "Get in, birthday girl. We'll hang 'em out the window!" Sallie giggled, and got in the car.

Breathing a prayer for favor and safety, I dialed the first number before they had left the driveway.

No, the District Highway Patrol Office could not order any vehicle to stop, simply to relay a message.

Westbound Interstate 20, Tarrant County Sheriff...

No.

An hour away, Weatherford Dispatcher. "You want me to do what, lady?"

I took a deep breath, "A school bus headed out on Interstate 20 for New Mexico has left behind a kid in Dallas. I need you to stop either one of two westbound charter school buses. Should be coming through your area right about now..."

"Well... we can try.... Okay, lady... hold on...."

A radio crackled.

"Hold on... an officer tells me they just passed him. He's in pursuit."

I collapsed on the sofa, while the dispatcher relayed the drama of our family freeway adventure like an enthusiastic sportscaster.

Unable to dispel the image of my heretofore law-abiding ex, barreling past a cop with overalls flying like a wacko flag from the window of that little brown car, I prayed the dispatcher's play-by-play would not include a speeding ticket.

A nervous bus driver faced his own private drama when those dreaded lights appeared in his rear-view mirror. "Yes, officer?"

Message delivered, the officer headed back east with siren screaming.

He spotted the station wagon, made a fast turnaround, pulled Ben over, and told him to ease off the gas pedal. The bus would wait for its passenger at Luby's Cafeteria in Abilene.

Mission accomplished—and with heartfelt thanks to God and to His compassionate guardians of law and children, I hung up the phone.

Sallie released her grip on the overalls to spread them over an empty seat in the bus. Between introductions and amidst gales of laughter prompted by her own dramatized teen view of the play-by-play, she devoured the take-out her new friends had thoughtfully provided. Outward Bound was a grand adventure, in spite of Sallie's spectacular arrival on the prep school scene.

Their hours together on the father-daughter freeway adventure were sweet icing on a quite untraditional birthday celebration.

On Sunday, the rest of us helped their father celebrate again.

And through the loving process of parenting, two people who had sadly discovered they couldn't live together, had at long last, become friends!

~Bettye Martin-McRae

28

Growing Up

*I*t had gotten to the point where my husband and I could barely speak to each other without arguing. This certainly wasn't helping our children—they felt caught in the middle, like they were the cause of our problems. We took care in assuring them that they had nothing do with our fights, but—children being children—they didn't believe us. It was up to us to be adults and parents, to do what was best for us and them.

We agreed that we couldn't stay together as husband and wife, but our children were still young and needed us to be parents—so we would remain friends, and keep our noses out of each other's personal lives.

When we separated, I made sure my husband took with him enough to start his life in comfort: sheets, blankets, pots and pans, and anything else he would need. I only kept one item of his, a heavy winter coat, since I didn't have one of my own. He agreed to pay the rent in our apartment until I could get a job that would pay enough to house, feed, and clothe us.

When we met at the courthouse, all our property had been divided, we had agreed on the child support, he'd pay $125 a month, keep insurance on both boys, and help out with clothing. Visitations would be anytime he wanted. When we sat before the judge without arguing about anything, he almost didn't grant our divorce, since we weren't trying to outdo each other. This wasn't normal! We confounded him further by agreeing to meet for lunch after leaving the courthouse.

After the divorce, my ex lived two blocks from our apartment. I would step outside; watch the boys as they walked that two blocks to see their dad. He would call me when they started back, and we'd both watch as they walked home. If I decided to fix a meal I knew to be his favorite, I'd send one of the boys to invite him for dinner. Many times, if he was taking the boys out to breakfast, he'd invite me to go along. I dated, he dated. In fact, he dated my best friend. We blew some minds by double dating once or twice. Everyone expected explosions, but that never happened.

I finally met a man who loved my children as much as their dad and I did. Still I didn't contemplate marrying Stan until he met my ex. They became good friends. My ex even warned Stan that if he wanted to stay married to me, he'd need to give me lots of room to be me, not to hold on too tight, because I'd bolt like horse that had been bee-stung.

When my ex moved, we moved to the same town too. When the boys played sports, my ex and Stan and I were there. It was so funny—people who knew that my ex was the kids' dad, watched the boys, looked at the two men, then looked at me and wondered. There was a strong family resemblance between both of them and the boys.

When Stan and I moved back to Abilene for better jobs, my ex soon followed. His family lived there too. Fortunately, Stan and I were both welcomed into my ex's family home, just as I'd been when he and I were still married. We were one big extended family and I loved it, since I'd never had the chance to get to know Stan's family.

Years passed, and when my husband's health failed, he had to quit his job at the post office. We moved to Oklahoma and started a business of our own, a charity-based used clothing store. We talked to my ex frequently. His health wasn't that good either and he had no one to take care of him. So we drove to see him and convinced him to move to Oklahoma where our boys and our grandchildren lived, and we could all help take care of him. He even lived with us for a month while he was getting settled.

Through his job, Stan was able to find my ex a really nice apartment. I helped him get his own business started, then introduced him to a friend of mine. They got married several years ago and we're still good friends.

My ex and I divorced over twenty-five years ago but we're still the best of buddies, and never once have we bad-mouthed each other to our children. I freely admitted to our boys that the divorce was mainly my fault; at the time I just wasn't grown up enough to maintain a good relationship. Sure, there were problems on both sides and enough fault to go around, but growing up for me came late in my life. Better late than never.

~Arlene Aoki

29

Unless Death Part Us

*J*used to think the phrase, "'Til death do us part" no longer had meaning once you'd gotten divorced. But ever since my former husband has been in intensive care, those vows have taken on a new meaning.

"Aren't you nice. I would never visit my ex in the hospital," the ICU nurse said during Gary's first week there.

I felt more confused than nice. When my daughter had called and said, "Dad was in a car wreck. He's in the emergency room," I knew what to do. Drive right over. Be there, for my children, for my former spouse, for his wife, Alice. And for me. After all, Gary was one of my first loves, my longest relationship, and the father of my children.

When Gary had to be "coded" and shocked back to life during his second week, I again rushed to the hospital. I sat in the waiting room with Gary's sister, her husband, and my children. We talked about a friend's wedding. What had they served and was the wedding cake chocolate? The conversation skated on the thinnest of ice. Beyond the canapés and chicken mousse, we were waiting, agonizing and wondering: Is Gary all right?

Finally Alice joined us and said Gary was stable. We could take turns going in to see him. My daughters went first. Then I went. The impact was palpable: this strong blustery man who I had known since I was nineteen—now wired to monitors, plugged like a kid with a pacifier to the ventilator. He couldn't talk, couldn't swallow and couldn't raise his head. I felt like I had walked into a sacred forest and seen the grandest, tallest, most venerable tree in the woods—felled.

"I need to see the wife. Are you the wife?" a bearded doctor with a tired voice asked.

"I'll get her." I hurried to the waiting room and beckoned to Alice.

"A doctor wants to talk to you," I said. She nodded and I started to follow her.

"Debbie, will you please stay in the waiting room?" she asked.

I froze, feeling like a child who's just been sent to her room. My face felt brittle; tears betrayed me. I felt hurt... then stupid. What had I been thinking? And what was I doing there? What was my role in all this? I was not the wife, not even some well-defined sibling or some staunch old friend. I was the mother of two of his daughters and I brought with me an uneasy web of history. I was one of the few people who knew Gary first as a poet and philosopher, a dreamer instead of a lawyer. But I had no responsibilities toward keeping him alive. I didn't have to come see him, worry over him, or take care of him.

Yet I felt oddly connected to Gary and to his new family.

I thought back to Gary and Deb, the beamish boy and the gleeful girl, who threw away everything—college, money, sensibility, and approval—to be in love with each other.

The ICU waiting area was now empty of relatives. I walked into Gary's room and slipped my fingers through his. He opened his eyes and squeezed my hand. The ventilator rattled; the heart monitor beeped. I wished I could help him and make all of his suffering end. I remembered advice I'd read: When someone is sick and you don't know how to help—send love. For a sweet moment, I held Gary's hand, like he was a trusting child and I was his temporary guardian. He had been a symbol of survival for me, a person who could solve any problem, save any situation. Now, he was the one who needed saving. I sent him love.

My daughter arrived. I whispered to Gary, "I'm leaving now."

He motioned for me to hand him paper and a marker. "Come back," he wrote.

I smiled. I had never really completely left.

~Anna Bern

30

When He Looked Like James Dean

The past is never dead, it is not even past.
~William Faulkner

When I walked into the foyer of the Little Brown Church for Bob's memorial service, I broke into a delighted, if incongruous, grin. Right at the entrance, my son Steve had posted a blown-up photograph of his dad at age nineteen: Bob, jauntily shrugging into a leather flight jacket, eyes squinted against the smoke from his Corona, looking cool and suave, the pure and perfect embodiment of the early 1950s.

Bob and I had been divorced for nearly twenty-five years. In fact, when Steve had called with the news, I did the math. If we hadn't divorced and we had remained in our genial but increasingly disunited marriage, and if Bob hadn't succumbed to lung cancer, we would have been celebrating our golden anniversary on June 18th.

Steve had already been to see his stepmother, whom Bob had wed once our divorce was final. There would be a memorial service in Long Beach, Steve said, and I would be welcome.

Though I'd not seen Bob since I had remarried five years earlier, I had continued to send birthday and Christmas cards, just as I'd always done. And I was aware of his many hospitalizations and painful decline. I knew that over the past couple of years, Bob had lost nearly seventy pounds, walked hesitatingly with a cane, and had looked closer to eighty-five than his actual age of seventy-three.

A career police officer, even after retirement Bob had remained active with the Southern California Juvenile Officers Association and the local Twelve Step program he had lead for decades. So I found it tough to picture how his deteriorating health had laid siege to his lifelong robust appearance.

Now, as I stared at the photo of the Bob of my youth, I recalled how we met. At seventeen in 1954, I had been the editor of the Compton College Tartar Shield; and Bob, a Korean War vet, was going to school on the GI Bill and taking a photography course. The photo lab was housed in the journalism building, so Bob used to joke about trying to lure me into the darkroom.

I took my seat in the chapel, and listened attentively as my son welcomed the crowds of people who had come to celebrate his father's life. Steve talked about finding the photo of his dad, and how he was astonished to discover how cool his dad had been in his youth, and how it was difficult for him to recognize that his dad had once looked like James Dean. The audience chuckled.

Steve talked a little more about his memories of his dad, and how his father had been smart enough to marry not one, but two bright and clever women. The audience laughed again, and I heard somebody in the back whisper, "I wonder if Terri is here."

Others stepped forth to relate their appreciative memories. As they talked, I reflected silently on how our divorce indeed had opened doors for both of us. Bob had found a more compatible woman, one who shared his interests, which involved police work and recovery programs, right in the town where he had been born.

Our divorce had freed me to seek and accept challenging new jobs. I joined the Peace Corps and went to see the world. I had heard gray wolves howl on the spring equinox in Mongolia, stared down a baby octopus while snorkeling in the warm Indian Ocean waters of the Seychelles, dined on armadillo at Macy's Café in Belize City and seen the Toledo, the castle in Spain I had dreamed of since childhood.

Whenever I returned to Southern California, Bob would take me to lunch and we would reminisce. He was content and fulfilled, and encouraged me in my adventures.

Steve asked if anybody else wanted to speak. I rose and approached the dais, and heard somebody say, "Why... it's Terri."

"With the exception of his niece, I have known Bob longer than anybody here today," I began. Then I told of our first encounter. I had exited from a rigorous Western Civilization test in late 1954, to find Bob standing outside the classroom door. He gave me a wolf whistle. Gratefully, I walked over and said, "That cheered me up." I stood on tiptoe and pecked his cheek. Bob had grinned and said, "If I get that for a whistle, I'm going home to get my bugle." The audience roared.

I picked up where my son had left off, recounting some of his father's earlier achievements, how he had been the quintessential optimist—and yes, as Steve had said—how his dad had been cool. "I'm happy to say," I concluded, gesturing towards the photo, "that I knew Bob Elders when he looked like James Dean."

Upon my return to Northeast Washington a few days later, I went to a local nursery and found an Abelia shrub named Golden Anniversary. Bob and I had been married for twenty-five years and had remained friends for an additional twenty-five. That chilly April afternoon, I planted the Golden Anniversary for us.

~Theresa Elders

31

Christmas Lights

The guardian angels of life fly so high as to be beyond our sight,
but they are always looking down upon us.
~Jean Paul Richter

*J*d had a fight with my husband. I don't remember what it was
about, but it was one of those big, nasty fights that made me
question whether or not I should have married him. He's my
third husband, by the way. His name is Xavier. He's one of the most
incredible people I'd ever had the privilege to know, and I felt blessed
to find him after my first two marriages had failed. I believed he was
my destiny, my first marriages being just practice for this—my one
true love. So, it is particularly upsetting having big, nasty fights with
him, because it makes me feel like I'm just not meant to be happily
married.

I was lying on the couch, trying to rest after a long, sleepless
night. It was already after noon, and I had not slept. My eyes were
red and swollen from hours of tears that just would not stop. I lay
there, staring blankly at the TV screen that still hadn't been turned
on, when suddenly I received a visit from my first husband. My dead
husband. Yes, yes... I know what you're thinking. I've had my share
of nut-jobs claiming to have seen angels. But once in a while, a sane
person comes along with a really spooky story, and, hey, wouldn't it
be cool if it were really true? Maybe, maybe not: that's always been
my attitude. No judgment, no faith—just hope.

My dead husband, Scott, had been my high school sweetheart.

We were together for twelve years, married for six. We were great friends. I thought, truly, that we would be together forever. Then things started to fall apart. Long story short: we simply got married too young. We loved each other very much, but it wasn't really "marriage" love, but "friendship" love. It's hard to know the difference at that age. He died three years after our divorce. I'd been told he had never really gotten over me.

Anyway... here I was, lying on the couch thinking about what I was going to do. Thinking about my marriage. Thinking about my failures.

"No relationship is perfect. You need to take the good with the bad, but pay more attention to the good." That's what he said to me. I didn't hear it with my ears; I certainly didn't have a vision of him sitting at my feet. I just sort of felt his thoughts in my head.

"Scotty, is that you?" I asked.

"Yeah," I seemed to feel him answer.

"Is that really you?" Was this real? Or was it just that I knew him so well that I knew what he would have said had he still been alive and talking to me. How could I be sure? Was it a dream? Had I, in my exhaustion, fallen asleep for a moment without realizing it?

Scott seemed to be gone from my head. My rationale had pushed him out.

"Are you still there?"

"Yes," the answer came instantly.

"Can you give me a sign?" I knew it was silly to ask. God doesn't give signs. You're not supposed to ask God for signs. He doesn't like it. He wants you to have faith. If God doesn't give signs, why should I think Scott could? Well, it certainly couldn't hurt to ask, could it?

I was trying to remain relaxed, to allow the thoughts to flow with ease into my willing mind. I was sure that was the key: relax. Let it come. Let it in. Welcome it.

Christmas lights! In my mind, I saw Christmas lights. Big Christmas lights, strung along the edge of a big picture window. Like the ones from when I was a little girl, the size of eggs—red, green, blue, and yellow, strung upon a green electrical cord. If one bulb went out, the whole string went out, and it could take hours to find which one was the culprit. You'd better make sure your test bulb was good, or you'd be in for a kind of mind-numbing frustration that is completely unsuited to the spirit of Christmas.

Well, that's odd, I thought. It's summer, for Pete's sake. It's ninety-eight degrees outside. Christmas lights? What does it mean? Is Xavier going to hang big Christmas lights this December? I know he doesn't care for the dainty white mini lights we have now. Do I have to wait till Christmas to know I'm not nuts? Maybe I should write this down. I'll never remember at Christmas. And I can't tell Xavier. I don't want to taint things by putting the idea in his head.

But what if it is true? What if Xavier hangs big Christmas lights this year, and I tell him that I knew he was going to do that because back in July my dead husband told me that he would. I need to write this down now, so I have proof, seal it in a dated envelope. Oh, this is just silly.

I put the idea out of my head and went on with the rest of my day. Xavier and I kissed and made up and decided to go out for dinner to help put things behind us. A new sports bar had just opened in town. We'd never been before. Chicken wings and beer sounded like just the ticket to lift us out of this bad place.

We sat down at one of the glossy lacquered tables. I was still feeling sullen and quiet. We still hadn't spoken much. I looked around at the scenery: the beer posters, the TV sets in each corner broadcasting sports, the waitresses in their skimpy orange shorts with control pantyhose underneath, the patrons, mostly men in baseball caps drinking beer. I looked out the window into the parking lot and something caught my eye. Around the large picture window was strung a row of large Christmas lights. The big kind like from when I was little. Festive for any occasion: Christmas, a sports bar, whatever!

Thank you, Scotty.

I looked across the table at my beautiful husband. Tears were welling up in my eyes once again as I remembered those words: Take the good with the bad, but pay more attention to the good. I always wanted to believe that Scott was my guardian angel, that he is the one who found Xavier for me because he knew we would be good together.

"What's the matter now?" Xavier asked me.

"Nothing." I smiled. "I just love you."

"I love you, too."

~Lynn Berroteran

32

Divorce is Not an End

$\mathcal{I}$t was ten o'clock on Sunday morning when the phone rang. "You guys up for breakfast?" the voice on the other line asked. "I'm going to Peggy's for breakfast and was wondering if you guys want to come."

"Sure," I answered and then turned over to hand Mark the phone. "It's Pop, he wants to go to breakfast," I told him. "I'll go wake Jessica up and get ready. You should too." Mark and Pop spoke for another five minutes, and then Mark also got up to get ready.

In less than an hour, we were at Peggy's for a late breakfast. The conversation turned to the usual topics: our daughter Jessica's drama in high school, her boyfriend, her friends, my family, Pop's family, and Mark's family. When breakfast was over, the waiter came with the bill and placed it on the table. Pop was about to pick up the bill when Mark quickly grabbed it. "I'll get this, Pop," he said and handed the waiter his credit card. "It's your turn next time, Dad," the waiter jokingly told Pop. We all looked at each other and laughed. We knew exactly what the waiter was thinking. This is not the first time that Pop's been mistaken as Mark's father—or mine. He definitely can pass as a father to either one of us. He is sixty-two, Mark is forty-four, and I am thirty-seven. I know there is nothing peculiar about mistaking Pop as our father because of his age—what people find peculiar is when we tell them that Pop is my ex-husband. People find it either amazing that we all get along or they find it totally strange.

For me, it's neither strange nor amazing. Although I cannot say we were free from the grief of divorce, it certainly was amicable. The first few years were the most challenging for both of us. He had a hard time letting go and did everything he could to make me change my mind. I was resistant and not willing to give in at all. It was not until after Mark and I started dating that Pop finally realized it was over between him and me. Although he never blamed Mark for our separation, seeing me with Mark made him believe that I had moved on and there was no turning back.

It's been almost ten years since Pop and I separated. A lot of things have changed since then, but one thing that remains is our successful relationship. I believe the reason for this success stems from having respect and the trust that we will be there for each other, even though we are no longer married. Added to this is our love for Jessica and wanting to make sure she is not affected in any negative way by the divorce. Having Mark for a husband is also a plus. He came into the family with an open mind and accepted Pop as a part of it.

This is what I had envisioned and had asked of God when I made my decision to leave Richard, who we dearly call "Pop." I knew at the time, that even though I wanted a divorce, I still wanted him to be a part of my life and my family. Divorce doesn't need to be the end of a relationship or destroy a family unit. Even after divorce, trust and respect between two people can remain intact as long as both parties are willing to work on it and concentrate on what is good, which in our case is Jessica.

~Clarissa Moon

Divorce
and
Recovery

A Broken Family
but Not Broken Hearts

*If the family were a fruit,
it would be an orange,
a circle of sections, held together but separable —
each segment distinct.
~Letty Cottin Pogrebin*

33

Loving Your Way Through Divorce

You should respect each other and refrain from disputes;
you should not, like water and oil, repel each other,
but should, like milk and water, mingle together.
~Buddha

My parents were married for fifty-eight years. When I got married, I figured my marriage would run a similar lifelong course. I could not imagine that I would ever divorce. I believed that couples rode out the hard times until the good times returned. So when my wife Helen told me she wanted a divorce, I was shocked.

Like many other men I have come to know, I didn't have a clue that there was anything wrong with our marriage. I routinely worked twelve to fourteen hour days, trying to make ends meet. When I would come home, I'd have nothing left to give. I'd have dinner, watch *Star Trek*, and go to bed. I was seldom angry or unkind. I was never verbally abusive, dishonest, or unfaithful. I just wasn't there. To me, winning at work was everything. I didn't understand how precious my relationship with Helen was until it was too late. I woke up to the problem only after she said "I don't want to be married to you any more."

That was about five years ago. Helen and I have since been in therapy. We tried dating. We separated. We did the things couples do

to their preserve marriages. Making it work was all the more important because we had two young daughters who were five and three
at the time.

I learned to listen. I discovered what was really important to her.
What colors she liked, what movies were her favorites, what her dress
and shoe size were. I became a student of Helen's interests—but it
was too late. Oh, she had given me plenty of warnings; asking me to
make more time for her and the girls, asking me to be more romantic
and spontaneous, or simply being more affectionate without it being
a prelude to sex. I never thought she would leave me.

Despite our prolonged effort, we divorced. Although we failed
to keep our marriage intact, we have progressed in other ways. We
quite unexpectedly became friends. We support each other. We rarely
hug—unless we are in one of those overwhelming moments in life
when we do what all good friends do. Then we will embrace and offer
a few comforting words of comfort and consolation.

Our divorce settlement has no agreements around money or
custody. We didn't want the courts to dictate what our obligations are
to each other or where our duties lie. Instead, we agreed to continue
to work as partners on issues related to property, finance, and our
girls, in much the same way as we have done for the past five years,
one step at a time. We sit down and talk. We remain committed to
each other in these respects and give paramount importance to our
daughters' well-being. We have agreed to always put our children
first.

About ten months ago, we decided it would be better for our
girls if we moved to the Midwest where my extended family resides.
Helen, who grew up in San Francisco, had come to love the Midwest
and my family (four brothers and sisters, ten nieces and nephews)
over the course of many summer visits. We decided to join forces
in this move. Though separated for three years, we agreed that we
would make the move and live together as housemates for eight to
twelve months, after which time I would find my own place. Such
an arrangement would be easier for our girls, make finding new jobs
less stressful, and certainly mitigate the impact on our finances. My

brother said, "Some people might look at what you're doing and think it's weird, but that's only because it looks strange to them. It shouldn't be the exception, it should be the norm."

Our relationship didn't die in a day and it wasn't rebuilt in a day. During the difficult early days of our separation, I told Helen, "When our girls grow up, or change or disappoint me, I will not become less committed to them. Why should I be less committed to you because you have grown and changed?" Divorce need not end a promise to remain committed to another's happiness. Now, what defines our new relationship is this aspect of lifelong commitment. It is this value that has guided us through this complicated transition.

Since returning to the Midwest, all four of us often have dinner together. We talk about school, friends, work, and what's going on in our lives. Not surprisingly, my youngest daughter, Mary, asked one night, "How come you guys aren't romantic any more?" We told her that we still love each other and will be her mom and dad forever, but that we aren't married anymore. She is only seven, so the answer was enough to address her question. But her comfort came not so much from our words, but from the actions she sees: her mom and dad loving and respecting each other. We are teaching our daughters love.

~Steve Hern

34

Trading Places

Better to bend than break.
~Scottish Proverb

"Don't you love Dad?" my six-year-old daughter asked softly. Bulls-eye, I thought. Aster's brave question merited all the honesty I could muster.

"No, I don't anymore, Sweetie," I replied, as gently as I could. With her baby face already streaked with tears, she burst into more gut-wrenching sobs. Her dad and I had just broken the news of our pending separation to her and her brother and sister.

"Mom, I know it's you," Aster pleaded. "Please don't do this to me now. I'm too young." She was right. As the spouse who initiated the separation and ultimate divorce, I bore the burden of the decision. Now, it stuck in my throat like a lozenge that refuses to melt.

I remember wiping the tears off Aster's face as we snuggled on her Little Mermaid bedspread, her head of tousled blond curls tucked under my chin. We stayed that way for two hours or more. Aster was inconsolable; no amount of hugging or kissing could diminish her pain.

This was excruciating—harder than telling my husband I wanted to separate, harder than knocking on my lawyer's door the first time, harder than almost anything I had ever done in my forty-six years on this earth.

Like so many couples, my ex-husband, Glenn, and I had a bad marriage but a good divorce. Our wise family therapist, a gentle Israeli woman, had counseled that our kids should not pay the price of divorce. We, the parents, should move heaven and earth to make it easier on our kids.

Acting on her suggestion, we decided to go where few divorcing couples had gone before. Instead of our children (then eleven, nine, and six) being shuttled between two households, Glenn and I would be the ones to switch places. Our therapist cautioned that this unorthodox arrangement would demand flexibility and an enormous amount of trust. Despite being a divorced couple, we are blessed with both.

Twice every month, I stuff my green Samsonite with my journal, Natalie Merchant CDs, and my cell phone charger before I head for Glenn's lakefront apartment in Chicago.

My ex-husband packs his briefcase and suits, and moves into our suburban apartment for five days. Instead of missing birthday parties, soccer games and babysitting jobs, our children stay firmly planted in their own home.

It wasn't always this easy. For the first six months after our separation, our three kids did the every-other-weekend shuffle. Going to Dad's meant sacrificing huge chunks of their lives. While they loved the city, they hated being away from their friends. For his part, Glenn would wrack his brain trying to plan field trips to please all three. But how many times can you visit the Lincoln Park Zoo with two teens and a preteen in tow?

After a few months of this trying script, we opted for us doing the switching. Now their dad could more fully participate in their lives. Our older daughter, Abby, can see a movie with friends, Aaron can toss a football with his classmates, and Aster can work with Dad to recreate the solar system with Styrofoam balls.

As for me, I can have my lakefront hideaway from which to launch my urban adventures. I can go biking (yes, I even use Glenn's bike), see a foreign film, or browse through a bookstore.

My friends understand, but divorced acquaintances sometimes shake their heads in disbelief.

"I could never do that," one divorced father of two admitted. "I would never trust my ex-wife in my place."

We recognize this may change when and if we find new partners. But we will cross that proverbial bridge when we come to it. For now, it works—beautifully.

I guess we're just lucky, but our kids are the luckiest of all.

Five years into our divorce, we continue to trade places. Funny thing, I am composing these very words in my ex-husband's apartment.

~Marcy Darin

A Mother Bear in Court

There are only two lasting bequests we can hope to give our children.
One is roots; the other, wings.
~Hodding Carter

On a gray March day, my world fell apart.

A police summons brought me to the door. Because I am visually impaired, I listened as a friend read the message that my ex wanted custody of our twins, Jason and Jeremy. In numb disbelief, I wondered how this could be happening. I had wanted my relations with my ex to be friendly for the sake of the boys. I paced the floor and cried. How would our two ten-year-old boys go through something like this? I had to get control of my emotions. The boys would be home from school soon. How was I going to break this news to them?

All evening my head hurt from trying to hold back tears. I struggled to find a way of approaching the subject. Finally, sitting on the edge of their bunk bed, I kept my voice steady and plunged in.

"Your dad wants you to come live with him."

"I like it here, Mom," Jason voiced. "I've got friends and I want to be with you."

"I don't mind visiting Dad, but I don't want to live with him," Jeremy added.

Ben, my oldest son, had come in the room and was listening.

A Mother Bear in Court: A Broken Family but Not Broken Hearts   117

"My friend went through this. It takes a long time in the court," he said. "By then you'll be older—like me—and then you can decide where you want to live."

"Dad's going to court?" Jeremy questioned.

"Yes," I answered hesitantly.

"You won't leave us... will you, Mom?" Jason asked.

The pleading in his voice tore at my heart. Shivers went up my back. "Of course, I won't leave either of you." I kissed them both. "We'll find a way to work it out."

I wished I felt as confident as I sounded.

We went on with our daily lives pretending nothing more would happen. This worked well until the letters started coming.

One afternoon, when the boys burst through the door from school, they were arguing.

"I don't want to sort the mail. It's your turn, Jeremy."

"I did it yesterday. It's your turn."

Jason reluctantly picked up the pile of mail and thumbed through it. He groaned. "Mom, another big, fat letter from the court. It seems like we get one every day. I hate coming home from school to read this bad stuff about you."

I felt a twinge of guilt because I couldn't read the papers myself to spare my children such trauma. Little boys shouldn't have to be subject to a tug of war like this, a nightmare that would take two and a half years to resolve. It was a cause I had not asked for, but I had to fight for my kids and their wishes.

Jason read some of it to himself. "Mom, this is junk. The attorney says that Dad is trying to get us away from you because you're blind and not a fit parent." He threw his arms around me. "Mom, you're the best ever. You give us everything we need and work hard for us. I love you Mom."

"Dad can't take us away from you even if you don't see very well. You take good care of us."

I thought about their comments while I helped them with their homework. I needed to believe them myself.

Later, I heard them playing happily outside. I walked around the tidy living room, folded their clean fresh laundry and smelled the meatloaf cooking in the oven. A sense of warmth overcame me as I looked at the pictures of my twins, which I could see if I put them close to my eyes. I would show the court my ability to function successfully as their mom. I would keep giving the boys all I had. I wouldn't let anyone break me or make me feel incompetent, I resolved.

The first time I sent them to visit their dad after this battle started almost broke me. The evening before they left, I jumped on the trampoline and played croquet as well as baseball with them. I was thankful I could see a little out of the corner of one eye. I wanted to engrave their images in my mind. I feared having them go to their dad's, afraid they wouldn't come back.

I attempted to be brave as I held them tightly before they got on the plane. My throat ached from keeping back the tears.

"My boys, take care—I'll miss you," I whispered.

"Mom, we'll be good," Jeremy reassured me. "And we'll come home soon," Jason added.

Back at home, in their rooms, I clung to their baseball caps and wept. I clutched their baby books to me. If only I could turn the clock back to when I rocked them in my arms. I smiled as I recalled the only way I could tell them apart as babies was to feel their heads. One had hair and the other didn't. I went over to touch Jason's football trophy and "Best Swimmer" patch. I felt Jeremy's achievement award and winning pine-wood derby car. Pride washed through me.

A week later, I welcomed them home with a lingering embrace, a plate of cookies with milk, and a big banner. While we snacked, the boys talked about their visit.

Jason said, "We had fun." Then he admitted with trepidation, "Mom, Dad says that one of these days we're going to live with him."

"I don't want to go!" Jeremy ran from the table and slammed the door.

"I'm gonna go hit some balls around." Jason headed outside.

I sighed. The only thing I could do was be there for my boys and make a safe haven for them to come home to. I would never again take for granted cheering for them in a sports event, having a birthday party, or attending a parent teacher conference—just in case it might be the last one. I would cherish playing basketball with them and tucking them into bed, because I didn't know if I would lose having these precious moments with them.

My mind flooded with memories: Jason as pitcher and Jeremy as catcher in the same game. I couldn't see them on the field, yet my sight impairment didn't stop me from yelling the loudest, after someone informed me of the plays. I remembered sleeping under the stars with them, being at the crossroads to hear about their day, playing red rover with them and their friends. The list went on and on. I would treasure them all and make the most of every second with them.

Finally the week in court arrived. I longed for it to end—yet I dreaded the outcome.

When it was my turn to testify, I approached the witness stand with determination. My nails dug into my hands. No one knew how my pulse quickened and my stomach knotted. I had to take in slow breaths and repeat over and over, "You're fighting for your boys because they want to live with you."

I prayed for calm assurance as I spoke with confidence, grateful I couldn't see the audience clearly.

I held my own even though the judge interrogated me.

"Please let Jason and Jeremy have a say in their future," I implored. "It may affect their whole lives. They've already been through enough."

The last day of the trial, the judge asked Jeremy and Jason to meet with him in his chambers.

"Don't worry Mom," Jeremy said quietly.

"We'll be okay," Jason added.

They had been brave troopers through the whole ordeal.

When the judge returned to the courtroom, he said that he had a weighty decision on his hands. He hoped to be able to sleep at night knowing he'd done what was best for the twins. It impressed me that he had listened to my sons. This was all I ever asked for. He sent the boys home with me.

I know it was God's miracle that we won—with the aid of Jason and Jeremy. They had declared boldly, "If we have to live with our dad we'll run away and become delinquents." A video showing the boys and my bonding must have reached the judge. The stirring testimony stating that it would be in the best interest of the boys to remain with their mother might have helped sway the judge.

Elated and relieved, I left the courtroom and didn't look back. The twins, their siblings, and I enjoyed a party together. We all felt free and spontaneous again. Jason and Jeremy held onto me like they'd never let me go. I clung to them also, my eyes moist. "I'm glad you get to stay with me in our home," I exclaimed.

"We knew we'd win if we stood up for ourselves and our mom," Jason piped up. "I'm glad the judge asked us what we wanted," Jeremy reflected.

Our ordeal would soon be over, but the boys and I would never forget it. What did I learn from one of the most horrific trials I'd endured? Perseverance, love between a mother and her sons, and trust in God. A mother will fight for her kids like a bear does for her cubs. And the children will lead the way.

~Pam Bostwick

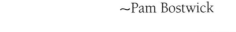

The "D" Word

Sometimes you can tell that your parents are going to get a divorce. All that fighting turns to calm, because they know that soon they will not have to put up with one another anymore. Sometimes you can't tell; it just pops out of nowhere. I was one of the fortunate ones because I knew that my parents were discussing the divorce. So when "the talk" rolled around, I was more prepared than some kids are.

Ever since I could remember, my parents fought about everything. I think we used to be one happy family, but that was so long ago I don't remember. When my parents told my brother and me to come downstairs so they could talk to us, I wasn't really worried. I had been getting good grades; I didn't do anything that bad… so it had to be about something else. Then it hit me… "Divorce!"

My parents did their best to make it sound like a good thing. But losing my mom wasn't a good thing at all. I thought I would lose my dog too, so I started crying as my dad talked on and on. I buried my head in my brother's shirt as he just sat there and told me it would be okay. All I could think was how can this be okay? Mom is leaving; my dog Keisha might be leaving. Our family is being destroyed!

They went on talking about why they were getting the divorce, and when things were going to happen. They made it seem so clear, like the pictures you take with a digital camera. But, it wasn't clear to me. The pictures were blurry, and I couldn't figure out why I couldn't take this, even though I suspected that it was coming. But thinking it was coming, and then getting the news full throttle, was entirely different.

A few months passed and they were divorced. My mom started packing her things a few weeks later and tried to find a house, which she did. I had to live with my dad, and still do, until my mom's house remodel is all done. She has been ripped off numerous times, so it isn't going along smoothly. Sometimes I can't handle not seeing my mom, since she and I were—and still are—very close. My brother moved in with my mom because he had problems with my dad and he can help my mom with her remodel.

I have to admit, it's nice seeing my parents not fighting for a change. When they are together, they are happier and they don't bicker about everything like they used to. So I guess I could say that the divorce was a good thing.

Now, as some of my friends are going through their parents' divorce, I can tell them about my divorce story and try to make them understand that divorce happens for a reason, but it doesn't have anything to do with you. It's not your fault, it's just that your parents can't live together 24/7. But they still love you no matter what. Always remember that they divorced each other, but they did not divorce you.

~Amber Lutz, 14

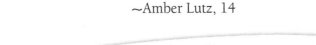

You Can Do This

Storms make oaks take deeper root.
~George Herbert

This was the big year—the year I turned fifty, the year my eighteen-year-old daughter started college, the year my younger daughter entered high school. The year I divorced my husband of nearly twenty years.

I was always a late bloomer. I didn't marry until I was thirty. At twenty-eight, when my mother was still alive, she told me she was worried that I wasn't married. I told her that it wasn't because I had never been asked, but because it had never been a great priority in my life. She passed away the next year, followed by my father five months later. My biggest regret is that my daughters never had the chance to meet them or know what wonderful people they were. They only know them through the photos I've shown, the life lessons that my parents taught me that I have tried to pass on, the silly stories about my childhood, how my parents raised me and my brother and sister, and how much I've missed them throughout all these years.

I had planned my divorce for at least two years before finally deciding the time was right, although it didn't go as smoothly as I thought it would. My husband refused to leave the house for weeks, and the tension became unbearable. I cried myself to sleep thinking about how my thirteen-year-old daughter—who wears her heart on her sleeve and has more compassion than most—would cope with this. When a friend told me her children had stopped talking to her for months because of her divorce, the thought haunted me for days. My older daughter understood completely, my younger felt torn between the two of us.

Finally, as moving day approached, I realized how adaptable kids really are. My thirteen-year-old came up to me and gave me a big hug. "You can do this, Mom," was all she said. And in that moment, I recognized that she understood the pain we had all been going through. Even though our journey was not yet over, I knew it would be all right. I had never given her enough credit for being an incredible person in my world—for her compassion, her strength and her grace.

I was sure of my decision. The struggle is what made us strong.

~Sachiko Iwanaga

38

A True Mother

Gratitude makes sense of our past,
brings peace for today, and creates a vision for tomorrow.
~Melody Beattie

I remember well the day I realized I had a true mother here in the United States, so far from my home in Germany. I had packed the last of the dishes for the move, when she called. Oh no, I thought. I can't talk to her right now. My heart was bleeding and I had no idea how to start a new life with my six children—without my husband. I was sure Grandma Towne would give me a hard time. After all, I was leaving her only son. Maybe I shouldn't say anything. I didn't want to lose her support and friendship. I had already lost so much. But I did tell her.

"Gary and I have separated. I'm filing for divorce."

Silence.

"Are you there, Mom?"

"Yes. I don't know what to say. Are you sure that's the right thing?"

"I've thought and prayed about it. I can't raise the kids with them knowing about the details of our troubled marriage." My voice broke.

"It's all right, Sonja. I understand," Grandma Towne said. "Do you need any help?"

That caught me by surprise. Mom Towne wasn't mad or upset.

Instead, she offered me help. "Sonja? Don't think you are divorcing me, too. If there's anything I can do to help you, I would like that."

Suddenly the sky wasn't as dark. I took a deep breath to steady my voice, but tears rolled down my cheeks, anyway. "Oh, Mom..." I said and couldn't say anything else.

"Why don't you bring the kids? I can keep them until you have your stuff together."

I wiped my eyes with the back of my hand. "That would make it so much easier. And... thanks."

"Everything will turn out okay. The divorce shouldn't make a difference in our relationship. You're like my daughter. Your children are my grandchildren, and that can never be taken from us. Go ahead and bring them. I'll keep them until your summer classes are over." And that's what I did.

Grandma kept the kids at her home in Colorado, while I finished summer courses at the university.

As time passed, Grandma Towne was always there for me. When the engine in my car exploded, she drove three hours to pick me and the kids up, and helped us to find a new car. She came to my graduation and helped me find a good teaching job not too far away. When I got remarried, she embraced my new husband and called him "son," just like she had taken me in as a daughter so many years ago when I had first married her own son.

~Sonja Herbert

39

Breathe

It takes a long time to grow an old friend.
~John Leonard

had to tell myself to keep breathing....

Thirty-one years of marriage ended with a simple signature on a divorce decree.

I can still remember that excruciating feeling of absolute despair, disbelief, hopelessness, and fear. What was I to do now? I was fifty-four years old and alone. I had been a part of a couple for the last thirty-three years of my life.

Well-meaning friends hovered around me, but I felt like closing myself off from the rest of the world. Solitude seemed to be an easier way to get through this, even though it was profoundly contrary to my usual outgoing personality.

I cried endlessly. At any given moment, I could start out with a whimper and end up with full-blown sobbing as I wallowed in my self-pity.

After the divorce, the world seemed filled with joyful couples. Everywhere I went, I saw people who appeared madly in love with each other. It pained me to see their happiness, knowing that my own love story had ended.

During this time, I was fortunate to have the support and love of my two grown sons, one married and one engaged. But, they both lived out of town and had their own emotions to deal with. Everything that they had thought safe and secure had suddenly crumbled before their eyes. My biggest fear for them was that they would lose faith in love and marriage. I was helpless in trying to figure out how to make their pain go away, especially when I was so focused on my own angst.

My ex remarried within a few months of our divorce. I found myself sinking even lower in shock and disbelief. Nothing made sense to me anymore.

I went to the library and checked out every divorce self-help book that I could get my hands on. I pored over them nightly as if the words could somehow heal me. I wanted to find answers to all of the questions swirling around me.

I found myself putting the onus for all of the marital issues and eventual termination of the marriage on my ex-husband. Temporarily, this gave me a false sense of self-worth and faultlessness. My incredibly loving friends supported my anger and grief and gave me permission to believe that the end of our life together was his fault. I clung to this "truth" during those difficult days.

I am not sure when my emotional shift occurred. Maybe it was when I joined an online dating service and saw that I was not alone. Possibly it was when I began to go out with other men again (which was quite daunting for someone who hadn't been on a date in over thirty-three years). Perhaps it was from reading through all the books I had surrounded myself with… or, maybe, I was just tired of being so sad and angry.

Whatever it was, I started looking at things differently. Instead of focusing on the emotional and physical breakdown of my marriage, I began to remember the happy times and priceless years that my ex and I had shared: growing up together, sharing the miraculous joy of starting our family, raising our sons and watching them become incredible young men, moving to our dream house, enjoying our wonderful friends as a social couple, being respected in our community, and… being in love.

It wasn't an easy transition, but it was necessary.

I let go of fear and opened my heart to possibilities. I learned that time was extremely helpful for the healing process. In evaluating my own role in the marriage's demise, I found the courage to face some of my issues with honesty. I found clarity in recognizing the empty loneliness that I had felt in the last few years of my married life but had been too afraid to admit. I began to accept there were going to be some things in life that I would never fully understand. I learned that moving on meant that I could forgive without needing to forget. I felt a sense of renewal as I began to direct my energy toward counting the many blessings and gifts in my life. While I could not change my past, I could look forward to a future filled with love, passion, and joy.

I decided to reach out to my ex-husband as a friend. I realized that one of the greatest gifts that I could give my children was to allow them to see their parents as human beings with flaws. We were not the image of perfection we had tried to portray for so many years. We may have made some mistakes along the way, but our lives together had been authentic and meaningful and good. We would always be family, and that would never change.

I came to accept the fact that my ex and I had simply drifted apart. We were moving in two very opposite directions and looking to the future with very different eyes. I faced the reality that, once our children were on their own, the commonalities needed to sustain a healthy marriage just weren't there. We had outgrown our earlier dreams and needed to pursue our passions individually.

Eventually, I found warm and accepting companionship with a new man in my life. I realized that my journey was full of new beginnings and it felt very liberating and right. Taking one day at a time, I again found laughter in my life and I began to extend myself socially again. For the first time in my fifty-four years, I realized that I was now a grown-up and it wasn't so scary anymore.

Last year, when our first grandson was born, my ex and I found ourselves sharing that indescribable joy of becoming grandparents. As we marveled together at this perfect little baby, our minds went back to the time when we were new parents. This was the circle of life and we would forever be a part of it. We told each other that we would always love one another, but that we probably made better friends than husband and wife.

We hugged and cried and laughed and cried some more... and, I began to breathe again.

~Laurie Max

Patch Work

The practice of peace and reconciliation is one of the
most vital and artistic of human actions.
~Thich Nhat Hanh

I'm a happy, first-time newlywed and the child of two people who, during my life, I've never once seen have a polite conversation with each other. My parents were too young when they married and had me. There's no way their marriage could have ever worked out. I had heard from others, that from the second the minister pronounced them husband and wife, the wedding guests started making bets on how long the union would last. Whoever said about a year or so, won. The only person who didn't win was me—their daughter.

But that's not to say that my parents' catastrophic mistake didn't teach me a lot of important lessons, the biggest of which was that even though players on both sides of the divorce went to sleep at night plotting creative, painful murders for each other, they still loved me. Seeing people, who truly couldn't stand one another, set aside their differences to make me happy helped me grow into an adult who realizes on a broader level that people must be tolerant, forgiving, and make compromises for the greater good of us all. Sometimes that takes a lot of creativity.

When my parents divorced, my mother was only nineteen, and my father was twenty-one. I was barely a toddler. My mother was a high school dropout. She had no life skills, no education, and felt like she had no hope. She lost her trailer home and had nothing but a dead-end waitressing job and a beat-up car that wouldn't go over forty miles an hour. My father moved back in with his parents, where he lived in their basement.

Sadly, circumstances forced my mother to leave me with my father and his parents. Their home had stability, and my grandmother stayed home to watch me every day. Although she was devastated, my mother knew deep down that her child would be better off in that environment. As it was, she worked all the time just trying to satisfy her landlord and put gas in the car. She felt like a failure, and her former in-laws certainly didn't help her self-esteem, because they thought she was an ignorant, trashy, irresponsible girl.

I was allowed to visit my mother two weekends per month, but my grandparents were extremely strict about the visitations. Once, my mother's beat-up car broke down on the way back, and she brought me home two hours late on a Sunday night. My grandparents took her to court and she lost visitation for a whole month. She was desperate and sad. She found a new boyfriend and moved in with him in a little pink house on the beach, which didn't help my grandparents' opinion of her. Now she was living in sin, too.

For my birthday, a relative gave me a teddy bear, but this was not just an ordinary teddy. My Teddy was pure white, like snow—a small polar bear with a purple satin ribbon. Teddy soon became the focus of my world. He was the one constant love I had and was the only thing I could bring back and forth between my two homes.

One morning, I woke up at my mother's house and Teddy was gone. The world had come to an end. I was inconsolable.

My mother eventually located Teddy under the house, no longer white, but now a sodden grey. Mauled by a German Shepherd, Teddy was dead—ears hanging, paws severed, purple satin ribbon chewed ragged. It was horrible. His left eye was so scratched up, he looked like he had cataracts.

I cried all day and refused to let my mother throw Teddy in the trash. Believe me, she tried. She thought I was crazy. Finally, and only because she was terrified I wouldn't love her anymore, she gave in.

"Don't tell Mom-mom that I let this happen," she told me, fearing my grandmother's wrath.

She thought my father's mother, who approved of nothing my mother did, would use this as one more example of how utterly unfit a mother she was. What kind of a parent lets their child's favorite bear be attacked and murdered by a mangy dog?

I was still sobbing and clutching the critically injured bear when we climbed the steps to Mom-mom and Pop's house. My mother knew she had some explaining to do.

This was her most dreaded hour. She hated those Sunday nights when she dropped me off, crying and snot-nosed at my grandparents' house. She knew it would be twelve more long days before she saw me again.

"The dog took Teddy," my mother explained regretfully.

In that one instant, something softened in my grandmother. My mother saw it and softened too.

"Come inside," Mom-mom said. She had never invited my mother inside since the divorce.

"Are you sure?"

"Yes. Now get in here out of that cold. You're lettin' all the heat out."

We stepped into the bright living room.

"Get your coats off and let me see that bear."

"It's pretty bad."

"There ain't nothin' that can't be fixed," Mom-mom said.

The two women, sworn enemies, worked together for hours, in the house where my mother was not welcome, to fix this bear. First they soaked Teddy in bleach. Then they ran him through the washer and tumbled him in the dryer. They cut up a pink washcloth and patched the ends of his paws where the dog had gnawed the stuffing out. It looked like he had paw pads. They found some felt in the sewing basket and my mom reconstructed the insides of Teddy's ears. Mom-mom found Teddy a new, golden ribbon and fluffed his fur with a comb. My mother had the brilliant idea of re-glazing his glass eyes with clear nail polish for instant cataract surgery. Teddy could see again!

Pleased with their results, my mother and grandmother showed me the new Teddy.

"Teddy ain't the same as he used to be, but he's still your Teddy and he still loves you just like you love him," my mother explained.

"And sometimes in life accidents happen. Things get messed up. Teddies get hurt, but we promise you, we will always be there to fix things as best we can," Mom-mom continued. "Do you still like Teddy?"

"Yes. I said. I like Teddy no matter what bad things happen to him. He is my Teddy like you are my Mommy and you are my Mom-mom," I said.

My mother left her former in-laws' house that night feeling like a shift had occurred. The women remained cold to one another for years, but they always had an unspoken understanding. They both loved me more than life. They knew they would each do anything to make me happy, so they couldn't hate one another. I watched these women ignore their own resentment and animosity in order to serve a higher purpose, and because of these strong role models, I learned what it means to really love.

~Victoria Fedden

No Regrets

*No language can express the power and beauty
and heroism of a mother's love.*
~Edwin Hubbell Chapin

The doorbell rang and I ran to answer it. I was expecting my friend to come by for me any minute. We would have to wait for my sister's return before we could leave. I was babysitting.

It wasn't my friend on the other side of the door. "Hello, Christine, this is my new husband." I heard the words and I recognized the speaker even though it had been a few years since I'd seen or heard from her. I was fifteen when she left. I would soon turn seventeen.

"Hello, Mother," I said. "You've gotten remarried?"

I stood at the front door but didn't offer entrance. "Is it all right for us to come in?" Mother asked.

"Uh... oh... yeah, sure... come on in," I muttered as I held the door wider for them.

"Where's your sister today, Christine?" She asked as she took a seat beside the strange man already seated on the sofa.

"I'm babysitting while she does her weekly shopping and errands." I answered. "She should be back soon and I'm going out with a friend of mine for a while."

"Well, I brought, Ross, my new husband, with me to meet you." Turning to the stranger, she smiled and said, "This is one of my daughters. Her name is Christine."

I knew Mother had finally gotten the divorce from my father that she should have pursued long before now, but her remarriage was a surprise. Why was she really here? Did she need money or help of some kind?

"Hello, Ross," I said. "I'm happy to meet you."

The next half hour was filled with catching up. She told me where she had been, and how she and Ross had met. I told her of the many homes where I had lived and assured her that I was happier living with my newlywed sister and her newborn than I'd ever been anywhere else. I showed her my room, which I had been allowed to fix up as I pleased. I told her about my school, my church, and described all my friends. Then she dropped the "bomb."

"It sounds like you are very happy here, Christine," Mother said. "But you are the only child I would dare ask this of. My other children are lost to me forever."

Oh, no.... I knew what was coming and I didn't want to hear it. Mother was right; I was happy and liked my life very much at the present. Still, I had to respect her enough as my parent to hear her request, so I asked, "What it is?"

"Ross and I are living in his home in Amarillo. It's near a high school and we would like very much if you could... or would consider..." her voice choked up, her eyes watered, and she glanced quickly at her new husband for support before continuing. "Ross and I would like you to live with us your senior year. I won't try to force you; it's your decision to make. But it would make me very happy if you decide to come."

So, there it was. It was my decision to make. My mother had lived a very difficult life. I don't know what helped her find the strength to finally follow through with getting a divorce from my father. Perhaps it was the fact that all her children had been taken from her and the only person she had to worry about was herself. Now, here she was, asking the impossible of me: to leave the only happy home I'd ever felt a part of. How could I?

"I know I'm asking a lot of you, Christine," Mother said. "Will you take some time to consider — before saying no?"

That's exactly what I did. I took the next few weeks before school was to start, thinking, praying, and soul searching. I had lived in so many homes—been passed around like a basketball on a court. I was loved here. I was happy. How could I leave for the unknown?

Finally, I made the decision to honor my mother's request. It was not an easy decision but I felt at peace once I made it, having had time to look at it from everyone's perspective.

My goodbyes said, I packed up only a few of my belongings and took a bus from Midland, Texas, to Amarillo to begin my new life. I had thought my days of moving from home to home were behind me. Would I find happiness here? I determined to make a strong effort to try. I remembered the old adage, "One usually finds what he goes looking for expecting to find."

I did find the happiness I went looking for while I honored my mother's request. Though it was one of the hardest decisions I've ever had to make, I have never regretted it. One month after my senior year began, I became a junior volunteer at the USO in downtown Amarillo. It was during the Vietnam War and helpers were badly needed.

I met my future husband at that USO. We have been married now for thirty-nine years and have three children, thirteen grand-children, and many foster children who have come and gone over the years.

Mother lived a long and happy life with her new husband. Both are gone now. My dad died soon after the divorce. Unfortunately, he never seemed to have found happiness.

Mother's divorce was the best thing she ever did for herself. And, as it turns out—for me as well.

~Christine Smith

A Little Child Shall Lead Them

It takes a village to raise a child.
~African proverb

My son and his wife divorced before my granddaughter, Lydia, was old enough to remember that her mother, father, and she had ever been a family. I was heartbroken.

It wasn't long before my ex daughter-in-law and my son were both remarried. All traces of the divorce disappeared. The two families blended in ways that many families are never able to do. It amazed many, yet pleased all, who witnessed the camaraderie extended to the families on both sides. It was after my ex daughter-in-law and her husband had their son, and my son and new daughter-in-law had their daughter, that the families on both sides broadened their love even further.

My son and his wife often have Lydia's brother or her stepsister (yes, Lydia's stepfather had a daughter by a previous marriage) over to their house to spend the night with Lydia or to play for the day. My ex daughter-in-law and my present daughter-in-law have been known to go shopping together or have a pizza night with all the kids.

One day, when Lydia was at our house, she was counting all her grandparents, cousins, aunts and uncles, and she knew them all—by name too—and on which side of the family they belonged. At her young age she has many loving relatives; she is lucky to be loved by so many. To think, in the beginning I had worried so about her!

Lydia's half-brother often calls my husband and me grandpa and grandma, while Lydia's grandma, on her mother's side, often dotes over my son's other daughter. It is amazing how people can get along when they keep the right objectives in mind; as it says in the Bible, "A little child shall lead them."

I came from a broken home during the fifties, and I seldom saw my father, as there was no love lost between him and my mother. I was proud to be a cheerleader in school, but my father was never at a ballgame to see me cheer. He never even came to my wedding to give me away. There was much of my life that my father missed, and my relationship with him was strained because of the animosity between him and my mother.

Today, Lydia has her own cheering section at her baseball and basketball games, led by her two mothers and two fathers. With the harmony her extended family puts forth, she is sure to grow up with self-confidence and the assurance that she is wanted, appreciated, needed, and loved.

When holidays come around, she doesn't have to wonder if she will receive a gift from her father—and be disappointed when she doesn't—as I did as a child. If she gets two of the same gift, there is no bother of having to exchange one; there is one for when she is at her mom's house, and one for when she is at her dad's house.

There are no fast rules or arguments about the amount of time she is allowed to see one parent over the other. She often even spends the day or stays overnight with her stepmom and sister when her dad is out of town on business. The doors are always open—and she knows it—and I am sure it brings her comfort.

When I think of the tears I shed as a child, and the insecurities I suffered even as an adult coming from a broken home, I am thankful my granddaughter is secure in the knowledge that she is loved and wanted by so many people.

In a world where there are so many hurting people, especially children, I am thankful for those families and parents who have put aside their differences and blended their families for the sake of the children. For our children are the future and it is their stability and security we must protect.

~Betty King

The Gift

"*D*addy, lock your doo-wer," one of my daughters says as we pull out of my ex-wife's driveway.

My six-year-old twins, already in pajamas, are buckled into second-hand car seats, their arms just long enough to flip the locks. My nine-year-old son is locked and loaded in the back seat between his sisters.

I get to have them from Friday night to Saturday night every week—a combination of neighborhood escapades and local lollygagging we call "Lazy Dadurday." And lazy it is. Not feeling the pressure to constantly take expensive and exhausting trips, we simply wake up late, enjoy our frozen waffle or Cheerios breakfasts, trek to the bookstore, the pet store or the pool, and just let it all hang out. My joy, and theirs, is simply to be together. Often our antics include my girlfriend, who shows them the kind of non-condescending respect and care I'd wish on any child, and they return her affection in spades. It also doesn't hurt that she makes French fries from scratch.

I lock my car door per my daughter's plea, and thank her for looking out for me. Beginning to feel the delightfully familiar weight of responsibility, I proceed down the long road that will eventually take us from their home to mine.

"Everything okay, guys?" I ask, glancing at them in the rearview mirror.

"Sure," offers my son.

"I mean with the divorce and all... do you have any questions, or worries, or anything?"

"Nope," he replies for all of them. But one of the twins clearly feels unrepresented.

"Why can't Mommy sleep at your house with us?"

I imagine the uncomfortable scene: my girlfriend, my ex-wife, me, four cats, three kids, one bedroom.

"Remember, you have two homes, one with Mommy, and one with me," I say, not answering the question. "You don't just visit me; you live with me, too."

I remind the kids that while other things in life may change, even crumble, a parent's love never does. The words sound pathetically trite in my head, but it's the most important thing to convey: not what changes, but what doesn't. Two homes. Eternal love. Endless Cheerios.

As the words come out, I realize that they're my own. I've weaned myself off my mom and dad's, my ex-wife's, Dr. Phil's, and anyone else's parental expectations. I've found my inner-dad voice and it tells me when it's okay to let my son stay up late and when it's not; when it's appropriate to be interrupted on the phone by a whining daughter and when it's not; when a tense situation calls for stern and consistent rules, or just an all-out, no-shoes-on, family wrestling match. Nine years after fathering a child, I'm confidently writing the story of my daddyhood from scratch, and it feels good.

My children are thrilled to see me when I pick them up, and just as excited to return home and share their adventures with their mother. There's no dark cloud between me and my ex, even when the kids are out of earshot. And my young daughter's innocent questions have quickly evolved from sad whine to curious query. Talking with them may be awkward, but so far requires no swooping therapeutic cavalry.

"Dad, let's play pod-racer," says my son a few miles from my garden apartment.

"Okay," I say, and select the Star Wars theme from my MP3. I maneuver around the other cars like a spaceship pilot, dramatically barking navigational orders all the way.

Once home, I hustle the kids from the car, holding their red overnight duffel on my shoulder and their hands in mine. As usual, the bag is overstuffed with art projects, stuffed animals, and board games they'll never play with while in my twenty-four hours of care, but I'm happy for all the pieces of themselves they care to bring along.

Once inside the apartment, the girls brush their teeth and then burrow their tiny bodies into small Dora- and Pooh-inspired inflatable beds. Meanwhile, I get their bedtime "sniff shirts." One is their mother's worn blouse from home; the other is my own T-shirt from the laundry basket. When they first started staying with me overnight, one of the twins asked for a mommy sniff shirt to help her sleep. When her sister requested a daddy version a week later, I couldn't run fast enough to grab it.

"Eeeeewwwwww," she says, giving it a strong sniff.

"Too stinky?"

"No. I like it," she replies matter-of-factly, putting the T-shirt to her nose and closing her eyes.

I make some popcorn, which my son eats ravenously while playing on the computer. I'm tempted to ask "So, everything's really okay?" but enough's enough. I'm really not looking for answers so much as affirmations anyway, and that's not worth an interrogation.

Eventually, he traipses into my bedroom and onto the queen-sized bed, and allows himself to be swallowed by the warm comforter. Before my girlfriend and I take our positions on the convertible couch, I peek into the room.

Watching them all sleeping silently, their bodies frozen in soft contortion, I know I should go to bed too. But I treasure the moment, just like I did after each of them was born. At the time, it came as a relief.

Now, it's a gift.

~Joel Schwartzberg

44

Lies Your Mother Told You

Dear Children,

This letter is in response to something that each of you, individually and at different times, said to me after your Dad and I told the two of you that we were getting divorced. Both of you told me that because of the divorce; everything you were brought up to believe was now a lie. In other words—I have been lying to you for your whole lives. Whoa! Wait a minute!

Should you wear clean underwear every day? Yup. How about looking both ways before crossing a street? Absolutely. Drink lots of water? Eat breakfast because it's the most important meal of the day? Wash your hands before you eat? Drive defensively? Tell the truth, even when it hurts? Yes, yes, yes, yes and yes. Where then, are the lies?

How about this one? I always told you that no matter how much your dad and I argued or disagreed, that it didn't mean we didn't love each other. It didn't mean we would get a divorce. That no matter what, we would make it through. Because... ta da! True love lasts forever. Is this the one?

Guess what? I believed it too.

I think I will never be able to look at a chocolate soufflé again without wanting to cry. It's what I had ordered for dessert on our twenty-sixth anniversary, romantic get-away, celebration dinner at our favorite restaurant. The soufflé had just arrived when Daddy gave me "The News." He didn't love me, he hadn't loved me for a long time... I must have known... people change; it's not his fault....

I wanted to scream, "NO! This can't be happening. Not us! Other people, but not to us! Not to me—I am a person who believes that true love lasts forever!"

As the words continued to come out of his mouth, I couldn't even look at him—I just kept staring at that oozing chocolaty goodness while my stomach heaved and churned, tears poured from my eyes, and I became a blubbery mess. Despite it all, part of me still wanted that soufflé—a voice in my head was saying, It's chocolate, you idiot! Eat it! But even the best chocolate soufflé doesn't stay looking so good when the whipped cream has tears mixed in with it.

Your dad and I tried to hold it together for a while longer—but it didn't work. And so... after almost twenty-seven years of marriage, we filed for divorce. Even though you are both adults, I know it was hard for you. It was hard for all of us, even though it was an amicable settlement. When you both accused me of lying to you, I started to question myself and what I had always believed. What had happened to true love? Is it really possible that true love can just dry up and blow away?

Now, almost a year after the finalization of the divorce, I have come to a conclusion. I don't believe that true love dies.

Your dad and I still love each other, but it has morphed into something other than a husband/wife kind of love. We share a history and our children, so we will always be connected in a way. I admire his energy and his dedication to making the world a better place. I know your dad cares for me—after all, I am the mother of his children and someone that he can depend on if he needs me. We just don't belong together anymore.

I love both of you, and I always will. Each of you took the best that Daddy and I had to offer and grew into two awesome and wonderful young women. You are beneficial to this planet, intelligent and caring, loving and supportive and a joy to know. I am so proud of both of you. I would call that true love, wouldn't you? Forever and ever?

And... who knows? I'm not too ancient yet and I'm not afraid. I may just be available to try it again. I am a person who believes that true love can happen—and when it does—it lasts forever.

Love, Mom

~Patty Hansen

Divorce *and* Recovery

Special Moments
and Everyday Miracles

Love the moment. Flowers grow out of dark moments.
Therefore, each moment is vital. It affects the whole.
Life is a succession of such moments and to live each, is to succeed.
~Corita Kent

45

What Should I Do?

*A*s I lost my moorings during the divorce process I desperately asked everyone, "What should I do?"

The divorce was inevitable and now I had the task of figuring out where I was going to live and how I was going to support my three children.

The advice I heard over and over again was, "Find a full time job and sell the marital house." It sounded like the wisest thing I could do. Plenty of single moms work full time—lots of children thrive in daycare. So, I put my house on the market. When I was married, I had chosen to be a stay-at-home mom and I had loved the hours spent home schooling and caring for my three children. Now I was faced with updating my resume and beginning a job search. It all seemed so simple actually, and made perfectly sound sense to everybody.

It was what I thought every single mom had to do—there was no other option.

I was making tremendous progress. I had an offer on the house, although I had no idea where I was going to move. I was one of two top candidates for a full-time job. And, although my three-year-old sobbed uncontrollably every time I left his presence, I still barreled forward, determined to do what I thought I should do.

I was asked to come in for a third interview for the job. I was confident that during this interview I would be hired and that this was more of a formality. But when I walked into the office, I received a very cool welcome. I was then told that I was two hours late for the interview. Although my calendar said the interview was to be at 3:00, the receptionist's calendar said it had been scheduled for 1:00. I didn't get the job. Then, to top off my day, when I got home my realtor called to tell me that the potential buyers had lowered their bid due to the home inspection. The new offer was too low for me to accept.

That night, after the children went to sleep, I sobbed. I felt like a failure, everything inside hurt, and I simply wanted my mother. I wanted her gentle hand to rub my forehead, and mostly I wanted her never-failing faith.

But, my mother had Alzheimer's disease. On the Saturdays that my children were with their dad, I would go and take care of my mother. Although she no longer recognized me and didn't really speak to me, on these days I would change her diaper, bathe her, dress her, and help her eat. Most of the time I felt grateful for being able to care for her. Yet sometimes it seemed unreal—even cruel—to be living a life where I would have to lose both my marriage and my mother in the same breath.

On this particular Saturday, I was merely overcome with sadness and fear. I had lost every iota of faith and had no idea what I should do. After I changed my mom and was brushing her hair, I began to cry and talk to her as I had done before she had Alzheimer's.

"What am I going to do, Mom? How am I going to support my children? I'm so scared." I looked at her with tears streaming down my face.

And then I saw something shift in her eyes. As clear as day she said, "Virginia dear, you don't have to do anything. Take care of yourself. Take care of your children. And leave the rest to God." She softly rubbed my forehead and smiled at me—then her eyes went blank again.

I received a miracle that day. My life, as hard as it appeared, changed. I decided to become the single mom that I wanted to be—not what I thought others expected me to be. And anytime it all feels like too much—I do as my mother told me.

I take care of myself. I take care of my children. I leave the rest to God.

He hasn't let me down yet.

~Virginia McCormack

Just Like a
Real Mother

Fathers, like mothers, are not born.
Men grow into fathers and fathering is a very important stage
in their development.
~David Gottesman

*J*don't recall standing in front of my fifth grade class and saying, "When I grow up, I want to be the divorced father of two girls, live on the poverty line, and be accepted—just like a real mother." If I had, I'm sure one of the nuns would have marched me off to the principal's office where I'd have had my thought processes realigned.

Still, by the time I turned thirty, I found myself in that very situation: a single father trying to function in a prejudiced world.

The girls were quite young when I divorced. Angela was almost seven, and Sarah not quite one. My own belief in social justice left me quite unprepared for others' reactions the first time the girls and I were out together and I needed to change Sarah's diaper. I walked into a changing room and ten mothers stared me down while they slipped sly comments at me.

"On your own, are you? You probably deserve it."

"Only a mother really knows how to care for a child."

"The men's toilet is down the hall—this is the mothers' room."

Even at the kids' school, the prejudice against a single father was oppressive. As a shift worker, the only volunteer committee I could attend regularly was the Monday morning "Mothers' Club." They stared at me the first day, obviously wondering what had possessed me to volunteer. By the end of the second month, I'd had enough of their misconception that the best parent is determined by breast size—and left.

Prejudice wasn't something with which I was unfamiliar. As a cop, every day at least one member of the community would suggest that I should be out catching "real criminals" instead of issuing them speeding infringements.

"Don't you have something else better to do?"

The correct answer to that was, "No, you have my complete and undivided attention at this juncture." Usually, it wasn't true. Sometimes, I'd be wrapping my mind around the ironing I had left undone at home, which one of the girls had softball practice, and what I was going to make for dinner. Just like a real mother might have.

As the girls entered adolescence and began to take on their feminine shapes, the prejudice against us expanded. We dressed up for the few functions we were able to attend, but as we walked down the street, the digs from passersby were along much the lines of, "An older man with a younger woman taking his child on an access visit."

In the best interest of the girls I ignored it. Just like any normal mother might have.

I hadn't realize how beaten I had become at "being a mother" until one of my friends invited me to a bridal shower. Although the bride-to-be and her betrothed were both friends of mine, for some reason, the matron of honor had invited a male (me) to the bridal shower. I showed up bearing an appliance gift for their new house, and learned that the "boys" were out, at the same time, having the bachelor party. I got an invitation to the bridal shower with the girls—and did not qualify for the bachelor party on the golf course?

Livid was an understatement, but paled significantly when the host dropped this one-liner on me.

"We thought you'd like to be here with all your friends."

I stopped breathing at the exactness of her statement. Most of my friends were women, married or widowed, but all with children. Over the years I had lost my masculinity to baby showers, carpooling, and Tupperware parties. The nights of going out to watch football games were now spent in front of the television because I was divorced and had no one to stay home with the girls. Invitations to motor sports events had been turned down because one of the girls had a sleepover. I had even thrown little girls birthday parties in my home, complete with fairy cakes and handmade princess decorations. I was just like a real mother.

My shattered ego and I were the last to leave the party. I had lingered, in the hope that the boys might return, and at least I could share in the post-game revelry. I was washing dishes for the host when she walked up to thank me.

"It was important to all the girls that you are here so they could see what real parenting is about. By your actions, you show that you're not only a father, but you have the softer side too, leading by example with actions matching your words. All our kids rave about you; they want to be just like you when they grow up."

"Excuse me?"

"They all want to be men who in the face of adversity, come through for their children. Just like a real mother."

I drove home and later that night, while ironing the girls' school uniforms; I realized that my divorce had given me something I could not have experienced any other way. The divorce let me be the parent to my children that I had always yearned to be.

Just like a real mother.

~Grant Madden

47

Not Alone

...your Father knows what you need before you ask him.
~Matthew 6:8

"Aunt Sharon, Grandma's gone." My niece Meloni gently broke the news of my mother's passing. It was 4:00 A.M. on Saturday. Only four days earlier, we had secured a hospice nurse to help Momma through what doctors figured were the final stages of her fight with stomach cancer. Now the sweet nurse met me, standing at the foot of Momma's bed, making all the necessary calls Meloni could no longer handle.

Sadness settled in with reality, even though Momma seemed to just be peacefully sleeping. She and Daddy had raised me to understand that death was actually a joyous promotion to everlasting life in God's presence. Daddy had passed away a few years earlier, so I knew that he and Momma were now rejoicing together. Thinking about that should have lifted the sadness a little, but it didn't. Instead, it turned inward.

I'm alone. The thought hit me in the pit of my stomach. My divorce, not quite two years earlier, had turned me into a single mother raising two pre-adolescent sons. During those last two years, I could call Momma when things got really hard or I was feeling particularly lonely. Mom liked to watch *The Tonight Show*, so I could always count on having someone to talk to, even late at night.

Now, as I stood looking down on her still form, the emptiness started to overwhelm me. My brother had his wife and my sister had her husband. I didn't have a spouse—and now, I didn't even have my mother.

Just then my pager buzzed. Who could be calling me at 5 A.M.? One glance at the number puzzled me even more. It was James, a gentleman I had just recently started to date. We'd met through a dating service, had talked on the phone several times over the past month, and had just met in person nine days earlier. Why was he calling at such an unusual hour?

All the details surrounding Momma were being expertly handled by the hospice nurse and I couldn't do anything else until my brother and sister arrived, so I went into the living room and dialed James's number.

He answered his phone on the first ring. "Hi James, it's Sharon," I said.

His voice was soothing. "I already know; your mother passed. I'm here for whatever you need." He heard the question in my silence and continued. "When I called your house and you weren't home, I knew." He hesitated slightly, and then continued. "This is probably the wrong time to tell you this, but there's no way I should feel you like this—unless we're supposed to be together."

Again, I was nearly speechless. "But how..."

"We'll talk later today. Concentrate on whatever you have to do and then call me."

By 2:00 that afternoon, the initial details were handled. All that was left to do was receive out-of-town guests and put together the program for the memorial service. Momma was never still while she was well and she would not have wanted us to sit around looking sad and moping for the next few days. Previously, I had asked James to escort me to a wedding that same evening and we decided to keep our plans. On our way home, James told me about his morning.

He had awakened in the night with one idea on his mind, "Call her." A glance at the clock brought him to his senses. There's no way I'm calling that woman at 4:00 in the morning. He tried to go back to sleep. After an hour of tossing and turning, the urge to call me had remained as strong as ever, so he obeyed. Not finding me home at that hour, his mind went straight to my ailing mother for whom he and his church prayer group had been praying. He paged me.

God knew that I would feel alone when I lost my mother. Before I could even ask Him for help, He nudged James at that very moment to give me the companionship I would need. Not only was James there for me during that very trying week—he and I were engaged the following month and we married in August of that same year. Contrary to my first thought that March morning, God saw to it that I was not alone.

~Sharon Norris Elliott

48

Without Ever Knowing

ivorce is hard on everyone. Sometimes we forget how hard it can be on animals.

Our son and his wife divorced a few years ago. Many of us in the family were devastated, including Missy and Dena. Missy is our Dandi Dinmont Terrier. Dena, a Rat Terrier, belonged to our son's family. Though the dogs are both terriers, they looked and acted nothing alike. The only similarity was that they both came from homes where they were loved like a member of the family.

Dena had been my son's dog, but when the divorce became final he decided Dena should stay with his ex-wife and their little girl. After all, Dena was very fond of my granddaughter and they would be staying in the family home.

In the past, when my son and his family took trips or would be gone for the day, Dena would come to stay with us. Though of different breeds and personalities, she and our Missy learned to enjoy the overnight slumber parties and became fast friends.

Chasing each other around the family room couch became a routine game. They nearly wore a path as they chased each other, first one way and then the other, barking and then veering out, making the chase include the whole house. Everyone stayed out of their way, until they found a spot to recover from their exhaustion, tongues hanging out. They made us adults chuckle and my granddaughter giggle.

Dena often came along when my son's family had just dropped

by for a short visit. She was, after all, a member of the family and Missy looked forward to her coming over.

Then the day came when the family separated and Dena's visits became less frequent. Eventually, they ceased completely. Missy knew things had changed. She didn't have anyone to chase and she often lay on the floor looking forlorn.

Life moved on and eventually both my ex-daughter-in-law and my son married new partners. They remained friends, which made my granddaughter's life less complicated. It also made life for us adults less stressful, as we adjusted to the changes in the family. We became accustomed to new people, and the absence of others.

One day, after our granddaughter's visit, we took her back to her mother's house. We had not yet been to the new home of my ex-daughter-in-law and her recent husband. We decided to take Missy along for a ride and thought she would enjoy seeing her old friend Dena.

When we pulled the car into the driveway, my husband took our granddaughter to the front door. Dena flew out! Missy was beside herself with excitement! There was a reunion in the driveway that day that was equivalent to any tear-jerker reunion you ever saw. Two friends who had been torn apart for no reason of their own, had been left wondering what had happened to the other. They had been given no explanation to satisfy their understanding.

The humans in their lives had mourned their losses and moved on with a new understanding of change. It made me realize that our animals mourn losses too, and most of the time, they are left to grieve without ever knowing what went wrong.

~Betty King

Stickers for His Dad

While we try to teach our children all about life,
Our children teach us what life is all about.
~Angela Schwindt

Our marriage was ending and I was overwhelmed with sadness and fear as I contemplated a life without my husband for me and our three children. Indeed, this was the most devastating event I had experienced in my twenty-seven years and my world was spinning out of control.

Though I fought hard to work on our marital problems—to forgive and see hope—my husband had other plans. He was my best friend, my first love, and my children's father. And now he was leaving. A year of unproductive counseling brought me to the dark place where I had stopped trying to save our marriage. With firm resolve, I began packing his belongings, and placed the boxes on the front porch. What happened next was the most painful, yet special, circumstance of my divorce.

My five-year-old son, Nick, had been watching me pack. I was too overcome with anguish to notice what he must have been feeling. Just how was he interpreting my actions that day? His daddy was his idol and hero, and the sight of those boxes no doubt troubled and confused him. All he knew was that his dad was leaving him and the safe little world in which he lived. Without hesitation, Nick quickly ran to his room for something to put into his dad's boxes. I was too distraught to ask what it was. It was not until years later that I found out exactly what his little gift had been.

Time passed, my children and I adjusted and finally recovered from the divorce. Their father maintained a good relationship with them and so they learned that though their dad and I divorced, he did not stop loving them.

Through the years, memories repeatedly returned of the day I packed my husband's belongings and moved them out of our home. I spoke of that day several times to family and friends because it was the hardest day of my life—a point in time when the realization of our failed marriage prompted me to make some hard, life-changing decisions. When recalling that day, I tried to imagine what had been so special to my son, what had been so significant in Nick's five-year-old mind that he ran urgently to get it from his room and place it into one of his dad's boxes.

Shortly after Nick's graduation from high school, he sorted the remains of his senior year and threw out his school papers and binders. I happened to see his notebooks in the trashcan and decided to retrieve one of his composition notebooks to read before I said goodbye to his high school years. In his English journal, he had written about his five-year-old memories of that sad day on our porch. It was a day he would always remember. I couldn't believe that I was actually reading my son's perspective on that day. In his handwriting, were the words that adequately described his confusion and feelings on the day his dad moved away.

He provided a thoughtful review of seeing his dad's things on our porch. I read about the sadness he felt for his dad and how, on that special day, he sensed his dad needed him and that his dad was losing so much. As I read his journal, I was so deeply moved by his story that my sadness of that day returned.

Nick recounted how earlier that week someone had given him a package of stickers. They meant so much to him—a childhood treasure. Though he was not sure why he wanted to give them to his dad, he was sure of one thing; his dad needed him and his stickers.

My son sensed his dad's loss and wanted to provide some relief. In his child-like reasoning, the stickers served that purpose.

And so it was that my five-year-old proved to be a good example that day—a child who had deserved to be protected and shielded from life's black moments was instead protecting and shielding a person he loved. I was so proud of our little five-year-old that day on that porch... and I still am. In the upset and pain of our divorce, our little boy was strong and kind, and responded to one of life's most wrenching events with gentle reminders of goodness and love.

~Catherine Armstrong

For a Lifetime

If I had to sum up friendship in one word, it would be comfort.
~Adabella Radici

One of the loneliest feelings in the world is the knowledge that the relationship that I had counted on to last a lifetime... didn't. It's during these moments—during the bleakest days of dragging through a divorce—that I find myself aching for a miracle.

Curiously, it's just these times when a friend seems to appear.

Sometimes it's a phone call from my oldest friend, Nancy. I've known her longer than anyone, and she has a talent for getting right to the heart of a matter. She always understands the very deepest part of me. When I hang up the phone, I always feel younger than the day I first met her.

Other times, I'm lucky enough to hear from Pam. I've known her for thirty years now, and I can tell her anything. It's amazing to me what comfort there is in that. And sometimes, what fun there is in that. Our conversations are often unusual, but they always leave me smiling.

Then there is Bea, a relatively new friend who understands a lot more about what I am going through than I ever would have guessed. She knows what to say and what not to say. She sends cards that make me laugh when I need it most. When it's often all I can do to get through the day, her positive attitude and infectious giggle never fail to act as a tonic, leaving me feeling uplifted and revived.

Fran is my old friend and jogging buddy who knows to pick up the pace on days when I need to run off the extra anger, and to stroll on days I just need to talk. She has a talent for finding cards that capture just the right sentiment so that I can have a reminder when she isn't around.

Nina never fails to offer wisdom, insight, and guidance when I need them the most.

Patsy has a talent for distractions and resources.

Jane sends e-mails that make me think. Margie sends e-mails that touch me deeply. Deb sends e-mail jokes that make me laugh until my stomach hurts.

At a time in my life when I feel stranded and alone, some friends make a point of "checking in" to see how I'm doing, and some make sure the children and I always have plans for the holidays.

There are the friends who know how to be there, and the friends who know how to listen. There are those who offer perspective and ones who know how to be silly. There are the ones who — bless their hearts! — are willing to rearrange their schedules in order to make precious time for me, all because they know just how valuable a real friend is.

Most amazing of all are the friends who teach me (usually by example, like the gentlest and wisest of teachers) how to forgive.

Every single one of them teaches me that even in the darkest of days, I can always make out the shapes of happiness if I strain enough to see. They teach me that not every relationship lasts a lifetime — but that we will always have a lifetime of relationships.

If anyone were to ask me what helps most in a divorce, I would tell them: friends. Good friends. They teach me that when I ask for a miracle to help me through the rough spots, I get friends who help me through the rough spots instead. And that makes them the miracle I needed all along.

~T'Mara Goodsell

A Bear with a Badge

Anyone who has looked a teddy bear in the face
will recognize the friendly twinkle in his knowing look.
~Harold Nadolny

"Hurry up! We're going to be late!" I yelled impatiently at my four-year-old son as I picked him up and almost threw him into the car.

The last few months had been a nightmare. I kept hoping I would wake up to find it was all just a bad dream. Without warning, my husband of thirteen years had left me. My world came crashing down around me. I was shattered. The concept of even beginning to pick up the pieces was as far away as God. Or so it seemed.

I had always believed in God, and could sing all the verses to "Jesus Loves Me." Where was He now? Where was all that love He boasted? I was all alone fighting for my life and for my son. Where was justice? Right triumphing over wrong? Fairness was a cruel joke.

I was taking my son to spend the weekend with his dad. Every time I left my little boy, it ripped my heart out and I dreaded the unbearable grief and agony.

On the way we made a brief stop at the mall. As we left, my son squealed with delight when he saw a sheriff's car parked out front. He ran toward it quivering with excitement. The deputy greeted us with a warm smile.

"What's your name?" he asked as he bent down to greet my son.

"Kevin."

"Nice to meet you, Kevin and Mom. I am Deputy Randy." Knowing every little boy's heart, he asked him if he would like to sit behind the wheel.

Kevin was in heaven. Propped up on his knees, he gripped the steering wheel and made vroom vroom noises. To top it off, the deputy let Kevin turn on the bright red flashing lights. Kevin beamed with ecstasy. My heart melted.

After helping him out of the car, the deputy opened the trunk, eyes twinkling and said, "I have something for you." He lifted out a big brown teddy bear wearing a sheriff's badge. He stooped down, and, looking Kevin in the eyes said, "This is for you because you are such a good boy."

All I can recall after that was fighting back the tears and driving in silence, as my little boy sat next to me clutching that big brown bear.

"Why did he do that, Mommy? Why was he so nice? Why did he give me this big bear?"

I managed to choke out the words, "I don't know. I guess he thought you were pretty special. And I do too. I love you."

"I love you too, Mommy."

Leaving him at his dad's that night was just as painful as every previous time, but somehow my burden seemed lighter—a little more "bearable."

The next day, I sent a thank you note to the deputy:

Dear Deputy Randy,

You will never know how much your kindness touched my son and me last night. Kevin's father left and we are in the deepest darkest valley we have ever known. The way you reached out to my little boy will never be forgotten. And the big brown bear will always be a treasure to him. Thank you for letting God use you to give us hope.

As I wrote that letter, I realized that God had been there all along.

I just wasn't looking. He showed his love through this person in a way that He knew we needed, in a language a four-year-old could understand.

Now many years later, I have learned that one way God loves us is through other people. And, for the last sixteen years, Deputy Randy has remembered Kevin with cards and gifts and visits—even a ride-along. My son is now twenty. He has graduated from the Police Cadet Academy and is working toward his college degree... and guess what still sits on his bed?

~Welby O'Brien

Photo Album

I promise you love. Time will not take that away.
~Anne Sexton

I finally put my wedding pictures in an album today. That would not be so remarkable, except for the fact that my divorce has been final for about six months. Looking at the pictures, seeing us so happy, excited and in love, I wonder how it all went so wrong.

Many people thought that we were crazy to get married, but we were in love. On our first date we knew that we wanted to spend our lives together, and eighteen days later we made it official. We eloped to Lake George, New York, without even telling our families. It was the happiest day of my life.

We had the ceremony on a hotel balcony with a Justice of the Peace and two friends present. I had never felt so nervous, excited, scared, happy and in love—all at once. The moment he took my hand I knew what I was doing was right. There was not a doubt in my mind.

Our blissful period did not last long though, and our relationship and marriage crumbled. I was devastated. I cried for a month straight, never leaving the couch in the living room.

Through the help of friends, I managed to bring myself back into the world of the living. The only way I was able to cope with life and put on a brave face was to hate him. I was out for blood. He had ruined my life, taken away my happiness. It was time for payback.

It was a bitter divorce. Expensive lawyers were fighting our battle in court. I was using the court to try to punish him. I made a big fuss out of small issues. It got so nasty that we weren't even speaking to each other. This was all fueled by my hatred, my hurt.

The last time I saw him was in court for the trial. That was when I realized that as much as I wanted and willed myself to hate him — I didn't. The man that was sitting at the other table was the man I still loved.

When the trial was over, I went home and cried some more. I cried for me, for him, for the love that was lost, and because my marriage was really, truly over. There was no fixing it. My marriage was gone. My future was gone. The true love of my life was gone. It was then that I put away the pictures.

Some time later, I moved from our townhouse and I rediscovered the pictures. Some were loose, some were in photo albums, but they weren't all together. But then, neither was I.

I decided that the pictures needed a home. I spent a lot of time placing and organizing the pictures until the album was perfect. It was a labor of love and tears.

Looking through the album, I have no regrets for what has happened, though I wish that the outcome had been different. Even with the divorce and the drama that came with it, I feel blessed. I am blessed because I found true love, though it was for a short time. I will always remember the feeling of true joy and love that filled my life and my heart. It was through a lot of time and tears that I was able to reach that level of understanding. It was not easy, but I learned that time does help to heal wounds. I know this, because it doesn't hurt like it used to when I say, "I still love him and always will."

~Emily Kate Capeles

A Living Miracle

I've learned to trust myself, to listen to truth,
to not be afraid of it and to not try and hide it.
~Sarah McLachlan

My granddaughter, Hannah, is turning four today. She is bouncing around the house squealing and laughing; excited about balloons, presents, and guests. The aroma of burgers lingers in the air from the supper we've just enjoyed. Family and friends visit as my daughter-in-law puts the final touches on cake and drinks. I relax, chatting comfortably with Cheri, a former best friend and neighbor, who sits on the couch between me and her boyfriend.

Just a routine child's birthday party, you might say. But to me, it's a miracle.

Emotionally and physically abused from the age of two, I had married at age twenty-six. I had buried those horrible childhood memories in some deep place and put them behind me. However, without knowing it, I had stepped into a marriage that repeated the nightmare of my childhood. Already beaten down emotionally, I was unable to stand up to the abuse I endured for the next twenty-two years.

I was always jumpy and anxious during the years of my marriage, but the sound of my husband's heavy footsteps coming down the stairs sent me into a panic. I knew what would follow—the evil in his eyes; the stench of his sweaty, filthy body as he trapped me face down and assaulted me; his heavy breathing. And the pain. Crying or pleading didn't help. I simply crawled into a tiny, safe place deep inside myself and waited for it to be over. After all, he owns me, I thought. Doesn't he have the right as a husband to do whatever he pleases with me?

When he wasn't assaulting me, my husband treated me like a slave, belittling and mocking me. "Get that garden weeded!" or "Get my dinner over here, now!" he would shout or growl. Even my children weren't spared. They grew up hearing, "Don't listen to your mother. She's crazy. We'll have to lock her up." His attitude towards me caused my children to lose all respect for me and they became very disobedient and rebellious.

Although I knew God during this time, I still felt totally alone. I had zero self-worth. I was imprisoned, trapped in a deep black pit with no way out. The only thing I lived for was my three children. I had to keep going for them.

"Renee, that's abuse. No one should have to live like that," friends told me. Little by little, I gained the strength to believe them. I finally had the courage to escape when my children were in high school. My friends helped me leave and go to a women's shelter. I will be forever grateful for their help and patience.

In the months following, I was still broken. I was terrified—of not making it on my own, that my husband would come after me, that I had sinned in leaving him, and that God wouldn't forgive me. I lived in sheer terror of what my husband would do to me if he got his hands on me. I tried to commit suicide numerous times. The agony seemed too big to deal with.

Gradually, in the years that followed my divorce, I was able to let God's love reach into the anguish in my heart. I realized God was not mad at me and never had been. I learned that I am God's precious daughter. I also learned He is the only one big enough to heal any pain.

Counselors guided me and my friends at church supported me. But God accomplished most of the healing in me. It wasn't always easy, but I resolved not to live in denial. I determined to look at my pain, feel it, deal with it, and trust God to heal it. As I talked to Him about everything and learned to trust Him, He worked within me—sometimes gradually, sometimes suddenly. Little by little, I gained enough self-worth to care for myself. One step at a time, I was able to let go of my fear and pain. As I refused to give up, my progress became easier and faster.

In the last several years, I have learned to draw boundary lines and to refuse to let others take advantage of me. I have discovered how to confront them kindly but firmly when they do. I am learning to be kind to myself too, by not expecting myself to be perfect and by not panicking over little things.

Now, I sit here at Hannah's birthday party thinking about how far I've come in the ten years since my divorce. I have a healthy relationship with my kids and grandkids. I am happy, at peace, and active in my church. I am able to honor and care for myself, setting boundaries and confronting as needed. I have healthy hobbies and I have even started up my own small business. My life has purpose and I want to live.

Just two years ago, I would run out of a store in terror if I even saw someone who looked like my ex-husband. Now, I am sitting on a couch, comfortably talking with his girlfriend. He—my ex-husband—is the man at the other end of the couch. He sits, with arms crossed, silent, and obviously nervous. But I am at peace—a new person with a new life, a person who has conquered fear. I am a living miracle.

~Renee P. as told to Evie Mack

54

The Last Time

Only in the agony of parting do we look into the depths of love.
~George Eliot

The last time I looked into his eyes, I couldn't see him. He was dying. The nurse said he couldn't hear me. I knew he could.

"Oh my love, stay a little longer," I whispered.

The only sounds in the room were the machines keeping him alive and his son's weeping as he held his father's hand, willing him to live.

I had gotten the call at work. My daughter's frightened voice asked me to go to her father's side; he had suffered a major stroke that morning and was not expected to make it. She lives at the other end of the country and was scrambling to find a flight. Her brother was on his way to the hospital and she didn't want him to be alone.

All the way to the hospital, I gulped deep breaths of air, my stomach threatened to turn, and my hands shook. I couldn't believe he was dying. Dying? He was far too young. Trepidation seeped through my mixed emotions as I approached the hospital. The waiting room was filled to overflowing with family, and ex-wives.

We had been divorced for many years, and I wasn't sure what kind of reaction I would receive; anger, disbelief at my presence, indifference. I needn't have worried. From the moment I entered the waiting room, they opened their arms and hearts to me. His brothers and sisters held me. We cried together. And I knew I was where I should be.

"David's on his way and Marlene is taking the first flight out," I assured them.

"Do you want me to go in with you?" asked my ex-brother-in-law.

"No, I need time to be alone with him."

When I entered the room, I was overwhelmed with grief. He looked so small, surrounded by machines, a myriad of tubes threatening to engulf him. My first reaction was to touch his forehead with my lips as I had done so many times with my children, looking for a fever. I shook my head in disbelief. Imagine... looking for a fever?

As I took his hand in mine, our son, David, came in and together we began the vigil—the final journey. David reached out to me and as I held him, his thirty years melted away. He was a toddler once again, needing solace.

Too soon, the doctor told him, "Let him go. There is no hope; his system is closing down." Such a terrible decision for a son to make; my heart broke as I watched him nod his head.

"Yes," he whispered, "It's time."

One by one, his family came in to say goodbye. The machines were turned off, the tubing removed and soon all that remained was the soft whisper of his breathing. The silence frightened me. I had to accept that we were no longer fighting, but accepting the inevitable.

I was surprised at the intensity of my feelings. I thought that I had divorced my memories when I divorced him, but there they were, turning back the hands of time.

I remembered the young man I had danced with and married; the arms that had held me with such tenderness and love; the young father who wiped his children's tears and kissed them better. I had not been in love with him for many years, but I knew that I would always love this man. I often wished that things could have been different, that our first brush with love had bloomed into the "ever after" kind, but fate had a different road for me to travel.

I leaned over and whispered into his ear, "It's okay, go to your father—he's waiting."

We sat on either side of his bed, holding his hands, waiting.

His breathing was barely audible. I lifted his hand up and said, "Okay, Da."

I am sure that his father took his hand and walked with him as they took the path home. He died holding the hands of love and for the last time, I whispered, "I love you."

~Shirley Neal

55

A Christmas Eve Miracle

Accept the things to which fate binds you,
and love the people with whom fate brings you together,
but do so with all your heart.
~Marcus Aurelius

I stood in the back of the church, bouncing my seven-month-old son while enthusiastically singing Christmas carols. I was one of nearly one hundred brave souls who'd ventured out in the winter storm to attend the Christmas Eve candlelight service. I wouldn't have missed it for the world. This was my first Christmas as a mother, and the significance was not lost on my feminine emotions. Interwoven throughout the season's celebrations were constant thoughts of my new family. It was a truly precious time, and I absorbed every smell, every sound and every sight, impressing the memories indelibly on my heart.

Partway through the service, and in the middle of a holy rendering of "Silent Night," I noticed a family: mom and dad on opposite ends with two very young boys sandwiched in-between. The boys were so very small, not more than four or five and full of wiggles and giggles. The grown-ups, sitting much like armed guards on either end, lacked their sons' joy. I knew little about this family other than the fact the mother left a couple months before, leaving her husband bereaved and broken. Upon seeing them together on Christmas Eve, I was hopeful they had reunited.

Unfortunately, it didn't take long for me to realize that this was highly unlikely. With a glance toward the wife, it became clear she resented being there. Unconcerned with whether or not she had reason for such animosity, I noted his grief-lined face. This was a broken man—thoroughly and completely.

How my heart ached for them, for the hurt that had led them to this moment and for the greater pain that was certain to follow. With my son still in my arms, I ceased singing and began to silently pray: A miracle, God! I ask for a miracle! This is what Christmas is all about, right? And if ever a family was in need of a miracle, it is this one. Do something, please? Soften hearts and mend wounds. And somehow, through the wonder of Christmas, bring this family back together again.

Christmas passed, and I never heard what became of the family that had so touched my heart. The days and weeks that followed filled easily with the responsibilities of caring for my husband and young son. It was a year of firsts—first holidays, first words, first steps, first birthdays. Thoughts of the broken family slipped readily from my mind.

Until my own family began to crumble. Ironically, I became a single woman six days before the next Christmas. Like stepping into the vision I had glimpsed the previous Christmas Eve, I was the broken and bereaved spouse watching the door close behind my husband for the final time. With a chill in the air of an otherwise mild day, he left without a second glance. I clung desperately to my oblivious one-and-a-half-year-old, as though he might be the next to leave. How could this happen?

As those six days passed painfully slowly, my despair deepened. Everywhere I looked, hand-holding couples and romantic symbols of the holiday season seemed to mock me and my loss. And then Christmas Eve came. I couldn't imagine how painful it would be. Only a year before, I had stood outside the glass looking in, thinking I understood but not having a clue. This year, it was my reality—and the searing pain nearly destroyed me. More than anything, I felt betrayed by my own foolish notions of true love. My childhood imaginings of marriage and family were painted in such vivid detail. Now I believed that those Cinderella-esque dreams had led me astray. "Happily-ever-after" didn't exist, at least not for me. I don't know if I was angrier at a world that perpetuated such a false hope or at myself for swallowing the lie so completely.

Days turned into weeks, and weeks into months. The responsibilities of caring for a child and maintaining a household eventually trumped my desire to drown in self-pity. I got a full-time job, enlisted the aid of daycare, and eventually developed the routine of a single mom. In time, my internal storm began to subside. I learned to smile again, buoyed by the laughter of my precious little boy and the love of friends and family. All was not lost. The sun still shone bright and my roses still bloomed. Life was good. But love again? That was out of the question.

Until... well, until I ran into him again—the father from Christmas two years earlier who was now a full-time single dad of two sons. We ran into each other at the same church where each of us had faced our greatest loss. Upon hearing of my divorce, he extended a truly empathetic hand of friendship. He understood the loss of self-worth, the grieving for lost dreams, and the sheer exhaustion of raising a son alone. With few words, but a healing presence, he infused me with courage and the hope that there was life—and possibly love—beyond divorce.

Within months, we were hovering precariously between the safety of friendship and the risk of relationship. Both afraid of opening our newly mended hearts, we did the cautious dance of intimacy and distance. It was during one of these uncertain moments, when our three sons were playing baseball at the park that the subject of Christmas Eve came up.

"I prayed for you, you know. On Christmas Eve. When your family was sitting in church together."

He looked surprised at my revelation. I continued, "I prayed for a miracle, for love to win. I saw how sad you were, and it nearly broke my heart. So I prayed."

He smiled, thankful I had been present with him in his darkest time, though he'd never known it. I didn't expect him to say anything, but he had a revelation of his own.

"The next year, you were the one alone on Christmas Eve." He paused. "I watched you, saw your pain, and remembered what it had been like for me the year before. And... well, I was the one who prayed for you that Christmas."

We sat speechless, humbled by the fact that years before we had unsuspectingly participated in something far beyond us. The threads of life's heartache, dark as they were, had been intentionally woven into the fabric of today, uniting the pain of the old with the exquisite wonder of the new. And in the unveiling of this truth, stubborn beams of light began to penetrate the thick guards of my heart. Love, real love, was not dead. Beauty would rise from the ashes of divorce, painting my life with rich color and filling it with fragrance once again.

I prayed for a miracle that first Christmas Eve — a miracle for a family I knew little about. Today, as the wife of the man who resurrected my dreams of true love, I now realize the miracle was granted. And not just for them, but also for me.

~Michele Cushatt

Life on the
Front Burner—
Now, It's All About Me!

Every new beginning comes from some other beginning's end.
~Seneca

Flashes of Brilliance

We can draw lessons from the past, but we cannot live in it.
~Lyndon B. Johnson

I stared at the walls, wondering what would become of me. After nearly three decades of marriage, I was on my own. My daughters were adults and busy with their own lives.

I had been nineteen when I had taken my wedding vows. I'd never lived on my own. My interests and activities had been shaped, first by my husband, then by my children. My role was to support, to assist, to make things work.

Now I had to make things work for me, and I didn't know where to begin. The most puzzling questions before me were: Who am I? What am I going to do with the rest of my life?

At first these seemed overwhelming. I felt hopeless and adrift. Being an avid reader, I began to read about others who had faced surprising life changes.

I decided to start over by laying a new foundation. I reconnected with my church and reestablished my spiritual relationships. I threw out old baggage. I moved. I got a new car. I wanted to cut all ties with the past. I wanted to remove all reminders of my pain.

As I stood poised to pitch my wedding ring, something dawned on me.

I could not rid myself of everything. My past was an intrinsic part of my present — and my future.

Flashes of Brilliance: Life on the Front Burner... 185

I had to embrace the person I was, and my life experiences, before I could rebuild. I needed a new perspective, and a symbol of my fresh start.

The wedding ring represented it all.

I went to the jewelers and had the diamond reset.

Somehow, the tangible evidence that a twenty-eight-year-old diamond could look contemporary and revitalized told me that I, too, could be renewed.

The stone had been close to flawless when we had picked it out. An accident several years ago had damaged it; a tiny chip marred the surface. But the new setting now hid the defect and the stone's facets sparkled with the best of them.

I began to stretch a little. I found a new job. I signed up for dance classes. I made new friends. I pondered what I would like to do with the rest of my life. Every day, the ring I now wore on my right hand nudged me to keep moving forward.

Since then, I've been able to accomplish a lot, and it hasn't always been easy. But my new life, like the new setting for my diamond that brings out the best in the old stone, it has a beautiful style and substance that is bringing out the best in me.

The flaws are irrelevant when the focus is on the harmony of the whole. And that's what my life has become today: a delightful blend of old and new, of memories and possibilities.

I'm on my own, but surrounded by love and support from friends and family, and anxious to explore those things I set aside when being a wife and mother took center stage.

I didn't throw away the memories, nor did I bury my past. Instead, I reframed them in a new context, a new setting of my choosing, and am let the resulting brilliance dazzle the world. The ring that reminds me will one day be an heirloom, while my choices become my legacy.

~Lynn Kinnaman

Warrior

y high-pitched scream was quickly followed by my three-year-old son's scream and then by my eleven-month-old daughter's scream. How was I going to deal with this horrible situation? There was a gigantic black bug running across the floor of the bathroom.

I married for several reasons, one of which was to find a life-long, resident bug killer. I agreed to change all diapers for the return service of my husband killing all bugs. Yet, here I was, not quite five years from the day we married, and my bug killer no longer lived here.

I had just gotten the kids out of the bathtub when I saw the huge nightmare of a bug. After the screaming stopped and I felt as if there was no longer any blood flowing in my body, I realized that someone had to do something about it. Because there was only one male in the house, my son, I thought I would give that a shot. "Oh, boy! You get to kill a bug!" I tried to be enthusiastic, but he saw right through my effort.

"I'm not killing it. You kill it." He huddled behind me, still dripping with water from the bathtub. My daughter was on my hip, still dripping as well, looking back and forth from me to her brother, her eyes wide and filled with a mixture of concern and amusement. After a little more begging, I realized that I would have to do something about that bug by myself.

After the screaming had started, it had taken up a temporary hiding place next to the bathroom cabinet. After frantically searching for a weapon, I found a bottle of conditioner and tried to smash it. I must have hit that multi-legged invader twenty times before I was convinced it was dead. Now, I had to deal with the crime scene.

While I searched for some tool to help me remove the bug, it must have seen its opportunity. It jumped up and tried to run away. I screamed, my son screamed, and my daughter screamed. Once again, I felt the chill of death as my blood stopped flowing. How could that bug still be alive? In a panic, I tried to smash it again, but this time, it was a moving target.

Now, you need to know, we had just recently moved into this house, and had noticed what looked to be evidence of a mouse in our very large linen closet. I had quickly determined that there would be no using that closet. I had filled it with rat poison and locked the door, never planning to open it again.

Well, wouldn't you know it—the bug went straight under the closet door. Now, I had to deal not only with the bug, but I had to open that dreaded door. I was starting to get a little concerned as well, that through all the terror, my daughter still perched on my hip, might just forget she didn't have a diaper on. This bug needed a speedy execution. I couldn't just leave it alive and hope it would die with the rats. With my luck, I would step on it in the middle of the night, or it would climb into bed with me.

I looked at my son who was alternately laughing, shaking, and crying. "I need you to stand by this door and watch the bug while I get a boot to smash him with. We don't want him to get away."

"Okay," he tentatively said. As he inched toward the door with his hands clenched together on his chest, he peered around the corner. Then, he ran back to the bathroom.

"Please. I have to get something to kill him, and I don't want him to get away."

"I'll get a big, big boot," he suggested.

"Okay. Thank you. You are such a big helper."

He scurried by the open door, squealing the whole way as if the bug was going to run out and get him. That was ridiculous. We all knew the bug was after me. He quickly came back carrying the biggest boot he could find in my closet.

"Oh, thank you. Thank you."

"Kill him!" my son shouted, as if he was shrieking a battle cry. I tried to annoy the bug with hairspray to get it to come out of the closet a little bit so that I wouldn't have to go in, but it would only run along the back wall. Every move it made was followed by terror on our end, all of us not knowing whether to laugh, cry, or just move out.

I realized that I was not going to be able to smash the bug, so I went to Plan B. I needed to trap it. I sent my son back into my closet to retrieve a shoebox. Then, just in case I caught that vile bug, I needed a quick exit strategy. I locked the kids in my son's room so that my ever-curious daughter would not follow me down the stairs. Then, the battle was on.

I summoned all of my courage and went into the rat closet. I propped the shoebox in front of the bug, and miraculously, he walked right in. Numb in my limbs, I quickly flipped the box over and put a lid on it. The bug was trapped, but I could feel it running around in a panicked state just on the other side of that thin cardboard I was holding. It may as well have been running directly on my hands. I ran down the stairs, threw the door open, and threw it out.

I don't know if my knees were shaking more or my heart was racing more, but the job was done. I had done it.

I hurried back upstairs to tell the kids the great news, and they treated me like I was like a great warrior returning home after a victory. "Yeah, Mama. You killed it! You killed it!" We danced around squealing with delight.

It wasn't fun to confront my fear, but it will get better. One thing I know is that I will always have a shoebox handy, and I can always hope that one day, my son and daughter will become little warriors too.

~Heather McGee

Climbing Diamond Head

The turning point in the process of growing up
is when you discover the core of strength within you that survives all hurt.
~Max Lerner

Michael, my three-year-old son, and I arrived at the Oahu airport anxious to be reunited with my husband. But our reunion was far from what I hoped. My husband picked up Michael and swung him in an exuberant hug. However, when I approached, his hug was stiff and brief. "What's wrong, honey?" I asked.

"We'll talk later."

That brief phrase sent shivers of fear through my soul.

The day dragged by with stilted conversation, and a stomach-churning sense of impending doom. I couldn't help trying to figure out what I might have done wrong.

I thought we were happy. Each day we'd kiss before going to work, each evening we'd fix dinner together, and then chase our son around the house to giggles and laughter. Each night we'd snuggle together as we spoke of our fears, struggles, and dreams. We had only recently moved to the beautiful island of Oahu, and we had spent each weekend at the beach or hiking the hour-long walk up Diamond Head.

Sure, there was the stress of the high cost of living, and being shy, I feared the new situation, new cultures, new people, but with my husband at my side I could face anything. My husband, ten years older, had much more worldly experience and I relied on him not only for companionship, but for his cooking and cleaning skills, for his ability to drive through the city traffic, and for his knack at being able to fit in wherever he lived. I did miss my parents though, so when my husband suggested I take our son and fly back for a visit, I thought it was a gift.

It didn't feel like a gift when I called my husband from my parents' house. He seemed distant in more ways than just miles. He cut the calls short; odd since we had run up hundreds of dollars in long distance charges when we were dating. Still, I put it out of my mind. With the trying to make ends meet in the islands, his brevity could certainly be excused. I tried not to worry—I knew we'd be back together very soon.

I couldn't even begin to imagine what had gone wrong in less than a week. Finally, we settled our son in for the night. Then he announced. "I'll be moving out, and don't be surprised if you get some divorce papers. I've found someone else."

The air whooshed from the room and I struggled to breathe—I felt like I was in a vacuum. It wasn't possible. He was my soul mate. The love of my life. How could I not have known this was coming? How could I not have seen? I ran from the house not just sobbing, but keening. The grief so overwhelmed me, that only the love and the responsibility I felt for my three-year-old kept me from dying that night of a broken heart.

My son reacted the same way. He would scream for his daddy each night, and I would hold him and share his tears, trying to reassure him that it wasn't his fault, that daddy loved him, that daddy would see him when he could—all the while wondering myself how I would get through the night. How would I concentrate on another day of work?

Some days I would find that I had dressed and taken my son to daycare, only to look down and realize I still had my slippers on. Other days I'd write appointments on my schedule and look at them later, realizing I had no idea who I was supposed to see, or where—that I'd only written in the time and my own name.

An ocean apart from family and friends, I was grateful for an understanding boss, who allowed for my frequent lapses of memory, and for a church that offered to provide babysitting and pointed me to a support group for divorced and widowed spouses. Still, I worried for my son. How would I raise him without a father? No one in my family had been divorced. How would I make ends meet in such an expensive place?

My son worried, too. "Mom, I guess we'll never go to Diamond Head again."

"Sure we will, honey."

"But how can we climb it without Daddy?"

That got my attention. My son needed assurance, even more than I did, of how we would make the long climb through life without my husband guiding the way. "Honey, tomorrow morning we're going to climb Diamond Head."

He looked at me unsure, but trying to believe that his timid mom might be able to take the lead on the climb.

The next day, I packed some drinks and cookies in a backpack and a couple of flashlights for use in the tunnels and stairwells that had been dug into the mountain. As we got into the car, I prayed I'd find the way through the city traffic, despite my poor sense of direction. With just a few wrong turns along the way, I managed to find the parking lot at the bottom of the old volcanic outcropping.

As we started on the trail, my son was off and running and I had to hurry to keep up. He slowed down as we came to the dark tunnels and he held my hand as we each took a flashlight to find our way. We followed the people in front of us, and shined lights for those who hadn't brought any. At the top of the mountain, we celebrated our victory with soda and cookies, feeling sorry for those who had made the hot climb and hadn't made preparations for something to drink at the top. My son offered to share his soda with another little boy who in turn offered to share his spam musibi, a Hawaiian treat.

That's it, I thought. We will prepare for our climb through life the best we can, we'll follow others through the dark places, and share our own light with those behind us. We'll celebrate our victories, share what we have, accept what others want to share with us, and when we are afraid we'll hold hands.

And so my son and I grew together. I learned to cook and clean, and eventually remarried. He grew into a young man who is always willing to share — be it a soda, a hug, or the knowledge that you can make it through a tough climb even when your guide unexpectedly leaves. We will always remember our climb up Diamond Head.

~G. M. Lee

Divorced and the Envy of Them All

It takes half your life before you discover life is a do-it-yourself project.
~Napoleon Hill

wenty-nine and divorced is nothing for anyone to be envious about, I thought. Turns out you never know what some people will envy. I was feeling sorry for myself, suddenly alone and empty, but I soon found out there is always a silver lining if you search hard enough.

The first thing on my agenda, after moving into my little apartment that Saturday, was to replace the dripping faucet in the kitchen. It had left a stain in the sink and the drip would certainly add to the water bill. Being on a tight budget, I couldn't afford to waste water. I soon realized that it meant I couldn't afford a plumber either. Determined not to give my ex anything to snicker about, I went to the library and checked out two books on do-it-yourself plumbing and proceeded to read the instructions for replacing a faucet. It didn't seem too difficult.

Famous last words. Removing the old faucet wasn't complicated, just time-consuming because it was corroded. WD-40, (not DW-40 as I had asked the nice clerk at Wal-Mart,) a lot of elbow grease, a few choice words, and learning to hold my mouth juuuust right finally resulted in the old faucet thrown into the garbage, two really sore knuckles, and a mess under the sink. I figured that installing the new faucet had to be easier.

Wrong again! Nothing fit the way the book or package said it would. I finally managed to hook the faucet up just the way the illustrations showed and turned on the water. Oh... that's what that funny little leftover rubber thing is for! After I turned the water off and mopped up the water that had sprayed everywhere, I started over and added the funny rubber thing—a gasket I came to understand—and tried again. So far, no leaks. Knock on wood.

I was so proud of myself—despite the fact that it took over five hours and a lot of hard work. In fact, I decided that next I could put down new linoleum to replace the nasty beat-up piece in my bathroom.

The next day, I returned the plumbing books to the library and checked out a book on flooring. The librarian's raised eyebrows and pursed lips did little to dissuade me. I was on a mission. It should have been a piece of cake after the kitchen faucet. Was I in for a lesson in futility.

After three hours, two false starts, and knees that screamed bloody murder when I touched them, I decided that I needed help... three hours ago. I couldn't afford to hire a contractor or professional floor person, so I enlisted my brother's help. He claimed he had to go to work (sure!) but volunteered a friend of his instead. After seeing his friend, Gregg, I eagerly started thinking of more projects that I might need help with.

Gregg was tall, dark, and yummy! Dark brown eyes and long lashes complemented his thick wavy brown hair and muscles. He would do just fine, I decided, even if he couldn't lay linoleum. But, it turned out that he could—and, he fixed my mistakes so they didn't really show at all. I cooked supper for him to repay his kindness and soon learned he wasn't interested in women.

Oh well, you can't win them all. He was still a feast for deprived eyes. And, he earned me some jealous glances from the other women in the apartment building.

Over the next few weeks, I became a regular at the local library and knew the do-it-yourself section like the back of my hand. I was on a first-name basis with the local hardware store and the Wal-Mart hardware area manager. Gregg was super-supportive and a great listener. I soon had a completely remodeled apartment with all the latest gadgets at half the cost of having it done by professionals.

Gregg still stops by to chat, but I'm so busy now we don't always have a lot of time. You see, since my divorce, I'm the envy of all the women in the apartment complex—as well as a lot of my married friends as well. If I have a plumbing problem, I can fix it myself and don't have to wait around for a plumber when I'm supposed to be at work. If my doorknob doesn't work, I can replace it myself and don't have to call a locksmith who charges enough to buy a small island in the Pacific.

In fact, I seem to spend most of my weekends helping other women repair or replace things around their homes—and some of them even have husbands. Because I'm so handy with my trusty pink tool kit, I've managed to save my hard-earned cash to buy new dresses and spiffy new shoes. Yes... they envy my shoes too.

So, before you let the depression of divorce drag you down, think about visiting your local library's do-it-yourself section and learning a new skill. It might come in handy and will probably save you some money in the long run. In fact, that was where I met my latest boyfriend, between the "how to repair windows" and the "how to install your own bay window" books. Tomorrow, after we finish painting the trim on my new bay window, we're going to the movies and then out to eat. After that, who knows? We may cuddle up and talk about a project for his place next. It's a nice-sized house that could use a woman's touch.

~Mary Alice Pritchard

60

Million Dollar Mermaid

The water is your friend. You don't have to fight with water,
just share the same spirit as the water, and it will help you move.
~Aleksandr Popov

My parents' divorce was final, and my mother and I were in the minivan bringing over the last of our things from our old house to our new one, twenty-five miles away just outside San Diego. Now that I was fifteen, the minivan seemed especially mini. We were dusty; there was grime under our fingernails, and dirt and sweat on our necks. We had been moving all weekend. My sisters were at the new house, unpacking, figuring out the layout of their new rooms, while my mother and I had gone back to the old house to check everything one last time.

Back at the old house, without the cars, boxes, and washer and dryer in the garage, our voices echoed as if we were in a cave. I remembered a family trip we had taken to the Carlsbad Caverns, all cool and dark, musty and acidic-smelling; my dad horsing around on the dangerous edges of the cavern with my middle sister and me and my older sister taking pictures with her new camera. My mother, silent and nervous in the dark enclosed spaces, only really relaxed when we got outside, and then smiling and even laughing as we picnicked under the cottonwood trees at Rattlesnake Springs, the water supply for the cavern. Now our empty garage smelled like car oil and laundry detergent, though the wood ceiling beams did somewhat resemble stalactites, if you squinted your eyes.

We left the garage and went around the house to the backyard, ducking under the bottlebrush shrub that, because of our negligence before the move, was now growing out of control. I always felt it should have been called toilet brush, because it looked like something you would use to scrub the toilet.

"I'll be glad to leave this yard behind," my mother said. It was split level, and covered with my father's various plants and shrubs and trees: bougainvillea, bird of paradise, hibiscus. My father had us memorize everything he grew, front yard and back. I couldn't look at a plant without either knowing its name, or at least what species it was. On each level, there was just a tiny patch of grass, barely room for a lawn chair or a barbecue. Now the plants were overgrown, some were dying, the grass was yellowing. My father had moved to a downtown apartment with his new girlfriend. Now, he only had a couple of cacti on the balcony. His green thumb finally, and easily, forsaken for the young, perky waitress he had hooked up with.

"It's not that I don't like plants or flowers," my mother continued. "But there was never any room to move out here. No yard for you kids to play in, no grass to tumble on." She pulled on the dry blade of a baby palm tree. She took in a deep breath and for a minute I thought she was going to cry or shout. But then she let go of the palm.

"I always wanted a yard with a swimming pool," she said, as we climbed back into the minivan. "When I was nine or ten, I became obsessed with Esther Williams, the swimming film star."

Somewhere, in the back of my mind I remembered vaguely, some aquatic, singing musical star in a flowered bathing cap who was always surrounded by synchronized swimmers. I'm sure we had probably watched one of her movies together.

"At the community pool," she went on, "which was called 'The Plunge,' I used to swim, pretending I was Esther. I would swim the backstroke across the water and pretend I was in a lavish MGM musical. I could do a dozen somersaults underwater without coming up for air."

"Esther Williams..." she said again, though it was more of a question, "Don't you know who Esther Williams is?"

"Oh, I think I know who you mean," I answered. "Didn't she have really broad shoulders and always came out of pools smiling with her arms outstretched?"

"Something like that," she said. "You know... they would put Vaseline on her teeth so that they would shine pearly white when she came out of the water. I used to have Esther Williams paper dolls, and an Esther Williams bathing suit with a small removable skirt."

"Hmm. Fashionable... Mom," I teased.

"Before you and your sister were born, we almost bought a house with a pool. It was a nice square pool, white bottom, with a diving board and a wooden deck. There was even space for plants around the pool, but your father said no. He said that chlorine from the pool water would get splashed onto the plants and into the soil and kill everything. The deck was three feet across all the way around the pool, and we could have built a small gutter, but your father still said no.... I don't think your father knows how to swim."

I had never realized that before. I remember that whenever we would go to the beach or lake, he would often only walk into the waves up to his knees. I had never thought to ask my father about it.

"That's weird. He couldn't have learned?" I asked.

"He didn't want to," she said.

We bought McDonald's, and brought it back to our new home. Andrea and Allyson, my sisters, were in the kitchen unwrapping dishes and setting them in the sink, which they had filled with water. After cheeseburgers and limp fries we made our way to our respective rooms. The first thing I did was plug in my stereo so I could listen to Pink Floyd's *Dark Side of the Moon* while I unpacked. Funny the things you find when you're either packing things up, or unpacking. I found a picture of my mom and dad between the pages of a Stephen King novel that I had only half read. The picture is on a boat, a ferry cruise, I think, from a trip to New York City a few years earlier. Now it was my dad who looked afraid and awkward, almost stiff, while my mother smiled, her cheeks full and red. Behind them, a skinny black railing or chain, I couldn't really tell, and then water, the harbor behind that. I thought again about what my mother had told me today. My father is afraid of water.

My older sister, Allyson, started pounding on her bedroom wall, which was right next to my bedroom. She was putting up a picture or a poster. I had the middle room, between the two of them, and I could hear Andrea singing to a Christian rock CD, in a soft, sweet voice, if a little out of tune.

I realized I hadn't seen my mother in quite a while. Her room was across from mine, and I thought she had been in the adjoining bathroom. I had heard the clink of perfume bottles and pills and deodorant as she arranged them in her medicine cabinet. But now her room was silent.

I peeked outside my room, into the hallway and called out.

"Mom?... Mom?"

"Where's Mom?" I yelled down the hallway to my sisters.

"I don't know, I haven't seen her," said Allyson, and then she poked her head out of her bedroom door.

"Maybe she's in the kitchen," said Andrea.

"I hope she's not crying again," said Allyson. "I hope she's not getting all emotional and stuff again." Allyson was seventeen, a senior in high school. Lately she'd been eschewing emotions for stoicism—thinking that this signified her transition to adulthood.

We checked the kitchen, but she wasn't there.

We checked the garage, the dining room, the living room. No sign of her.

Through the open window we heard noises from outside. Water slapping. Small waves breaking. She was in the backyard pool.

We opened the sliding glass door and stepped out onto the back patio.

The sun had long since gone down, the edge of night had made everything blue and gray and shadowed. The deck lights and the pool light needed new bulbs, but we could see our mother's shape, her body, bobbing and floating, diving. The backstroke, the breaststroke, the crawl. She somersaulted four, five, six times and then slowly rose from the water, arms outstretched, shoulders broad and square. We could just barely make out her smile, the glint of white teeth.

~Rob Williams

61

Jack and Jannie

Beauty is not in the face; beauty is a light in the heart.
~Kahlil Gibran

As I walked along the lushly wooded path of the state park, a couple walking ahead of me drew my attention. A little yellow dog, which may have been part Cocker Spaniel, scampered between the legs of the slowly moving couple. They were holding hands and I heard their laughter drift back on the slight wind that was blowing that day. The woman, I noticed, walked with a pronounced limp. I caught a glimpse of her porcelain skin as she turned her head to look at her male companion. She tucked her golden blond hair neatly behind her ear and gave him her full attention, and her smile seemed to light up her face and everything around her. There was something about the couple that intrigued me, and I observed them walking ahead of me with fascination. The couple strayed from the path and I passed them by. Their laughter was somewhat soothing, and I was sad to see them go.

It was a beautiful day, although slightly overcast, but that seemed to match my mood. I loved this park. It held a certain mysticism and healing power just by breathing the air that came off the Atlantic Ocean on one side and the intra-coastal waterway on the other. Huge, majestic oak trees with their arms stretched over the well-manicured landscaping of native fauna lent an air of comfort. They seemed like wise keepers of the history they have witnessed, and a past that has been long forgotten by human memories; an epic history like wars, natural disasters, and generations of families who lived and died in the space around them. I was there among the massive trees and breathing the fresh air to try to get a fresh perspective on the current turmoil in my life, which would surely seem a small thing in comparison to what these beautiful trees had endured.

I had thought myself healed and recovered from a marriage that had lasted way too long. I had accomplished what I thought impossible just five years earlier; I escaped and started my life over with a child and nothing but the clothes on our backs. Although years of emotional trauma had worn me to an empty shell, I picked up the pieces and had started to gain confidence in my own inner strength. My life was falling into place. Laughter was starting to replace the fear and sadness I used to see in my daughter's eyes, and happiness was something that I finally felt deep inside my spirit. Life was an adventure filled with possibilities and not dread.

I had recently met someone who started breaking down the walls of emotional protection I had built over the years, and he was helping me to trust again. He was someone who opened my heart to the potential that happiness in a relationship was a possibility. He made me laugh, made me talk, and made me feel safe enough to open up to him. But there was something missing. I realized that he was investing more of himself than he was getting in return. I had come to the sad realization that we were at a roadblock. I could continue to experience the comfort and security he had come to represent, or I could face the fact that the feelings just weren't there, be fair to both of us, and move on.

Knowing I had made my mind up to end the relationship, my pre-divorce pattern of thinking was taking over. The big "life" questions kept running through my head. Is there truly a happily ever after? Is there truly a person out there who could love me for me and I could love back with the same intensity? Does true love really even exist? I needed to get myself centered, clear my head, and in the quiet of the park actually listen to my thoughts.

As I meandered down the dirt path where butterflies flitted among the fragrance of wildflowers, I found myself nearing an old log cabin that had been converted into the park museum. As I went inside and began reading about the park's history, I noticed the woman I had seen on the path earlier. She came inside alone, and I saw her companion and dog standing outside. I smiled at her and she smiled back.

"We can't bring the dog inside, so he's letting me come in and look around first," she said with a thick speech impediment. I realized then that she was not only slightly physically disabled, but that she might also have a mental disability. She kept wringing her hands and glancing toward her companion. I could see that she was feeling sad and insecure that she had to come in alone.

"The dog won't bother me in the slightest bit, and we are the only people in here. Do you think we could sneak her in for a little while?" I asked.

The woman smiled so big that I couldn't help but laugh out loud. She opened the door to the cabin and said, "She don't care, Jack, come on in!" Her companion carried the dog in his arms as he walked in, nodding his head in my direction. I wasn't prepared for what I saw when I could see him face to face. When I was walking behind him on the path, it was impossible to see Jack's physical affliction. He was extremely disfigured from what appeared to be a fire or a chemical burn. His face, neck, chest, and arms and, in fact, all visible skin on the front of his body looked melted, and it was mottled with white and red scars. I tried to school my reaction, smiled brightly, and held out my hand, "I'm Dawn," I said.

Despite his frail appearance, his handshake was firm, and his huge smile tightened the scarred skin on his face as he said, "I'm Jack and this is my wife, Jannie. We've been married for eight months!" He put his arm around his wife and the pride and love shone in his eyes. She blushed shyly and then laughed. She petted the dog's head and said, "And this is Tobi. She's our baby."

Jack and Jannie were inspiring. Their friendly manner was contagious, and at first we made general small talk. Then they talked about how they had moved from a big city to a small beach condo because the area of the city in which they lived was not safe. Jannie's blue eyes filled with tears as she told me how a neighbor had attacked her. The neighbor woman had beaten Jannie senseless in broad daylight when she was waiting for the bus to take Jack his lunch. Jack had tears in his eyes, too, and he gently stroked Jannie's back as she talked about how the woman who beat her had been verbally harassing Jack and her every day, making fun of them by imitating them and calling them names.

At the end of her story, Jannie smiled widely and said, "It all worked out, though, because the police caught her." She hugged the dog close to her as she said, "Tobi saved my life! If it weren't for Tobi, I know my neighbor would have killed me. Tobi knocked the woman down and protected me."

Jannie told me how Jack had run the three miles to the hospital from his job at the post office when he got the call about what had happened. "He didn't even wait for the bus!"

"I wanted to get to her and be with her as fast as I could," Jack said. I couldn't imagine the physical pain that running three miles in his condition must have caused him. Jannie's eyes kept seeking out Jack's, and she smiled each time he looked at her.

Our conversation lightened, and we exchanged other pleasantries about the park. They even showed me the many tricks that the amazing Tobi could do. As they left and I watched them disappear down the path, tears clouded my eyes. These two people had endured unfathomable physical pain and mental anguish made worse by cruel people. They had found a safe harbor with each other where there was love, respect, and kindness.

What touched me was the way Jannie looked into Jack's eyes; there wasn't a doubt that she was confident in his love and acceptance. He made it obvious that she was the most beautiful person in the world to him. By the beaming smile she bestowed on him, it was clear that she felt the same for him, too. They saw through the painful physical handicaps to each other's souls and their love was based on what they saw deep inside. They related on a level that so few people have the capacity to ever see, let alone experience. Meeting them and seeing them interact was life-changing for me. I smiled as I realized that for those two people, at least, true love did exist.

Were all of my "life" questions answered that day in the park, when not just quiet contemplation cleared my head, but a sweet, adoring couple touched a place deep inside my heart and soul? The answers were not easy. I knew I had to say goodbye to my current relationship. That, of course, made me very sad and I knew the sadness would not go away for a while. I knew in my heart I wanted to wait until I found what Jack and Jannie had. The sweet couple, just by being in that magical park at that particular time, taught me what to look for. Will it happen in my lifetime? I'm not sure; it might not be meant for me. But I am willing to wait and be content to live my life to the fullest until it does. Who could settle for anything less after experiencing the beauty of Jack and Jannie?

~Dawn Smith Heaps

62

A Sign of Hope

Hope is that thing with feathers that perches in the soul
and sings the tune without the words and never stops... at all.
~Emily Dickinson

When my sister found herself facing an unwanted divorce after more than two decades of marriage, our family was devastated. For hours, I sat and listened as she talked about her fears of the future, the struggle of just getting through a single day, the deep sadness that surrounded her and her daughter, knowing that the place they had always called home would soon only be a memory. I did my best to offer comfort. Together we prayed for strength to push forward.

I was with her the morning the movers came. Watching her walk through the house one last time was gut-wrenching. She stood quietly in the doorway of each room, knowing she wouldn't be coming back. She later told me that she was trying to soak up all of the happy times for remembering in the years to come.

Under an early morning sky, we closed the front door for the last time. The sound of it shutting behind us rang out with a stark finality. The end.

You know that feeling of hopelessness when you've done all you can do and nothing changes? That's how I felt that day.

Climbing into the car, neither of us spoke, but our grief was palpable. I wanted desperately to feel a single ounce of hope, anything to help make our long trip bearable.

As we turned east, the sun was just beginning to clear the horizon. The sight of it there—pink and perfect—lifted my spirits. At least it isn't raining, I remember thinking.

It seemed like an odd time to take pictures, but I reached for the camera in my purse and snapped a picture of the sun, then a quick one of my sister's solemn profile.

"What are you doing?" she asked, looking at me as if I were a stranger.

"As sad as this day is, I must document the moment," I told her, certain that one day we would look at these photos and marvel at how far she had come.

At the time, such a day seemed beyond our reach, but I knew that just as sure as the sun was rising pink and perfect in the east, it would rise again tomorrow and the next day and every day after that, for as long as God ordered it. And while I wasn't certain what tomorrow held, I had absolutely no doubt who held tomorrow, nor that my sister would make it through this difficult season.

With that assurance in my heart, I reached over and squeezed her hand as we drove into the warm and steady light of a new day.

~Dayle Allen Shockley

63

Clarity

How beautiful a day can be
When kindness touches it!
~George Elliston

My husband and I finally came to an agreement to settle our divorce and I thought I would be able to get back to living my life and enjoying my babies.

Then, after I had given him substantially more than was his, he decided he wanted more. Because it seemed as if the demands would never end, my first thought was to tell him I would see him in court. However, I was so tired of living in this state of limbo and not knowing if things were ever going to just settle down and be normal again. The bad thing was that he knew that.

I was pretty sure that I was going to just take the deal and be done, but I called my attorney and said, "I have to think a little. I haven't had much sleep, so I just want to make sure that I am making the right decision. I'll call you at 3:00 to let you know what I have decided." I knew that any additional money cut from my budget would make my life and that of my children even more difficult.

I looked at the big, blue eyes of my children and said, "Let's go for a drive." My daughter was asleep before we were very far from the house, but my son enjoyed the sights. We drove to the scenic, southern part of the county where the road, shaded by the trees, rose and fell with the hills. The drive was relaxing and pretty, and I hoped that maybe it would clear my head a little. We drove and drove.

We had driven until it was about thirty minutes past lunchtime. "Baby, are you hungry?" I peered into the rear-view mirror to see if my son was nodding in agreement.

"Yes, Mama. Hungry, hungry, hungry."

There was a small town just ahead with a little restaurant that had always caught my eye, but I had never stopped. I decided that today would be as good a day as any to try the little restaurant that looked like a grandma's house. Grandma always makes you feel better.

"Okay. We'll stop up here and eat."

My daughter was just waking up as we pulled up to the cozy restaurant surrounded by huge oak trees. As we stepped onto the wide front porch scattered with rocking chairs, I was hopeful for a peaceful getaway.

We walked in and were told that we could seat ourselves. The restaurant was an old house, reborn, with many rooms to choose from. We walked across the creaky hardwood floors and through the rooms until we got to the sun porch that I thought, surely, looked like the happiest spot in the place. My son commented on the quirky decorations. "You don't put chairs on the ceiling," he laughed, and we talked about all of the other funny things we saw.

There was a table just off in the other room, but within viewing distance, where a group of mainly silver-headed ladies was seated. Some ladies were decked out in festive hats and others with rosy-cheeked smiles. They looked friendly and happy, enjoying a lunch date with their friends.

The kids and I ordered, and became enveloped in the little world we had stumbled into. We looked out the windows and talked about the green trees, the birds, the squirrels, and the soothing shade. I was very much enjoying our respite from the overwhelming stress that had consumed me the past couple of days.

The waitress approached our table. "The ladies at that table," she said, motioning toward the group of smiling faces, "said they want to know all about that perfect mother over there with her children. Is your husband in the Air Force?"

"No," I answered, flattered by the compliment. I scrambled for how I was going to answer this question without making anyone feel awkward for asking. "He just doesn't want to be married anymore."

Her face looked shocked, and she said, "I'm sorry. I'll let them know so that they can keep you in their prayers." Tears welled up in my eyes. These days, people only had to show the slightest concern, and I fell apart. With much effort, I managed to keep the tears from tumbling down my face.

My children and I enjoyed our meal and lazily took our time. I knew that when we walked out the door, I would have to snap back to reality. The 3:00 deadline was quickly approaching. I didn't have the absolute clarity on my decision that I had hoped for, but at least we were enjoying ourselves.

When we finished eating, we paid our thirteen dollar bill. Then, just as we were rising to leave, the waitress came over and handed me an envelope sent by the group of ladies. It read, "Beautiful Family. Prayerful Good Wishes." I walked over to tell them thank you without opening the envelope. The bulge inside told me all I needed to know. Tears streamed down my face, and I couldn't even begin to control them. They had no idea the message that they had just given me straight from God. He is always there to take care of us, and sometimes He sends silver-haired angels to see that the job is done.

When I got home, I opened the envelope. Inside it was $72. I called my attorney and said, "I got some clarity on the settlement offer at lunch. I'll take his deal." I didn't second-guess my decision at all.

~Heather McGee

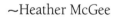

64

Journey to Peace

The journey is the destination.
~Dan Eldon

"What do you want?" My ex-husband's question resounds in my head as I sit alone on the Great Wall of China.

"Peace," I whisper. Tentatively, I say it a little bit louder. Nothing changes. No one notices. I turn and glance at the crumbling wall as it meanders across miles, extending as far as the eye can see. "Peace!" I shout out. To no one in particular, but really to all the souls who have traveled this wall before me.

How did I get here? How did I wind up on the other side of the world, on a centuries-old fortress wall, all by myself? Never in my life had I been on my own.

Raised in a happy, love-filled home, I left at the age of twenty-two to marry my college sweetheart. I was already five months pregnant.

Our marriage was a journey filled with vistas, valleys, and plateaus. The plateaus were typical of any married couple busy raising children. The monotony of work, clean, take care of the kids, and sleep. But the vistas, our happiest moments, were when the whole family was together, on vacation, around the pool, or enjoying dinner together sharing our highs and lows of the day. The valleys came at the end—one after another. Disappointments and dead dreams became deep crevices that we couldn't seem to find our way through.

We were the proud parents of two boys, spaced five years apart. I stayed at home to raise the kids while he worked in the music industry. His career choice caused much friction between us because he worked long hours and was gone for extended periods of time. I had always wanted him to work a typical nine-to-five job. But friends and family thought we were the perfect family. One friend said that if you looked up "nuclear family" in the dictionary you'd find a picture of us.

So again, as I sit in the warm sun on this ancient wonder of the world, I think, How did I get here? Once more, my thoughts turn to my marriage.

Fifteen years into our marriage, we had another unplanned pregnancy—after being on birth control for ten years. My husband was unhappy. He didn't want more kids. I was thrilled. I had always felt like I wasn't done having babies and had begged my husband for more. I longed for a daughter. I dreamed to experience that special mother-daughter bond that I shared with my own mother. My dream died when I miscarried the baby. I was devastated. I felt like I was in quicksand, constantly struggling to keep my head up so I wouldn't drown. As I railed against God, my husband confessed to me that he was relieved that I had miscarried.

I looked at him—the man I had pledged to love for the rest of my life—and thought, God forgive me. I cannot live with this man for fifty years. That was the day my marriage died; and along with it, all the dreams I had for it. Everything unraveled from there. Two years later, I was divorced. After eighteen years of marriage I was now single. My parents, both sets of grandparents, my brother—all were married to their life mates. I was the only one who had failed.

My family and friends were supportive and loving, but my sense of failure and guilt was overwhelming. Life for me and the boys changed dramatically. After staying home all those years I now had to work full time. My oldest started his freshman year in college. With a car, a job, and the independence that comes with being eighteen, he filled his time with friends, school, and work. The younger one went through the eighth grade in a fog; spending a great deal of time at his friend's house where they still ate dinner together as a family. Now, home alone for more than eight hours a day, even the dog seemed depressed and neglected.

How did I get here? Those were words that my ex said had reverberated through his head the morning of our wedding. Again, I contemplate the series of events that led me to this very moment — sitting atop this ancient monument.

After struggling through my first few months as a single mother, one day, reality finally hit me and I lost it in the middle of a grocery store parking lot. As I was loading the groceries into my car, one bag tipped over and a jar of spaghetti sauce rolled out, fell to the ground and broke, splattering sauce everywhere. As I looked at the crushed glass, splintered into a thousand pieces, I thought, that is my life. It will never be the same. I broke into tears, sobbing deep soul-aching tears. Eventually, I pulled myself together and drove home to make dinner — because that is what single parents do. We don't have a partner to take over when we need help.

A couple of months later, my parents mentioned that my father was going to China. The cost was less than a thousand dollars. I decided that if I could get the time off work, I would withdraw the money from my savings account and go.

So here I am, Thanksgiving Day, sitting on the Great Wall of China. I wandered the fortress wall for a couple of hours. Finally I sit and survey my surroundings. I swing my legs over the edge and contemplate my journey to this place. In my journal, I write:

Never would I have imagined that I would be here, sitting on the Great Wall of China built in 221 BC. Today is Thanksgiving in America.

I am thankful, ever so grateful for this moment — the sun is shining, the wind is blowing, I am alive and at peace. All is well within my soul. I am all right. My boys are good, healthy, and beautiful. I am blessed. In spite of the twists and turns my life has taken, happiness and peace are now in my heart.

Thank you Lord for my life, for my health. For this opportunity to go to China with my father. I take a deep breath, let it out slowly... I am alive, I am awake. God is love, love is God.

This wall is one of the great wonders of the world, and I am experiencing it by myself and that is perfect. It is the way it is supposed to be. The wind is now still. The sun is bright.

Look what I have accomplished this year:

- *Bought my first house*
- *Saw my oldest son graduate from high school*
- *Went out on my own after forty years (twenty-two years with my parents then eighteen years with my husband)*
- *Completed a marathon plus two half-marathons*
- *Interviewed for my first job in nearly twenty years*
- *Sat on the Great Wall of China*

I throw a coin over the wall. It's good luck if you make a wish. I wish that I will always feel this same sense of peace.

And I finally realize the question is not, "How did I get here?" But instead, it should be a statement, a declaration, a philosophy and a mission:

"I am at peace. All is well, and I am at peace."

~Marie Williams

65

Sleeping Alone

Freedom is the greatest fruit of self-sufficiency.
~Epicurus

After twenty-one years, it was over. Despite values, intentions, and best efforts, I was getting divorced. The decision had been made and the heartache accepted.

My ex and I had both stayed in the house as the painful (but peaceful) changes had come about. Those last months sure hadn't been a happy time, but it seemed the right thing to do at the time. My ex was still arranging for his new living space as the property settlement was finalized. September came and our last daughter was off to college. For me, it was eerie and tense.

And then he moved out. Empty nest with a capital E.

When the brightly colored rental truck pulled up in the drive, I was full of anxiety. I sat at the kitchen table as he carried his boxes out to the truck, and the couch, the chairs, a dresser. It was strange to watch half of the furniture go out the door. But fair was fair. I had agreed to the split. It had seemed the right thing to do. I didn't realize how much it would hurt to see those symbols of our twenty-one years together pass before me on their way to who knows where.

After the front door slammed shut, I went to the living room window and watched the truck wheel away. The truck's gaily decorated side panels reflected the late afternoon sun, and they seemed to mock the dark misery inside me. Who could be happy at a time like this?

The house felt so empty. I reflected on that thought. The truth was—it wasn't. "I" was still there, and so was one aged and slightly maniacal cat.

I sat, eyeball-to-eyeball with the incorrigible feline, and I could swear he was grinning at me. It made me laugh. Laughter echoes in a couchless, half-empty, newly-divorced house. I decided it sounded kind of good.

I lit a fire in the fireplace. It wasn't even cold out, but I had one of those easy start logs and it just felt right, especially since I didn't need to take my ex's allergies into consideration any more. The fire crackled and felt good, even though it was a bit warm.

No problem, I thought. If it gets too hot, I can turn on the air conditioner. Who's going to complain? After all, it's my electric bill now.

I danced around the living room to an Enya CD, only narrowly escaping trampling the surprised cat, who was not used to such frivolities lately. No one dances in a house that is waiting for divorce, it seems. It's funny to realize how quickly dancing can return. Like riding a bicycle, you never forget how, and the mood was finally right. I had never really danced alone. I had danced as a teen. I had danced at my wedding; I had danced with my husband at events. I had danced with the kids. But not alone. Why was that? I danced up a storm, and decided dancing alone was quite all right.

When it was bedtime, I ascended the steps in the quiet of the night. My anxiety had returned. I had slept alone in my bed for months, with him in another room, so what was the big deal?

Staring at the ceiling, I listened to the night sounds. Or lack of night sounds. It was so quiet. There were no children in their rooms, no snoring man down the hall. Even the cat had disappeared. I was alone.

Had I ever been alone? Growing up, I had been the second of six children. Sharing with siblings had been a way of life. I had left home for college and there I lived with three roommates. I left college for marriage, and then had my children. This was—literally—the first night I had ever spent really alone.

I couldn't go to sleep and my mind kept churning. I thought of the many nights I had "walked the floors" with a fussy baby. I thought of the many nights I had waited up for teenagers to come home. I thought of the many nights of restless anticipation when someone in the family had a big day ahead of them. I thought of the nights I had cried myself to sleep as the divorce became real. Some of those nights had been hard, but I had always done what seemed to be the right thing.

I didn't set the alarm. I could sleep—if I could sleep—as long as I wanted to. It was a nice thought. I was waiting for no one on this particular night. There was no snoring. No disturbing noises. There was no one to worry about. There was no one to cater to, except me. Could I cater to me?

And that's when things changed. The oppressive silence became nurturing peace. My life had not gone according to plan, but I was okay. In fact, I was better than okay. I was beginning a new phase of life, and I could look at it as scary or I could look at it as an adventure. It would be my adventure, no one else's. I didn't have to be lonely, because at that moment, I knew that the person I was with was pretty interesting, strong, loyal, and brave.

And soon I was sleeping. Alone. Peaceful and happy.

~Christine Bush

The Journey Home

One joy scatters a hundred griefs.
~Chinese Proverb

I'm not sure at what point I knew I was setting out on an important journey. I'd been to dinner with Jane and Paulette many times before. Nothing seemed out of the ordinary when the waiter approached our table and greeted us with, "Hi, I'm Rico." But the waiter held a steady, trance-like gaze upon me while adding, "And it'll be my pleasure to serve two, such beautiful ladies this evening." That changed everything.

"Two beautiful ladies?" I pointed to myself first, then at my two friends who were seated on either side of me. "Is one of us not-so-beautiful?"

Even though the waiter's boyish face turned crimson red, he never took his eyes from me. "Forgive me. I... I'm sorry," he stuttered, clearing his throat and revealing an Italian accent. "I think I meant to say three, not two. It's been one of those days."

"I know the feeling," I told him.

From the time my feet had slipped out from under the covers and hit the floor that morning, an avalanche of self-pity seemed to be waiting for just the right time to tumble down on me. I had received a call regarding an off-Broadway play I'd written and staged, to learn that it didn't wow potential producers enough to take it to the next level. And afterward, as I loitered about the city trying to figure out my next move, I was accosted by an old lady and her dog.

As I approached them, her mangy poodle charged at me, barking and showing its teeth. The woman pulled the leash taut and laced into her slobbering, little pooch with, "Daisy, stop. It's nobody."

Yup. Nobody. That's me, I thought, huffing and puffing up the three flights of stairs to my dingy studio apartment. It was the only place with four walls I could afford since I'd left my husband. I couldn't bring myself to call it home, but it was my port in the storm. This was my first birthday alone since the divorce.

Air. I needed air. I wrestled open the window, giving way to a rattle of traffic and city buses on the street below. Then I turned from the peels of paint scattered on the sill and made a beeline for the freezer. Armed with a spoon and a pint of pistachio ice cream, I sank into a kitchen chair. I slid off my shoes and kicked up my feet. Devouring ice cold spoonfuls that didn't satiate my hunger, I felt as aimless as the little piece of fuzz I noticed drifting in the breeze. I watched it, all caught up, suspended amid a shaft of light that spilled in from the window. The poor thing had nothing to cling to. Is this what my life has become? No husband, no children; no white picket fence; still pursuing passions and banking on dreams; staring at peeling paint and identifying with fuzz?

Before I could succumb to tears, there was a knock on the door. When I opened it, I found the smiling faces of Jane and Paulette. "Happy Birthday," they crooned in unison, bearing gifts and flowers. They were perfumed and ready to party. At any other time, I would've been thrilled by such attentiveness, but the words "happy" and "birthday" seemed an oxymoron this year.

"C'mon. You only get one fortieth. Let's celebrate," Paulette said.

I cast a litany of beseeching: "I-don't-feel-good, I've-got-a-headache," but Jane countered with, "What you need is a night out. A bottle of wine, dinner, and some birthday cake is the cure for what ails you."

They wore me down until I found myself seated between them at Café Italiano—a restaurant that swelled with the sound of Pavarotti, the pungency of garlic, and silver place settings that reflected elegance well beyond my means. It wasn't so much the lavishness that made me feel uncomfortable, it was more the waiter. He persisted in gawking at me from behind the cappuccino station.

The next time he appeared at our table, he held up a bottle of wine we'd ordered. "Who'll do the tasting honors?" he asked.

Jane looked to Paulette, who suggested, "Why not the birthday girl?"

The waiter gasped, his olive complexion whitening. "The birthday girl?"

"Yes, that's me," I told him. "It's the big four-oh."

"Forty?" He fixed his eyes on my face. "Today?" His stare was piercing, as if he were looking straight into my soul.

I answered him with a nod.

"I can't believe it." His voice cracked. "I just can't believe it."

"Well, neither can I," I told him, watching how the corkscrew quivered in his hands. His Adam's apple bobbed and tears lit his eyes.

I turned to Jane, then Paulette—searching for them to explain things. But they both just shrugged, looking as baffled as I felt.

"It's... it's just that you look so much like my sister." There was desperation in the waiter's voice, a sense of urgency. "And you're probably not going to believe this, but just last night I had a dream about her, and at the end, she said, 'I'll see you tomorrow.' And here you are. You're the spitting image of her."

Embarrassed, I could feel a hot flush rising in my cheeks. Other patrons were looking on. Even the crew of waiters elbowed each other when they spied Rico's sudden blaze of emotion.

"And that's why it's just so eerie," he said. "Because today would've been her fortieth birthday, too."

"Would've been?" I asked.

"She died in a car accident when she was twenty-four."

Sadness unfurled as a shiver in my spine. Jane, Paulette and I sat there, transfixed by that waiter. He was completely overcome—his shoulders rounded, he'd swung his tear-streaked face to the floor.

My heart seized and humility narrowed my throat. "I'm sorry. How very sad."

Jane and Paulette echoed my sentiments, and then another waiter stepped in. He put a hand on Rico's shoulder and gestured that he'd take over. As Rico was escorted away, we were all stunned amid a brittle silence. I flipped open the menu, seeking the words printed inside, reading them as if a prayer that would bring us back to the moment.

"What just happened here?" I asked.

"Something beautiful," Paulette answered. "Something mystical, I think."

"Yes, when you walked in," Jane said, "I think you brought that man's sister back to life."

Staring into the faces of my friends, reality gripped me, and the tedium and anxiety of my existence fell away, replaced by a swell of gratitude. We reached for our wineglasses. And when we raised them high, I toasted Jane and Paulette—and the memory of a stranger whose heart I swore was beating among us.

There were appetizers and entrees and even cake for dessert, but there was no sign of Rico. As we were leaving, I spotted him tending tables in the courtyard outside and quietly approached.

"I just wanted to say thank you and so long," I told him, leaning in to kiss him on the cheek.

"I should be thanking you," he said, drawing his arms around me. Before he let me go, he uttered softly, "Happy birthday. Live two lives—one for you and one for my sister."

Later that night, when I slipped under the covers and rested my head on my pillow, I realized that while I'd given that waiter a memory and vision of his sister, he, in turn, had given me the gift of realizing that my story wasn't over. There were chapters, maybe volumes, yet to be written—beyond un-produced plays and protective dogs, peeling paint, and drifting fuzz. I understood. I had finally come home.

~Kathleen Gerard

67

That's Life. Live It. Feel It.

The morning steals upon the night,
Melting the darkness.
~William Shakespeare

Imagine waking up every day feeling like a child on Christmas morning. Every day. This was my life. Two beautiful happy little daughters and a gorgeous loving partner. He had boundless energy, and contagious enthusiasm—just like Tigger. He was a perfect blend of charm and a love of life. If a child were to depict my life, it would have been bordered by joined up red hearts. This was my world. It was like a picture you would stick on the fridge to warm your soul.

"Anyone hungry?" He would ask. "Yessss!" the girls would reply in unison. "Coats on then," he would say, and off he would go, with a little girl on the end of each of his hands, into the woods to build a fire and cook lunch.

I would often witness the scene as if I had risen above my body, looking down onto it, and feel wrapped in a blanket by so much love and happiness. He was their scoutmaster, leading them off on treks along the coastal path, crouching around rock pools with nets and buckets, taking them snorkeling at night to see who was awake underwater after dark.

But children grow away from their parents. That is a parent's job. The parent is the facilitator, equipping the children with the skills to make them self sufficient, and then the parent becomes redundant. The transition is not always a smooth one. You make them independent of you, but who makes you independent of them?

The girls grew up and went in search of new mentors. Their peers became their advisors and their entertainment managers. Pop stars, film stars, and sporting heroes became their new idols. Real or perceived authority figures became their enemies. I watched as their relationship with my partner deteriorated. I watched him disintegrate—and with him, the whole family. "Please make an effort with the girls," I would plead. "You always take their side," he would scorn.

"Please make an effort to get on with him," I would plead to the girls.

"You always take his side," they'd reply.

I was powerless to stop the course of events that was unfolding. I could have written the script, but I was not directing the production, which was changing from a romantic comedy to a horror film. What started out as a happy family ended in one daughter being driven away by her unhappiness, and me leaving my partner. I was left alone with my elder daughter who felt overly responsible to me, whilst having to come to terms with her own sense of loss. I'm her mother; I should be supporting her, not her supporting me. I didn't make a good consolation prize. My old friend, Guilt, a frequent visitor in those days, now had his feet firmly under the table. I tried to pinpoint the exact moment from which things escalated, to rewind and rerecord, a torturous exercise. Who changed the channel when I was out of the room?

It was after one particularly sleepless night that I walked down to the beach to watch the sun rise. Just to see if it would. My world had ended; had everyone else's? The sun did rise. It should have reassured me, but if filled me with despair. How would I get through another day? It was Christmas morning. The irony was killing me.

As I sat on the shore, the sky changed from grey to orange, then pinks and pastels. I drew my knees up under my chin, clasped my arms around my legs, and wept and wept and wept. I could not accept what had happened, outwardly saying "No, no, no." I sighed loudly, and shrugged my shoulders in an attempt to regain control. I looked up to a magnificent sky, where birds filled the air, starting their day. To the right I could see a man clambering over the rocks. He had long blond hair, tied in a ponytail that fell midway down his back. Denim shirt, black jeans, and construction boots. Although it has now been many years, I remember the image as though it was yesterday.

I was in a remote spot, chosen for this reason. I hoped he would go away. "Please don't come near me," I prayed into my knees. "Please go away. Pleeeease…" I said with my eyes shut, hoping when I opened them he would have disappeared. But he made a beeline toward me. A dolphin made from bone hung from a shoelace around his neck. He had high cheekbones, clear blue eyes, and a smile that made his face look like it was floodlit. He was close enough to see that I was distressed, sitting in my checkered pajamas with a coat around me.

It was then that I experienced my first miracle—a truly altruistic act of kindness from one stranger to another. He did not ask me for my story, or offer any (practical or otherwise) help. He couldn't have helped anyway (or so I thought). He simply extended his hand and as I took it, he said to me, "That's life. Live it. Feel it."

He didn't say anything else, just looked straight into my eyes and held my gaze. I didn't say anything, and didn't move toward or away from him. This moment may have lasted thirty seconds, or two hours, but it had the significance of a lifetime. He then walked away, clambering back over the rocks the way he came.

Call it a breakdown. Call it a breakthrough. In that instant I felt spellbound. Whether he had witnessed me dancing naked on the beach—or as he did, consumed by grief—it appeared to him to be the same thing. I was alive, a living, feeling being, and that was something to celebrate. The capacity to experience pain is also the capacity to experience joy. I was fortunate that I cared so much to care so much. I should have been grateful, not sorrowful.

When the man had disappeared completely, I gave thanks for all those happy years. I named everything I was thankful for. I imagined that I was holding a gift in my outstretched hand, said thank you, put it down, and put out my hand to receive the next one. In so doing, I was able to let the sorrow go and feel positive about the now, instead of feeling negative about what had passed.

I saved my biggest thanks for last as I looked over toward the rocks, and although I didn't see him again, I haven't stopped thanking him... whoever he was, wherever he is.

~Joy Summers

Divorce *and* Recovery

New Fish
in the Dating Pond

*There are two kinds of sparks, the one that goes off
with a hitch like a match, but it burns quickly.
The other is the kind that needs time, but when the flame strikes...
it's eternal, don't forget that.*
~Timothy Oliveira

68

A Match Made in Mud

Life is a celebration of awakenings, of new beginnings,
and wonderful surprises that enlighten the soul.
~Cielo

"Divorced, overweight grandma with lots of baggage seeking Christian male with college education, financially secure, non-smoker, non-drinker, no small children and a great sense of humor."

Okay, so I never did place that ad. Your self-esteem is bound to take a hit when your twenty-four-year marriage fails. I had enjoyed being married and was open to it again.

With encouragement from a friend, I joined a dating service, one that didn't use photos or videos. After a few weeks, I was introduced to Doug. We saw each other off and on for ten weeks. Doug had warned me that he was "slow to warm up." He had not touched me: no hand holding, no arm around me, no kissing. I believed that "being slow to warm up" was just an excuse to cover the fact that he found me totally unattractive. Maybe it was time to ask the dating service for another introduction.

The agency I worked for was gearing up for its annual mud volleyball fundraising event — not an activity I heartily embraced. It was too labor-intensive for the small amount of revenue it generated. But, I inherited it when I had accepted the position of executive director.

I warned Doug that on mud volleyball day, a hot Saturday in July, I would be busy all day. If he wanted to see me, he could drive out to the fairgrounds where we had converted the outdoor arena into six mud pits. I had asked that he bring me a large iced tea, heavy on the ice. I really didn't expect him to show up.

On the day of the event, things went pretty much as I expected. The mud was deep. It sucked the shoes right off your feet. You could taste it and feel the grit between your teeth. From my narrow-minded conservative perspective, I found the games disgusting and demeaning both for the players and the organization. Several hundred players and volunteers were in mud up to mid-thigh. Anyone unfortunate enough to fall was covered in mud from head to toe. I stayed as far from the mud courts as possible, trying to maintain my administrative air. If I could find an excuse to run an errand, make a bank deposit or do anything else, I would leave for a while.

After driving into town for more ice, I was feeling pretty smug to still be mud free at noon. I pulled my little teal Geo Storm up to the beverage concession stand to unload the ice. As I stepped out of my car, someone grabbed me from behind! One of my volunteers had me in a full embrace. He was fresh out of the mud pit. He rotated my body around his until I was completely covered in mud: front, back, and sides! I must have looked like a giant chocolate bunny whose ears had been eaten off.

I couldn't maintain my executive edge like this. We had arranged to have two water sources on site for cleanup. One was a children's wading pool with a garden hose that ran incredibly slowly. A long line of children were waiting for a turn with the hose. I didn't have time for this unless I forced my way to the front of the line, pushing and shoving hot, tired, and dirty little children aside.

The second alternative was much faster. I walked to the far end of the mud courts down near the parking lot. I stepped up onto the wooden pallet and nodded my readiness. Within seconds, the firefighters had the fire hose aimed in my direction. The cold, forceful blast against my body took my breath away and nearly washed me right off my feet. I knew I could never turn my back on that fire hose! I would have to be satisfied with a clean front and a muddy back.

As I stepped off the pallet, I saw Doug walking towards me, a 32-ounce iced tea in hand. Do I run and hide? Do I meet this disaster head on?

My pride was shattered, my administrative air washed away without a trace. But, oh, how I needed that iced tea! I went for the tea.

Certain that this day would end my relationship with Doug, I sheepishly showed him around, introducing him to a few of my staff and volunteers. He was always a few steps behind me with a perfect view of my muddy backside. I was relieved when he left. It truly was a long, hard day.

About 8:00 P.M., when I finally took refuge in my own comfortable home, I played the messages on my answering machine. There were the usual calls for my son and from telemarketers, and the one I dreaded most... from Doug. "Hey Karen, this is Doug. When you get home give me a call. I have a couple of questions for you."

I was too tired for this. But if he wanted to end the relationship, I wanted to get it over with. Surely there was room in this day for a little more trauma. So I called.

When he answered on the second ring, my voice sounded irritated, even to myself. "This is Karen. You said you have a couple of questions?"

Doug's first question was, "Do people really pay money to do that?"

"Don't ask me why, but they do. And your second question is?" I said with more impatience than I had intended.

I was certain Doug's second question would be the one that was designed to let me down easily. So I was not at all prepared when he said, "Do you know how good you looked today?"

The perfect ending to a horrible day.

The perfect beginning to a lifetime together.

~Karen R. Hessen

69

Gone to the Dogs

Never, never, never give up.
~Winston Churchill

Determined not to repeat the matrimonial mistakes of virtually all my other family members, I didn't get married until I was forty-five. But, even so, I got divorced two years later. The five years since then have been some of the roughest of my life. But I decided within a couple of years to move on and continue my search for a life companion.

I used to think that people who complained about the rigors of dating at an advanced age were a bunch of losers. Now I know better. I went to church, I joined a Toastmasters chapter, I met a lot of interesting women through my work, but, at the end of the day, I always ended up alone. The traditional methods of meeting someone just weren't working, especially since so many women my age, while also divorced, had responsibilities with their children and grandchildren — something I didn't have. So I tried Internet dating, also with no long-term success. As so many of us do, I decided to give it a rest and just try being alone for a while.

One day, I saw a woman walking her collie. I recalled my childhood and the stories I used to read of Albert Payson Terhune's collies at Sunnybank Farm in New Jersey. I recalled how Lad of Sunnybank, Treve, Gray Dawn, and the rest of the collies had more adventures than any dog at my house. I loved those books, and spent many an hour escaping a sad and abusive childhood through them.

As I thought about the books and the collies, I decided to go online and look up Sunnybank collies. I was surprised to find an in-depth site about the dogs and their owner, Albert Payson Terhune.

After spending some time perusing the site, I decided to sign the guestbook, which had posts from readers around the country whose lives had been touched by the stories of these magnificent collies so many decades ago. As I read previous posts, I saw one from a woman who, coincidentally, lived in the same city as I do. On a whim, I decided to send her an e-mail just to say "hello" and share my affinity for the dogs.

She wrote back to me, and it turned out that we actually lived in the same zip code. We wrote a few letters back and forth and found that we had so much in common: We were both Christians, we were both writers with non-profit backgrounds, we were about the same age, and we were both divorced, she twice. We finally got around to a couple of phone conversations and then a cup of coffee at a Starbucks, where we sat and talked for hours.

Within a few weeks we began a romance in earnest, which, unfortunately, only lasted about six months before we both admitted it wasn't meant to be. But it was a glorious six months, with more coffee, lots of movies, quality time with her delightful dogs, and days and nights that neither of us will ever forget. Today we are still friends, and I even do holidays with her and her relatives, some of whom wish I could have been her next husband.

Thanks to the Sunnybank collies and their website, I know that love, or at least friendship and companionship, are still out there somewhere, no matter what age I am. And now I know that Winston Churchill was right; as with anything in life, we should never, never, ever give up. Friendship, companionship, and love can be discovered in the most unlikely of ways and when we least expect it. So I'm leaving my door open and the light on for them. They might be coming up the sidewalk right now, perhaps on a leash.

~Rick Moore

70

The Perfect Match?

*S*ingle again after eighteen years of marriage. Ugh! Basically, I'd been married my entire adult life. I got married at twenty-two, and I was now forty-one. How in the world does a woman in her forties date? Where would I even meet men? Pretty much everyone I knew was part of a couple. I wasn't in college anymore, which is where I had met my ex. I didn't want to do the bar scene. What to do? What to do?

A number of people told me I should try online dating. "It's just like shopping!" my girlfriend told me gleefully. "You just go on the website, browse through the photographs, and click on the one you want."

Well, that didn't seem too painful. Okay, I decided, I'll go for it. I figured I'd start with the site that I had heard the most about. A lot of people will be members. Might as well put the odds in my favor for meeting an eligible bachelor.

I signed up, answered all the questions, even wrote a little biography about myself. The only thing missing was a decent picture to post. I decided to have one of my friends take a digital photo of me. In the meantime, I went ahead and charged three months to my credit card and clicked "submit."

I signed on the next day, and to my delight had several e-mails waiting for me. Wow! And I had thought guys were so visual. I didn't even have a picture posted, but several guys were interested in me anyway. I replied to the e-mails, and a couple of days later finally had a picture taken to include in my profile. Once I uploaded my photograph, I decided to start my own search.

I kept it very generic. Didn't use the "advanced search;" just checked off the boxes for "female seeking male," "age range 35-45" (what can I say, I like younger guys) within "20 miles of my zip code." I clicked on "search" and sat back, anxiously waiting to see who the mighty match-making gods would fix me up with.

Take a wild guess. Who do you suppose turned up as the Number 1 match for me? Does the song "Escape" ring a bell with anyone? You know, the one about "If you like piña coladas..." Yep... of course — my ex-husband was the number one man who the match-making gods thought would be my perfect match. What kind of sick game is this? I leapt from my desk chair and paced around the house, mumbling "This is so wrong. This is so very, very wrong!"

I wasn't jealous, which I was glad about. It just seemed so icky and weird. So, even though I'd paid for a three-month membership and had only been a member for a few days, I decided to cancel.

Here's the rub. Even though you cancel your membership, your profile is still available for others to see unless you request that your profile be hidden. Something I didn't realize until the next day when I received an e-mail from my ex. "Fancy meeting you here," he wrote. A modern-day twist I suppose on that classic '70s song.

But my version doesn't end up with the guy and the girl realizing that they were really meant for each other all along. Instead, I realized that sometimes the match-making gods simply get it wrong.

~Marie Williams

71

Love Was Just a Phone Call Away

*I*t took less than a week, more than a few pots of tea, the occasional glass of wine, and lots of teary-eyed support from a couple of neighborhood ladies to pack into boxes what could be salvaged of my eleven-year marriage. As the weight of each memory crushed the backseat and crammed the trunk of my aging Pontiac, my war-torn heart, lit with the promise of a newfound future, soared with its first glimpse of hard-earned freedom.

I was a penniless, degreeless, thirty-four-year-old mother of two rough-and-tumble young sons. My self-esteem was dangling precariously by the skin of its teeth. As far as I could see, the only thing I had going for me was the unfailing support and endless generosity of my parents, who promised they would always be there for me. They never once let me down.

Almost two years later, Pa and Grandma threw Rough and Tumble into the back seat of their shiny new car and headed for the Sunshine State. Their timing couldn't have been more perfect. I was tired of sitting alone in my rented house night after night, so I had just begun to dally in "Sincerely Yours," a dating column in my local newspaper. Feeling like a desperate housewife well before her time, I placed my free ad and agreed to pay $2.00 a minute to pick up any messages left on my voice mail. Surely it couldn't add up to much? Right?

Wrong. The first time I called, there were over sixty messages waiting in my inbox. In the privacy of my kitchen, I spent hours of kid-free time screening would-be suitors. Finally, after determining most of them unworthy, I had a list of twelve potentials I deemed interesting enough to arrange a face-to-face meeting with at the local coffee shop. Always one to err on the side of caution, I confessed my situation to my sister, who was thrilled to both monitor my safety during comings and goings, and live vicariously through my secret rendezvous with the dates we affectionately referred to as my "johns." However, when she hinted that she'd love to sit in, incognito, on one of my meetings from a nearby table, I told her in no uncertain terms to back off and place her own ad.

Our excitement was short-lived. There wasn't even as much as a whiff of chemistry between me and any of my chosen few. My hopes of finding someone who even bore a close resemblance to Mr. Right were spiraling out of control almost as fast as my phone bill. The day the boys returned home, I received a bill for $400! To what end? I berated myself. For half of that I could've bunked in with my parents and the kids and sipped margaritas by the pool all day!

As I wrote the check, I swore off the phones for good. There was only one, as yet, unheard message so I played it. Certain we had nothing in common as I listened to Number 13's quiet, steady voice, I jotted down his number and tucked it into my kitchen drawer for a rainy day.

A couple of weeks later, I decided I might just as well get my money's worth and give him a call. After a short and less than sparkling conversation, he suggested that we meet. I hesitated, but he was insistent. (A little bit stubborn about it actually, but as it turns out, that's a whole other story.) Oh, what the heck? I thought. What was one more thirty-minute meeting in my not so exciting life?

His name was Paul. He described himself as tall with dark hair, which was perhaps a little less in abundance than it once had been. He would be wearing jeans and a blue jacket, and said I should look for him in the lounge of the restaurant where we agreed to meet.

The rain was coming down in buckets that night, I had a massive

PMS headache, and my ex was late picking up the boys. I rushed in late to the restaurant and was already checking my watch to see when I could make a quick exit. Shaking myself off, I searched the bar. I didn't remember describing myself as a shaggy, wet dog but I must have, because he seemed to know me right away. Hey, I screamed inwardly as he walked toward me. Now hold on just a minute, I thought as I struggled for air. Why hadn't he mentioned that he had the most come-to-me-baby smile I'd ever seen? And those dimples... If a girl wasn't careful she could lose herself in them. As I caught my breath, I swore quietly to myself, furious that I hadn't dabbed on a bit more vanilla musk, wore a more cleavage-friendly sweater, or worked a little more diligently at taking off those extra ten pounds that had recently found a loving home on my hips.

Throughout the meal, which due to a bout of prepubescent butterflies, I barely touched, he kept the conversation flowing easily. When I got home, I reported in to my sister, devoured two peanut butter sandwiches, a couple of cookies, and a huge glass of milk... and never looked back.

Six months later we traveled to France. One evening, while sitting at a candlelit table at a pretty hillside inn in Nice, Paul proposed over a fluffy cheese omelet. "Would you like to get married one day?" he asked.

"To you?" I replied, frowning. Well, how was I supposed to know what he meant? To this day he still says stuff that confuses the heck out of me.

We were married on a harbor island cruise two years later. After a long custody battle, I became a full-time mother to his two sons, and for the last fourteen years he has been a wonderful role model and devoted stepfather to Rough and Tumble, who are now in their early twenties. He held tightly to my hand throughout a long and complicated pregnancy and never let it go, as I brought our lovely daughter—the spitting image of her daddy—into the world eight years ago. He stayed by my side through the agonizing years of my parents' devastating illnesses and deaths, and spoon fed Jell-O to my oldest son when he was in the intensive care unit of a trauma hospital after a car accident that nearly took his life two years ago.

I guess you could say we made it, and although it's true that you never know what lies ahead—I'm certain that whatever it is, we'll make it through.

~Debbie Gill

72

Six Simple Words

A dmittedly, each of us carried baggage—enough for a seven-day cruise. And, we knew we had more than a mere suitcase to lose this time around. We were vulnerable, wary, and utterly terrified that we might stumble yet again. The sting of divorce still smarted as if the wound were as raw and as deep as the beginning of the end. Without question, the ugliness had shaken us both to our very cores and caused us to question and to doubt and to mistrust—even our own instincts.

It hardly seemed fair for all that fear and skepticism to have tainted one of life's most joyous events: falling in love—again. Granted, having fallen short the first time around, we truly recognized and valued the second chance we had been given for "happily ever after," and we savored the connectedness, intimacy and passion of it all—but with an unmistakable degree of guardedness. Not allowing ourselves to let go completely—to freefall without so much as a thought as to where we might land. Sadly, it prevented us from listening solely to our hearts.

That is, until my husband-to-be uttered six simple words in response to my what-if-ing our relationship to death: "What if my daughter couldn't make a healthy adjustment? What if we seriously question our decision five years down the road? What if we start experiencing some of the same problems that destroyed our first marriages? What if life throws us unforeseeable circumstances?"

The words, "We'll lean on each other," rolled off his tongue as if he had never been surer of anything in his life. "That way, neither of us will fall and we can support each other through thick and thin until whatever faces us has passed."

Needless to say, I married that man more than a decade ago and have never looked back—except to reflect upon our good fortune and the weightiness of those special words spoken seemingly yesterday. Undoubtedly, when our twin daughters are old enough to understand the significance of, "We'll lean on each other," I'll be sure to share with them just how important those words were to me, for they allowed me to trust... again.

~Melinda L. Wentzel

73

Dating and the Single Mom

hen I got divorced, I thought about child support, custody, and my ability to weather the split, but I never once thought about dating. I just assumed it would happen—eventually.

A year passed. That's 365 days and what seems like twice as many nights without so much as dinner and a movie.

"I could fix you up with Killer," a friend volunteered. "It's just a nickname—and he has a snowmobile." While contemplating how I'd ever introduce him to my mother, my son started waking up at 2:00 A.M. I stumbled over the haystack-size piles of unfolded laundry as I took the sixteen steps to his room, wondering how I would ever date or be intimate again when I might be interrupted by: "Mommy, I have a booger." Somehow, Killer didn't sound like the kind of guy that could handle it.

When I was single, I had a list of thirty-four qualities I was looking for in a man: tall, funny, successful, wants kids, and is a good dancer, were some of the things on my wish list. Now I had a new list with only one criterion: can help a small child use a tissue.

I reversed my policy on personals and answered one. It read: "Take a chance on a decent, responsible man, 43. Non-smoker with a good heart." It was two weeks before we could get together. In the meantime we exchanged twenty-five e-mails, each revealing another detail of our lives. As soon as he got out of his SUV, he started complaining about the price of snowshoes, the price of the cheese he'd packed for our picnic, the cost of gas... you get the idea.

A friend counseled, "Just go slow and remember, it isn't you. It's every bit as depressing as it appears." My next blind date, a 6:30 A.M. breakfast, proved her right. Before I even sat down, he started reading the newspaper and ate two soft boiled eggs without looking up, just like we'd been married for twenty years. It was, indeed, depressing—even if my married friends insisted I was lucky and it was a luxury to be able to sleep alone at night.

It was time to go on the offensive. I'd run my own personal ad. I hesitantly entered the newspaper office and began, "Communicative male..."

The woman on the other side of the counter began to laugh. I looked up and she laughed even harder. She grabbed a tissue and started dabbing her eyes as she said, "That's an oxymoron. Lemme tell you about my fiancé." I left.

I tried a party. When you live in a small mountain town, people think it's fun to have outdoor parties in the winter. I bravely stood outside in a blizzard, endured a blowing wind and smoke from a bonfire. After one hour, in the initial stages of hypothermia, I left. On the way out, the hostess said, "Why leave now? Bow-Wow-Chow, the dog trainer I wanted to introduce you to, isn't here yet."

I highlighted my hair. I strapped on ankle weights and did leg lifts. Surely rock-hard cellulite would counter the fact that I was a hormonally challenged, forty-eight-year-old woman. It didn't work. The next date lasted just twenty minutes.

Desperate, I consulted a specialist in Feng Shui, the ancient Chinese art of paying someone to rearrange your furniture. She arrived in a black Saab turbo, her briefcase bulging with mirrors, bells, and wind chimes. She placed a ba-gua (pronounced as if you're gargling) chart on top of a floor plan of my house. "I see the problem," she said in her clipped British accent. "It's the loo... I mean the toilet. It's positioned right in your relationship sector." I did as I was instructed: kept the lid on the toilet down and bought red bath towels.

The bath towels must have been the key, because my next fix-up was perfect—a New Age Nick Nolte look-alike. David burned incense incessantly and although he had no furniture he seemed to have an endless supply of CDs of monks chanting. Instead of working, he spent his day in meditation so I figured he could handle my consumption of EstroPause. But after a few dates, David announced he was redirecting his sex drive into his third chakra and left town.

Maybe it's time for Botox and a few more red towels.

~Joanne Palmer

Team Fix-It

Cooperation is the thorough conviction
that nobody can get there unless everybody gets there.
~Virginia Burden

I settled into an easy chair across from my hiking buddy Don, just as Joel, my eleven-year old son, wandered into the living room. My sense of wellbeing suddenly morphed into single mom guilt. Maybe I should have taken him with us, though he'd seemed content playing with a neighbor.

I introduced Don and Joel. We chatted for a few minutes about Forest Park and then Don thanked me for the hike, shook Joel's hand, and left.

"Do you like him, Mom? Do you like him?" Joel asked the minute the door closed.

"Of course," I said. "Don's great."

"If you like him, why don't you marry him?"

"Don and I are just friends," I explained.

Neither Don nor I were interested in dating. Besides, I thought to myself, I've been divorced less than a year. My first priority was getting my three kids and myself settled in our new home and new lives.

A few weeks later, my friend Craig helped me haul some old carpet to the dump. Afterward, he stayed for lunch. Tami, a junior in high school, Ben, four years younger, and Joel gathered with us around the kitchen table for sandwiches and root beer. After lunch,

Tami and Ben wandered off. Joel cleared the table, Craig found a dishtowel, and the three of us did the lunch dishes. Craig gave Joel a high-five for a job well done and left.

"Do you like Craig?" Joel immediately asked. "Do you like him?"

"He's a terrific friend."

"If you like him, why don't you marry him?"

His question, now getting old, set me to thinking. Why was Joel so anxious for me to marry again? After all, he could walk to his father's house less than a mile away any time he chose.

Days later, a letter from my father in California echoed Joel's sentiments. My father hoped I would meet someone soon who would take care of the house, the kids, and me—emphasis on the house. Without a man around, things would go to pieces.

How helpless did my father think I was? I was standing at the kitchen counter, tearing his letter into small bits, when Joel wandered by. "Don't you think you kids and I are doing all right?" I asked him.

"Sure."

"Don't you think the house is all right?"

"Maybe right now. Dad says we'll start having trouble pretty soon. No offense Mom, but you aren't mechanically minded."

Mechanically minded? True, I couldn't fix anything in the world with a pocketknife and a paper clip like my ex. But I had average intelligence and skills.

I was explaining all this somewhat indignantly to Joel when the doorbell rang. It was Rick, our neighbor. "I'm about to mow my lawn. I can get yours while I'm at it," Rick offered. "It's not a big deal."

I looked past him to the lawn. Wow. When did it get that long?

I assured Rick that I'd get the job done myself, closed the door, and took a deep breath. My ex had taken the lawnmower.

The very next weekend I found a simple push mower at a garage sale. As I pushed it up the hill of our front yard, I began to appreciate the extent of our lawn. I poked my head through the front door and called for reinforcements. Ben came outside and created a pattern of rectangles over half the upper section. Then he informed me that the blade was too dull to cut well.

I was impressed with Ben's insight. I had just thought I wasn't pushing hard enough. Together we took the mower to the local hardware store to be sharpened. There I learned that we could buy a new power mower for about the price of sharpening my medieval relic. Ben and I both listened carefully as the salesman explained how to prime the starter, pull the cord, and check the spark plug. A steep learning curve for me, but Ben understood it all.

That night, as the kids inhaled turkey tacos, I did a Steve Martin impersonation. "We're Team Fix-It," I said. "You all inherited your father's talent for fixing things. Together we can maintain or repair anything."

Less than a week later, I had a chance to test my claim. I was making chicken enchiladas when Tami came in the kitchen, clearly agitated. "Mom, there's a buzz on the phone so loud I can't understand anybody."

"Remember how you hooked up your own phone at the house your father built? I'm sure you can fix our phone."

When her father had built our house, he had done the initial wiring for a phone in Tami's room, but felt no urgency to actually hook one up. Tami did. She studied a phone box, then stripped the wires in the wall, slipped them around the screws in the box, and tightened everything down till she had a stable connection. She plugged in a phone and promptly called a friend.

"You meant that Team Fix-It stuff?" Tami murmured, and started testing phones and jacks. When she found the bad jack, I, her ready assistant, went to the store for a new phone box. She wired it in and voilà, we had a quiet line.

Just give us a problem and we'd figure it out.

The water company complied. They sent a water bill for an astronomical amount. I called the company, assuming a mistake. They advised me to see if the needle on the water meter dial was spinning out of control.

Water meter? My confidence plummeted. I didn't even know where it was, let alone how to fix a plumbing problem. Still, I wasn't about to run an ad in the personals:

Wanted: Male, forty to fifty, intelligent,
articulate, athletic. Likes to fix houses.

I enlisted Ben and Joel's help. We located a concrete box by the street just to the left of the driveway, lifted the lid, and found the meter—with the needle spinning.

Ben and I checked every faucet and every pipe we could get to in the house. We checked the outside faucets. Nothing. Joel went into his room and lay down on his bed. Was that team spirit? But a few minutes later he came out and explained that since the problem wasn't in the house, it must be in the sprinkler system. It was probably a loose sprinkler valve in the green box by the back porch.

"You sure can solve problems in your head," I told Joel as Ben opened the lid of the box, tightened the valve, and the water meter needle stopped spinning.

Over the next few months, the kids and I worked together to keep the house running. When male friends came by, Joel no longer asked if I wanted to marry them. In fact, the kids and I were thinking of printing up family business cards:

Team Fix It—Up To Any Challenge

We are going to be okay.

~Samantha Ducloux Waltz

The Dating Game

Take spring when it comes and rejoice.
Take happiness when it comes and rejoice.
Take love when it comes and rejoice.
~Carl Ewald

There I was, single and divorced at the age of thirty-five. I had been married for seventeen years and didn't know what I should do. My daughters were teenagers and busy with their own lives. I was heartbroken, not only because my family life as I knew it had ended, but my daughters would leave every other weekend to visit their father. Weekends alone. Silence.

Most of my friends had family lives and couldn't go out or get together with me. I was lonely and felt so rejected. All of my dreams and goals were gone. The dreams of what the future would bring for "us" were now over. My life had changed—but how could I change my dreams and goals? How could I heal—and change my heart?

I decided I needed to start dating. I joined an online free dating service. If you fall off a horse, you get back on, or you will never ride that horse again. Didn't this have to do with dating as well?

For my first date, I told quite a few people where I was going and felt safe with the location. We were to meet in the evening. I was as nervous as a teenager. Our eyes met as he walked in. He was so incredibly beautiful. The perfect gentleman. We spent a lovely evening together, and I couldn't have felt luckier when he e-mailed telling me he wanted to see me again. We talked online in an instant message and in mid-sentence he disappeared. I never saw or spoke to him again. This left many images in my mind as to what happened. I called him Mr. Perfect. But, I decided to give this dating thing another good try.

The next date was Mr. Truck Driver. He drove a semi and was often gone for long periods of time. He was recently divorced himself. He really helped me see the light in letting go. I had many dates in which I would come home and share my stories with my girlfriends. My friends were often begging me to meet them at the local coffee shop to share my dating stories. I went out with Mr. Coffee, Mr. Actor, Mr. Denial, and so many more. Then Mr. Paramedic came into my life. I met him at a singles dance. We danced and talked all evening. He asked me when I would be coming back and I told him the following weekend. Again, we talked and danced all night. We decided to go out on a real date. I really had a nice time. I went out with him a few times and he showed me his house and introduced me to his father. After my shock at seeing that his father lived in a trailer in a very small backyard, Mr. Paramedic explained that his father had pulled the trailer from West Virginia and was living in the back for the time being.

One Saturday, he had just worked an eighteen hour shift and wanted to know if I wanted to come over and watch a movie and have a glass of wine. I thought it sounded wonderful. When I arrived, we sat down to wine and dinner. A great start right? Well, when I entered the living room, to my horror there was fly-tape hanging from the ceiling light fixture. Mr. Paramedic explained that his father put it there because he saw a bug.

Fly-tape? I hadn't seen fly-tape since I was a small child and saw it hanging in a barn. The front door was open to let a breeze in. I stood in the middle of the room talking and as the wind blew into the room, the fly-tape above me flew and touched my head. I screamed as the tape stuck to my hair and all four feet of it fell on my head, arms, and hands. It was incredibly sticky stuff and difficult to get out of my hair. Mr. Paramedic was only concerned about his hands getting sticky. I didn't know what to do. My hair was quite long and I was in a bad situation. I decided to get into his shower and thought maybe some conditioner would help brush this out. I ended up with a rat's nest on top of my head. I left and went to a friend's house. Three women and I worked diligently to get this out of my hair. We tried everything, as they laughed with tears streaming down their faces. They said it was like *I Love Lucy*. Finally, we found that cooking oil worked.

Mr. Paramedic called me three days later. Why, you ask? Should I have expected him to ask how my sore head was—or if I even had any hair left? He called to tell me he didn't think we were working out. Ya think?

I was determined I would not stop dating just yet—besides my coffee friends were depending on me. I couldn't let them down now, could I? My last date, I called Mr. Geek. We went out to dinner. We had a lovely time. I wasn't attracted to him, but at least I didn't have to worry about investing in a wig. I knew things were not working out when he sent me an e-mail on Valentine's Day. I opened the e-mail to find a picture. He had scanned a Slim Fast coupon and wanted to know if I wanted him to bring it with him next time we went out.

I was completely finished with dating. I came to the conclusion that I was quite happy alone. I went on with my daily life smiling and at peace. After all, I did have the memories that made me laugh as I thought of all my dating experiences. What I didn't expect was for Mr. International to come into my life. I knew him online and we were only friends. One day, he called me and wanted to meet. I didn't have any plans for the day so we met for dinner. We spent a great deal of time together for the next two months before he left the country. The day he was to leave I handed him my special necklace of the Sacred Heart, which I wore daily. He said, "No. I'll tell you what. You keep it, and when you're ready, you mail it to me. When you do, I am coming back and marrying you."

Need I say we are married now? I still have all the memories of dating and look back at how much I grew while finding myself. Once I stopped dating, the right guy came into my life with as much joy and laughter as life could bring.

~Brenda Crawford

A Kid's Perspective

When my husband and I got our divorce, we had been living in a small town, so to "get away from it all," I took our two children and moved to another city. I was concerned about the effects these two major events would have on my children, so I went to a doctor to talk about it. He told me that if the move or the divorce had unduly disturbed the children, the first place it would show up would be in their schoolwork. Gratefully, I acknowledged that they had settled down well in the new environment, they were beginning to make friends and the results of their schoolwork were more than satisfactory. So no problems, right?

HAH!

I can still remember the horror I felt one day as the kids and I got on a city bus and I heard my son, in that loud little voice, that only seven-year-olds have, announcing to the male driver, "Hi, this is my mommy. We live here, but my daddy doesn't. My daddy has a girlfriend, but my mommy doesn't have a boyfriend, do you, Mommy?"

I could feel my face burning as I stumbled to the back of the bus as the other passengers—and the driver—seemed to get their laugh of the day. As for me, I never took that same bus again!

However, my son had obviously given a great deal of serious thought to our situation, as a couple of years later as he and I were waiting for the elevator in our apartment building he turned to me and said in a very solemn tone of voice, "Mom, I think you ought to get married again. And Dad ought to get a dog."

Who knows what thoughts run through the mind of a child? Certainly not me!

~Dorothy M. Clifton

77

Post-Divorce Dating

No love, no friendship can cross the path of our destiny
without leaving some mark on it forever.
~François Mauriac

In the aftermath of my divorce, I felt there could be nothing more unappealing or futile than the thought of dating again. Why bother? I'd already met the love of my life—my soul mate, even though we were now divorced. Anyone else would surely be a letdown.

My single friends wouldn't hear of it. One of them had just met the post-divorce man of her dreams through an online dating service and insisted I give it a try. I obliged by creating a profile that sufficiently hid my reluctance and portrayed me as somewhat witty. I was surprised to receive quite a few responses. Instinctively I rejected prospects with typos or grammatical errors, envisioning a plethora of other defects lurking beyond their lack of writing skills. The one I settled on turned out to be a Chris Farley look-alike, whom I found endearing until he admitted to shaving eight years off his age. Then, when he bragged that in preparing for our date he'd actually gone to the trouble of flossing his teeth for me, any remaining appeal had vanished. And so I concluded, that instead of sitting through another excruciating dinner with a stranger, wishing I were home catching up on my taped episodes of *Guiding Light* or weeping over my video of Princess Di's funeral, I'd rather go out by myself.

Because of my years traveling on the road for business, I felt quite comfortable exploring the town alone. One particular night, I went to see a band at one of the local casinos here in Las Vegas, where I'd come to start over after my marriage ended. Almost immediately after I entered the showroom, a tattooed biker-type with a goatee and shaved head who looked like a cross between Billy Bob Thornton and Charlie Manson came and sat next to me. Though I could tell he was itching to converse, I kept to myself and sent a flirty smile to the bass player, pretending he was my boyfriend.

"Have you seen this band before?" Slingblade asked, his gravelly voice matching his appearance.

I nodded in his direction, avoiding eye contact, sure that if I had looked at him straight-on I'd find a swastika etched on his forehead.

"My name's Paul. Do you want to dance?"

"No, I don't dance," I answered in his direction. "But thank you."

He nudged my arm as the band started to play the next song. "C'mon," he said. "Let's dance."

I turned to him and saw he was more handsome, his eyes much kinder than I had expected. Though he had an intensity about him, I also detected a vulnerability. Plus he held his drink with his pinkie in the air—really, how dangerous could he be? I gave in.

We seemed to move well together, and during one of the slow dances I realized it had been almost a year since I'd been that close to a man. He smelled nice and his shirt was soft. We danced nearly every song and lingered for a while afterward as the band packed their instruments.

"I'd like to take you out Saturday night," he said.

Oh, no. A familiar sense of dread came over me. "You mean, go on a... date?" I hesitated, and then remembered I'd been having more fun than in recent memory. I gave him my number.

Paul followed through and picked me up Saturday night promptly at eight o'clock. "Here, I brought you something," he said, handing me a pamphlet entitled, "Understanding Post-Traumatic Stress Syndrome."

Surely, it's some kind of warning signal when your date arrives at your door, not with flowers in hand, but a brochure detailing a chronic mental disorder. I suppose the gesture was rather considerate; I might have been spared untold turmoil had my ex-husband entered my life with the appropriate paperwork. To be fair, I could have reciprocated with a handout of my own, entitled "What You Should Know about Incessant Nagging."

"I have PSTD," he explained. "From Vietnam. I wanted to be honest with you."

"Post-traumatic stress disorder? Hmmm... I should tell you something, too," I said, and then with a teasing smile, added, "Men don't usually get that until after they've been with me."

We both laughed and it didn't take long to realize that neither of us was ready for anything beyond a superficial exchange; his condition haunted him with the carnage he'd seen and I had yet to let go of my ex-husband. And so we simply enjoyed each other, with no agenda for the relationship.

Paul was a blast to hang out with and I reaped the benefits of his many connections in town. We dined in four-star restaurants and got the best tables at the comedy clubs he took me to—everyone he knew seemed willing to comp us in exchange for a few bucks passed in a handshake. Paul's son, who managed one of the ultra lounges on the Strip, made sure we were well taken care of; bouncers would unhook the velvet ropes just for us; and doting waitresses, who came to know me by name, served complementary cocktails or sometimes came over just to say hi or show off a new boob job.

I admit that some of Paul's PTSD behavior took some getting used to. I found out the hard way not to trigger his startle response and learned to cough or clear my throat when approaching him from behind. Reports of the day's casualties in Iraq often prompted him to hole himself up with the blinds closed and I wouldn't hear from him for days or sometimes even weeks.

I'd never been around anyone whose life had been defined by war. During the Vietnam era, I was young and absorbed in important issues like impressing boyfriends and scoring a fake ID. Sure, I saw snippets of battles on the six o'clock news—we weren't bombarded by round-the-clock cable broadcasts back then—and that was the extent of my exposure. Paul's stories of his platoon rushing through rice paddies amid mortar explosions and flying debris touched me profoundly. The scenes so embedded into his psyche seemed to emerge through the tattoos on his skin.

Unquestionably, my life is richer as a result of getting to know Paul. No, he's not my soul mate, but had I refused his offer for a date, I would have missed the opportunity to make a good friend. I think most people are meant to be experienced from the periphery rather than the epicenter, and now when I date I try to enjoy the moment. The man probably won't be another love of my life—even if he flossed his teeth beforehand—but maybe we'll end up good friends.

~Linda O'Connor

Single, With Children

"Nursing mother seeks Prince Charming. Ready-made family includes two kids, two cats, and leaky basement. Endless patience required. Must be able to eat macaroni and cheese every day. Divorce in progress."

My early days as a single parent were some of the loneliest of my life. Adult relationships — love, sex, conversation, and intimacy — seemed hopelessly out of reach. Hugs from little people who leak from all orifices are wonderful, but there's only so much drool one person should be required to absorb. As a single mom, I longed for someone to tell me I was sexy, pour me a glass of wine, and massage my feet. My ex, who's a devoted dad and one of my best friends, faced a similar dilemma. He had the kids two nights a week, and every Saturday night, because we split weekends down the middle to accommodate our religious differences. He also cared for his ill parents.

Finally, after ten years of single life, he is engaged to a wonderful woman. I am also still single, and looking back over our separation, when our son was three and our daughter just fifteen months old, I'm amazed to see how well it all worked out.

To maintain an active presence in our kids' lives, my ex uses the flex time his job offers to leave three hours early once a week. As the "parent on duty," he supervises the kids when they do their homework, chauffeurs them to various activities, and feeds them dinner. Many nights, he goes back to work after returning them to me. On weekends, he tries to balance errands and lawn maintenance with meaningful time with the kids.

So what's a lonely mom or dad to do when dating becomes more like job-hunting than *The Love Boat*? For years I couldn't even afford a babysitter. My friends and family were vigilant to make sure I didn't enter yet another doomed relationship. I felt like I had "LOSER" flashing in red neon on my forehead. The swingin' life of childless singles looked glamorous until I realized that meeting them involved finding something unstained to wear that still fit, and then standing around at parties where no one else talked about children.

I tried dating for about six months. Pre-mommy professional experience was pretty flimsy conversational material because I didn't have a career track or an income. And odd as it may seem, the child-free don't want to hear about temper tantrums or toilet training.

One guy I dated predicted he'd be a "great father," but he wasn't on speaking terms with anyone in his own family. He only wanted to see me alone and thought my mother should babysit. He favored my daughter and belittled my son. In return, they exhibited their rowdiest, messiest behavior when he was around. Once, a well-placed kick from my son had him rolling and groaning on the floor for twenty minutes.

"But Mommy," said my wide-eyed, darling boy, "he asked to see my karate kicks."

After understanding that the guy who didn't like my kids was still unmarried at forty-four because he was too selfish to really care about another person, I returned to the personal ads with some new insights about how their wording reflects the goals of the writer. I realized that all the phrases people use to describe what they want out of a relationship (fine dining, Broadway shows, travel) sound good, but they're fantasy, not what makes a relationship work.

Fine dining and travel may be what we like to do, but they don't sum up who we are. After all, who doesn't like good food or vacations? In addition to being generic, these activities are also what we do to escape from everyday life. Sure, take me to restaurants and shows, but I also need you to show up for the daily grind. What are you going to be like when we can't go to flea markets or have candlelit dinners? How do you react when the sparkling conversation you cherish is tarnished by endless interruptions? What are the behaviors that help a red-hot romance survive as it shifts to encompass the stresses and emergencies of raising children?

Unlike child-free dating relationships, those that include kids may have less room for flexibility and compromise because of the children's schedules or needs. A single person walking into a ready-made family can feel like a swimmer caught in an undertow. A parent may struggle with how his or her desire to be with the new partner conflicts with childcare responsibilities.

The added hubbub, sleep deficits, and general disorder that life with children entails can increase the temptation to whine, snap, and gripe. It's not relaxing when the kids all talk at once, especially if idealized visions of orderly evenings still dance in your head. Practice, however, can improve the situation. Both parents and their love interests need to brace themselves for the hurricane and be prepared to be flexible and patient.

The arrival of the date (a fresh adult) can impose order upon chaos simply by providing a cheerful distraction. Being wowed by everyone's story of the day, helping to set the table for dinner, or even just giving the struggling parent a hug can set the entire household on the right track for the evening. Kids should not be made to feel unwanted or secondary once the date arrives.

Single parents know that life is mostly unromantic. Candlelight and soft music don't matter nearly so much as remembering to pick up milk from the store. No one can feel the heat of passion all the time. Impromptu picnics on the beach need to translate into an ability to improvise when conditions veer from the ideal to the disastrous. Common courtesy and good manners, mutual goodwill and patience, thinking about your partner as well as about yourself—this is the stuff that dreams are made of. Even when you can't afford dinner and a movie.

~Elizabeth Breau

My First Love

You, yourself, as much as anybody in the entire universe,
deserve your love and affection.
~Buddha

Dinner finished and both my sons decided to return to their uncompleted homework. As I cleared the dishes from the table, my mind prepared the agenda for the evening: clean the kitchen, put out the garbage, take the dog for a walk, and fit in a moment to relax on the couch before bed. But, as all mothers and wives learn over time, agendas need to remain flexible in order to inject the unexpected, and tonight would present the epitome of the unexpected.

My husband and I proceeded with our rehearsed dance of post-dinner clean up. I put the dishes on the counter while he proceeded to move them to the dishwasher. And then, out of nowhere, he said, "I can't do this anymore." I responded with my usual acceptance of his lack of interest in the dish dance and told him to go do whatever else it was that he needed to do and I would finish on my own. He said more emphatically, "No, I can't do this anymore." He gestured his arms repeatedly in an outward motion from his body, pointing his fingers toward me and then back at himself. Mindlessly, I continued to place dishes in the dishwasher and began to run the water in the sink for the pots and pans.

"Deb?"

"Yes?"

"I said that I can't do this anymore. You and me."

Numb. His words felt like a semi slamming into my chest at 100 miles an hour. Paralyzed. I couldn't speak.

Later, the wisdom of others told me that I must have known, or at least seen the truck coming at me from a distance. But, on this night, at this time and in this place, I had no idea that my husband, my first love, was asking me for a divorce.

In the span of the next five month period, I attended my sister's wedding, bought a home, signed a separation agreement, hosted my son's French exchange student, celebrated my son's sixteenth birthday, changed titles on deeds, got a mortgage, lost twenty pounds, refinanced a car, maintained a façade of "everything's okay" and, finally, moved from the marital home.

Four months later, my son left to go to France for his portion of the exchange and I was able to breathe—into a paper bag. I was hyperventilating. I cried for three days straight. I tried to make sense of the whole mess. But, nothing would make sense. And I came to realize that it really doesn't need to make sense.

Love is a funny character in a book that is written by an often pathetic author, who is idealistic instead of realistic, and enjoys the melee of passion and apathy and the thrill of an unfulfilled destination called fate. The book has been written hundreds of times with ample editing, subject change and plot alterations, but there appears to be no prediction about the ending—except that the heroine in this particular story could learn how to chart the course of this tale toward a horizon worthy of the triumphant spirit of her new found depiction of love.

Years of caring for others had caused me to ignore my own needs. Oddly enough, I came to the realization that I did in fact have needs. I needed to feel warmth and love. I needed to feel accepted and that I somehow belonged. I needed to feel respected and honored. I needed to feel happy and content. But, most of all I needed to feel that the one person in the whole world who should love me the most would love me the most, regardless of the mistakes that I've made. Someone who could accept my faults and praise my strengths and make me feel everyday that I was the best that I could be.

My search began with the typical path chosen by those leaving a significant relationship: dating. Your social circle shifts and your married friends are happy that they now have a new "single" friend to introduce to their newly divorced friends. The thought of having a new relationship was enticing. And the thought of starting the relationship process all over again from the beginning did seem exciting. Everything is new again; the first date, the first kiss, the flowers and the dinners in romantic venues. Holding hands with someone new seemed more exciting than the last three years of my marital bedroom practice.

However, there was usually something missing from these short term affairs. My love life was becoming a *Seinfeld* episode of "man hands," "close talkers," and "low talkers," notwithstanding the occasional episode of *Sex in the City's* bad kissers, adulterers, and noncommittal types. Some were funny, others were smart, some philosophical with upscale taste, and some just basically gorgeous and wonderful to hold. But, ultimately none gave me the satisfaction that my heart was craving. None could make me happy or give me fulfillment. I decided maybe I was better off alone.

And alone I was. No invites to dinner or social events included that proverbially announced and "guest." My cats became my confidants and heard about my day's events and the hardships of being a single woman in today's world. I became engrossed in the art of "puttering," cleaning drawers that didn't need to be cleaned and reorganizing cupboard after cupboard. I took tennis and horseback riding lessons and learned to speak French. I started to read more and speak less. I discovered meditation and learned quickly that I really wasn't that good at it. Nonetheless, I still tried.

And then one day I was standing in front of my dresser mirror and caught my reflection. The soft light of the bedroom gave my skin a warm glow. I cast a flirty smile to the mirror. My image returned with an alluring grin. The reflection was far from perfect but, it was me. And what I had come to learn of myself was wonderfully endearing.

I was socialized to consider the needs of others as paramount to my own. Not the best approach when ultimately I am responsible for my own happiness and fulfillment. Some lessons take time to learn. And although I don't think that I will ever come to the point of forgiving my ex-husband for the disruption that he created in my life, divorce and time have given me the ability to forgive myself for not choosing to be my own first love.

~Deborah Batt

Chapter 8

Divorce *and* Recovery

You and Me...
and Kids, Too?

*Family life is full of major and minor crises—
the ups and downs of health, success and failure in career,
marriage, and divorce—and all kinds of characters.
It is tied to places and events and histories. With all of these felt details,
life etches itself into memory and personality. It's difficult to imagine
anything more nourishing to the soul.*
~Thomas Moore

No Furniture

There are few things in life more heartwarming than to be welcomed by a cat.
--Tay Hohoff

Stepmother. The word has ugly connotations and a bad history to boot: shades of Cinderella and every maligned innocent child whose father ever brought a new woman into the household.

The reality is that life isn't exactly a bed of roses for stepmothers, either. What you have to understand about us is this: we are entering, by definition, a house of grief. The death of a marriage is as difficult to endure as the death of a loved one, and takes as long to mourn. Even in those instances where one's new husband wanted his divorce, the ghost of the first wife—of the biological mother—never really goes away. A stepmother's very presence in the home is a daily reminder to the children that they are not going to get what they want above all else—their parents back together.

Paul married the first woman he'd ever dated. He was a geek, an MIT graduate who knew that he wanted a family, and was deathly afraid that if he didn't marry her while he had her, so to speak, he'd never have another chance at marriage. Not the most auspicious beginning.

He was content enough during their years together—or so he thought. When they made the difficult decision to separate, he was amazed that his migraines miraculously disappeared; he'd assumed that all marriages were like theirs, and was amazed by the relief he felt when they were no longer together. They had two children before that happened; the younger was not yet two years old when they separated.

By the time Paul and I met, he'd been divorced for two years, and his former wife had already remarried. We felt... how can I phrase it... that we had been looking for each other our whole lives, that every misstep we'd taken along the way had been worth it, as it had brought us together in the end.

His children, of course, felt differently.

The fact that their mother was already remarried did not keep them from blaming me for keeping their parents apart; the fact that their father was happy with me was not their concern. The evenings I came for dinner were strained. "Daddy, tell her I want more milk!" My attempts to charm them with museum visits, long afternoons at playgrounds, and gifts of books did nothing to change their minds.

And then, after six months of dating, to their disgust the moving truck brought me, all of my worldly goods, and my cat Spike to live with Paul and the two of them—Jacob, then aged six, and Anastasia, who was almost five.

Paul's guilt over the divorce and what it had done—or might yet do—to his children had led him to be permissive in his interactions with the kids. They could do whatever they pleased, whenever they pleased; there was no fixed bedtime, no foods that had to be eaten, no worries about interrupting or saying "please" or not getting what they wanted. I had the distance necessary to see that Paul wasn't doing them a service by trying to be their friend, and before long he was able to understand and agree with what I was gently pointing out to him.

The children were aghast: not only was I there all the time now, but I came with baggage: Rules! Manners! A closed bedroom door! Furniture was rearranged or—worse—thrown out. Toys could no longer be strewn throughout the house.

To say that the children were not happy with the new regime is an exercise in understatement.

From the beginning, Jacob and I were locked in an ongoing, exhausting form of mental combat. We argued over everything; no issue was too small to discuss, to analyze, to take to heart. "You're ruining my whole life!"

I finally thought I understood why we were such adversaries, though, and it was because we had so much in common. The reality was that we shared the same secret unspoken wish: we both wanted the other one out of his father's life. And while I was more discreet than he about this desire, it was nonetheless real.

We'd been struggling for about nine months when Paul suggested that we adopt another cat. Spike was clearly my family, and made it clear that he only had time for me; it would be good, said Paul, for us to cement our new family with something that belonged to all of us. So we trooped down to the local shelter and came home with Kirsipuu, named for the wearer of the yellow jersey that particular day in the Tour de France bicycle race.

Spike never forgave me.

My cat had come from the solitude of living with just me — and I'm a pretty quiet person — to the chaos of living with two small, active, and very noisy children. In no uncertain terms he let me know that adding someone of his own species to the mix was simply asking too much. He hissed and hid and yowled at regular intervals.

And eventually, found his way into Jacob's room — and Jacob's heart.

I was passing the doorway to the kids' room when I heard my stepson talking. Pausing just out of sight, I listened. Jacob was sitting on his bed, stroking a surprisingly docile Spike. "I know what it's like for you," Jacob was telling the cat, his voice soothing. "They just move her in and nobody asks you if it's okay with you and suddenly you have to see her all the time, even when you don't want to."

A pause, filled only with the sound of Spike's purr.

Jacob took a deep breath and leaned in closer. "But you know," he continued, "you have it better than I did. At least she didn't bring furniture!"

It was a beginning....

~Jeannette Cezanne

My Ex-Husband's Wedding

*I*n May, my ex-husband is getting married. Again. This will be trip number three down the aisle for this self-proclaimed gift to women. I was wife number one.

Young, uneducated, naïve... I guess the list of reasons I married him in the first place is endless, and ultimately, why the marriage failed. We share between us the gift of three beautiful children—the oldest, now nineteen and away at college, a high school senior plus a freshman. The three of them have had the advantage of both parents remaining actively involved in their lives. Although they have physically lived with me and my husband of ten years, their dad has lived only minutes away. Some people assume that as each child reaches legal age, the contact between their father and me will decrease. So far, that theory has been disproved.

An interesting relationship has developed during the many years that we have been divorced. During his second marriage, the situation was tense. The woman was certain I was Satan in the flesh. Of course this had my ex-hubby intricately re-scrutinize my morals, religious beliefs, and the contents of my refrigerator.

My husband and I tolerated the various stages with which my ex experimented. In addition to the Holy Roller phase, we were privy to his health-nut mode and his Save the Earth campaign.

During the health-nut mode, our kids would come home

complaining of casseroles concocted of who-knows-what, and speculating that I was feeding them things that would probably kill them by a week from next Tuesday.

Save the Earth found the children deeply concerned about the chemicals seeping into their pores from the horrible laundry detergent I used to wash their clothes. If I kept this up, a week from next Tuesday looked like an unnaturally long lifespan!

When wife number two hit the road, we saw a slow, but eventual return to reason. He found his calling as a painter, and became an entrepreneur. His business is quite successful. He stopped scrutinizing the contents of our cupboards and the kids' stomachs and realized (even admitted) that my husband and I had done a very good job of parenting. His religious beliefs took on a true spiritual aspect. And he met and made plans to marry a bright, pretty, and very nice young woman.

Do I harbor any leftover feelings of resentment, anger, or hostility? No. What point would that serve? Our children know, and for the most part understand, that things were different years ago; their dad and I hadn't a clue about making a relationship work, nor the barest means with which to try. We've both made our mistakes, learned from them, made some of them again, learned a little more, and wound up today in successful relationships with wonderful people.

Do I fear that his third marriage might wreak havoc on our settled lives? Not at all. His fiancé has shown a sense of self-worth, integrity, and respect for the relationship that remains between my ex and me. She understands that I pose no threat to their marital bliss and she knows I have no intention of interfering in their lives. She is not out to reinvent motherhood or correct all the faux pas I've made. She's not intimidated when circumstances require me to engage in lengthy phone conversations with her future husband.

What do the children think? They're thrilled for their father's happiness. They are fairly decent judges of character and they think he's made a good choice. Our daughter will be a bridesmaid and the boys will stand with their father as he takes his new vows. Do I feel sidelined by this role my kids will play, or second fiddle to the excitement and anticipation of this wedding celebration? Heck, no! I don't have the time or the energy to waste on such trivial nonsense. Besides, I'll be much too busy planning what dress to wear and what might be the proper gift to buy. My husband and I checked "chicken" on the response card for the wedding dinner, and happily mailed our reply.

~Maggie Kelly

"That's Fluffy, my fifth wife from my seventh life ... or was she my seventh wife from my fifth life? ..."

82

Father's Day

Standing at the kitchen sink washing dishes, I dread the next time Jenny or Laura approach me, certain that the next thing that comes out of their mouths will be, "Mom will you...?" I don't think I can stand to hear another request from a teenager.

Laura graduated from high school this month. The ceremony and the celebration are over. She'll go to college in the fall, moving to a campus a couple of hours drive from here.

Today is Father's Day and I wonder if Jenny and Laura will think to consider their stepfather as part of this celebration. If they do, I'll cry because they thought of him. If they don't, I'll cry because his role in supporting them will be one more thing they've taken for granted.

Yesterday's mess from feeding over fifty people at Laura's open house still looms on the kitchen counters. After her party here, Laura went to her friends' graduation parties and came home long after we had gone to bed. I assume that she and Jenny have slept in this morning because they needed a pit stop between yesterday's flurry of activities and today's visit to their dad's where they will stay tonight.

"If we stop feeding them or giving them a place to sleep, do you think the girls will ever come to visit us again?" I ask Todd.

"You've raised two wonderful daughters," he assures me.

As I massage the dishes in the warm soapy water, I hear him in the living room telling Jenny that she might want to talk to her mom. Then I hear Todd typing on the computer in the office, probably finishing some weekend work.

Jenny comes over and asks if I would join her in the living room. I shake my head and look down at the suds. Standing next to me, she sees my tear-stained cheeks and red eyes. She tugs at my arm the way she did as a child and begs me to join her.

Too tired to protest, I dry my hands on a kitchen towel. Walking over to the couch, I can't figure out what to say and the tears begin again. She sits on my lap. "Please stop crying and tell me what's wrong," and begins to cry herself, which I haven't seen her do in a long time, unless she's been angry.

"I'm just feeling overwhelmed with all that we've had to do in the last few days to get ready for Laura's graduation party." I don't mention how I wish they would acknowledge Todd on Father's Day. It wouldn't mean anything unless they did it on their own.

"I'll wash the dishes on Monday, after I get home from Dad's," she offers.

"Thanks," I say in a high-pitched voice. "I'll take you up on that."

"Do you want to watch Laura and me wrap presents downstairs?"

I don't feel like watching them wrap gifts for their father so I decline the invitation and retreat to my bedroom.

Laura comes into my room, probably because Jenny sent her upstairs. Even though the tears have stopped, she can see that I've been crying.

Sitting at the foot of my bed, she asks, "Are you getting your period?"

I grab a pillow and throw it at her. She's right. We both laugh.

"Thanks for helping with my graduation party—I mean for organizing the whole thing."

"You're welcome." The recognition helps lift some of my emotional cloud.

"Why don't you come down and help us wrap presents?"

"No thanks. I don't think I'm up to it."

"Pleeeeease." Like the exhausted parent of a persistent child, I give in just so she'll stop begging.

Downstairs I see Jenny sizing up wrapping paper for two identical Marshall Fields boxes laid side by side. Inside each one is a polo shirt, one salmon colored and the other navy blue.

"Do you think Todd will like it?" Jenny asks, pointing to the salmon colored shirt."

"I'm sure he will." My voice cracks and my eyes spring another leak.

"Mom, what's wrong?"

"Nothing," I squeak out. "Nothing at all."

~Tracy Gulliver

83

One "Step" at a Time

After relocating from Michigan, my second husband, our four-year-old daughter, Brett, and I were preparing for our first Thanksgiving in Florida. My stepdaughter, Christine, invited us to her in-laws' to celebrate and meet the whole family. One of the guests was, Diane, Christine's biological mother and my husband's ex. When Diane was introduced to Brett as "Christine's mother" she was extremely confused. She looked at me and said, "But Mom, I thought you were Christine's mom."

It was time to sit down and explain the "extended blended family" concept.

"Before Dad met me, he was married to Christine's mom. I am Christine's stepmom. She is my stepdaughter."

My daughter looked at me and asked "Mom, were you ever married before?"

"Yes, I was actually." She eyed me for a few seconds than smiled and said,

"Oh, I get it. Dad's your stephusband."

~Patricia Holdsworth

84

Third Time's a Charm

Siblings are the people we practice on,
the people who teach us about fairness and cooperation and
kindness and caring—quite often the hard way.
~Pamela Dugdale

Three divorces between us—my two and his one—plus four toasters, two and a half sets of multi-patterned dinnerware, fourteen forks, sixteen knives, twelve teaspoons, and seven frying pans. My new husband and I surveyed our combined worth. We both had owned our own homes before deciding to marry again. Surely in all of that pile of stuff and more, we had everything we needed to set up housekeeping.

It wasn't that we didn't have the right things to begin our new life together—we simply had too much of everything. Even after filling up two trash bins and several boxes for the rescue mission, we still had too much stuff for one house and one family. We heaved what was dilapidated into the garbage and took stock of our remaining treasure. The questionable pile looked ready to teeter over. Extra beds, couches, tables, sheets, pillow cases, blankets, toasters, knives, and a three-foot-tall pile of pots and pans.

Decisions had to be made. Whose personal stuff should we get rid of? His or mine? Was his stuff in better shape than the items I had acquired during my lifetime? Were his irreplaceable mementos more important than my doodads?

He owned a hoard of manly things that he "needed": wooden

salt and pepper shakers, TV trays, leather this and Naugahyde that. Everywhere I looked, his fishing gear: hooks, shiny white and yellow line, slinky rubber worms, bobbers, can't-fail bait, piles of maps, books and magazines, and—lest we forget—the picture of him hauling in the big tuna! My new husband began to dig his heels in a bit. I began to worry—I'd seen a stubborn streak like that before. Couldn't I see how important these things were to him?

Yes, I could. I relented a bit.

On the other hand, didn't he understand that I wanted to decorate my new home with lacy, embroidered things, silk flowers and ruffled bed skirts? He balked, and then his facial expression flashed a look of partial compromise. I pleaded my case. We ended up compromising, room by room.

We still have some of his wooden and leather thingies—and he'll always have an ample supply of fishing gear. But now they don't reside in the living room with the china bowls, embroidered pieces his mama made and the oil paintings from my mom.

We also dealt with engineering issues of children and relatives. When we surveyed the situation and put the two family histories side by side, we realized that to properly assemble our puzzle would require time, hard work and a bit of finesse.

Neither of us knew exactly how the grown-ups would get along, but we did have dissension between our children. Vincent, my son, and Suzanne, Gordon's daughter, were at odds with one another. On many days, the children's bickering made my head hurt. Although my husband and I tried to love them equally and show no favorites, an ongoing—and growing—rift between them threatened to rock our little boat.

Most of the time Vincent ran—full bore—to prove his might. He superseded Suzanne by three whole years and towered above her.

Suzanne looked like a diminutive, dark-haired china doll on top of a music box. I worried that she might break if anyone squeezed her too tightly. She would let out a pitiful, "oh-aren't-I-a-poor-little-baby" whine and draw our sympathy for some horrible misdeed Vincent had done to her. Initially, neither Gordon nor I saw that her shenanigans put us at a disadvantage and caused us to issue punitive judgment against her bigger and older stepbrother. That is, until the day I caught Suzanne in the act of faking it. I still remember the moment that she knew that I knew. She smiled her first big girl "I-know-how-to-play-this-game-now" grin at me, and laughed. I realized then that Suzanne would be just fine.

Yes, our families and children have their own histories and needs. That doesn't change, whether a family grows up together from birth or they meet in a stepfamily situation. The four of us grew more intertwined as the years went by. My husband and I saw the challenge as keeping problems to a low roar and discovering ways to be happy while orchestrating a bright and healthy future for all of us.

Thankfully, we've been married for twenty-six years now, and I can say is, "We really did it. We're a true success story."

Not too shabby.

~Cinda T. Crawford

Bringing Up Amy

Other things may change us, but we start and end with the family.
~Anthony Brandt

We were a diverse—and perhaps perverse—group gathered at the restaurant that day: my daughter, whose high school graduation we were celebrating, my ex and his new wife, her two sons, my sister, my girlfriend, me, and the Chihuahua puppy smuggled in the stepmother's purse. Although our divorce had been civil from the start, it had taken a while for us to be able to sit happily as a blended family at this table in Muncie, Indiana.

It had been my idea to seek a divorce. Mike had been stoic and outwardly supportive. From my daughter, however, I would hear the breathless tales: "Daddy uses your old clothes for rags." "Daddy sold the chest of drawers you thought you would get back when you moved." For my part, I smiled with gritted teeth and remarked that he had those rights. After all, the divorce decree had granted him everything still in our former home. One year after the divorce, for my birthday, Amy bought from her father a lamp I particularly missed and proudly presented it to me. I had loved that lamp, a gift from a now-deceased aunt and assumed it was gone—along with the chest of drawers, the clothes, my college luggage, and other items I had not taken when I left the house.

When Mike and Liz first started spending some time together, Amy was thrilled. Liz did all the fun "mom things" I didn't have time to do, since I had a job that sometimes required twelve-hour days. Amy would come home with leftover treats, recipe cards, and scraps of fabric with grand plans to go with them. As her father and Liz got more serious, Amy had some difficulty making the jump from "only child" to "only daughter."

When Liz found out she was pregnant, Amy's first reaction was not a positive one. Eventually though, she grew excited about the idea of a baby, and when Liz had a miscarriage a few months into the pregnancy, Amy was devastated.

Any divorce is a balancing act of who gets which holidays, which weekends, which tasks. Amy spent her junior and senior years of high school three hours away from home in order to attend a public boarding school for exceptional students, the Indiana Academy of Science, Mathematics and the Humanities. There were required home weekends as well as the standard school breaks when she had to be picked up from her dorm by 6:00 P.M. on Friday and could not return until 4:00 P.M. on the Sunday the break was over. Mike and I tried to be fair in divvying up who had to take off work and who had to get home late on a Sunday night. Sometimes sickness or a work emergency would require a last minute change in plans, but in those two years the shuttle never broke down. Well, once or twice we might have had to ask Liz or my girlfriend, Jean, to make the drive, but we still had it covered. Through our combined efforts, Amy had the opportunity to attend this excellent program.

When extra support was needed, we were there as well. When family members passed away, we helped Amy deal with the logistics of getting to funerals as well as providing her a shoulder to cry on. When my nephew passed away unexpectedly at the age of twenty-five, Mike was there, both to offer his condolences to my sister and to be a good daddy to our mourning daughter. One holiday season, when it looked like I might be alone, Liz and Mike invited me to join their feast. I wasn't quite ready for that, but I appreciated the offer.

Graduation finally came, and after sniffling through the ceremony, we made our way to the restaurant for a late lunch, each of our cars full of Amy's belongings. That is how we came to be the blended family, contraband dog and all, trading stories and experiencing mass fits of coughing whenever the puppy whined, as we celebrated Amy's initiation into adulthood.

We came together a few weeks ago again when Amy, about to be a junior in college, moved into her very own apartment. There we stood, laughing and sharing stories, petting the communal cat on the lawn of the big old house now divided into apartments. This time we were joined by three of Amy's friends from the Academy who had come from across Indiana to help her move.

As we admired the flowers and garden sculptures, I thought about how fortunate Amy has been to have had a family like hers, with the ties both of blood and friendship. There have still been difficult bits to get past and missteps made by both sides, but we have made certain that she has had what she needed. We've moved past animosity, and if what Mike and I have reached isn't quite friendship, it's still shared parenthood. Maybe the next time Liz invites me to Thanksgiving dinner, instead of begging off I'll ask her what she wants me to bring.

~Jenny Austin

An Adjusted Fit

After my daughter received her engagement ring, I needed my mother of the bride dress to wear at her wedding. I purchased a long mint-green gown off a sales rack for twenty dollars. It was my size. Once I tried it on at home, it didn't fit perfectly, but I figured losing five pounds before wearing the dress would alter the fit. Then, my husband saw it on the hanger. He hated everything about the dress. I put the bag over it, placed it in the back of the closet, and instead I wore a yellow gown I found on the Internet.

Eight months later, my son began dating one of his co-workers, a divorced woman with children. "Three," he said holding fingers in the air.

I was from what we called a "normal family" background. My parents had celebrated their fiftieth wedding anniversary. I had over thirty years of marriage. At first, I never considered how my son's new relationship could matter to my life. Dating, after all, is just about checking things out. Plus, their dates seemed rather sporadic.

As his interest in the woman increased, I suspected my life would change. Not only would I need to adjust to one more addition to the family—but four. Once I met the three children, I began to truly understand their impact on my life.

Determined to make my way through change, I planned to handle whatever came up with grace. But I was not prepared for the children. I admit it. And while I did understand they are entitled to all their emotions, wasn't I also entitled to display any of my own? I am an adult, but also a mother. When one of the children complained about my son not purchasing her something, I was quick to speak out about the hungry children in Africa. After my tirade, I felt horrible. I had no friends to turn to for advice. No one in our circle of friends was divorced and all their children were still single.

I decided I had to be myself. Just as I expect adults, friends, and family to accept me as I am, so must these children. I am entitled to express my opinion. I certainly expressed plenty of opinions to my own children while they were living with me. Why should I expect myself to act differently now? I realized I had to show the three children who I am—just as they are entitled to be who they are—while we adjust to each other.

As we started to plan my son's wedding, I received the news that my daughter was expecting. In one year, I will be an official grandmother to one child, and a stepgrandmother to another three children.

But I will not tell the three children to accept me as another grandmother. After all, they already have two. I am perfectly comfortable letting them call me by my first name. If they decide to call me grandmother, I will welcome the name. Because of my own family background, I cannot understand all the emotions the children are going through. But I can offer opportunities to them; take them to a movie, the library or to lunch.

Each one of my grandchildren will matter to me. I will try to support them however each of them needs me, while I also remain true to myself. That is, after all, who they need me to be.

I picture myself wearing that mint green dress hanging in the depths of my closet to this wedding. I might finally take advantage of that bargain price. Perhaps if I shorten the length or the sleeves, somehow alter its appearance, my husband will like it better. But if I do order another one off the Internet, it will not matter. All that matters is that as a family, we remain who we are as we adjust to each other, while we find the way to fit.

~Linda Hanson

87

Never Letting Go

Becoming a stepmother had been so exciting. Marriage was something I had always wanted, but gaining four beautiful stepchildren had made it all the more meaningful. Then as our marriage deteriorated, the memories of happy times spent with the children were almost impossible to bear.

Jade, the five-year-old—and the youngest of the four brothers and sisters—took the divorce much harder than the rest of them did. It was easy for the three older children to say goodbye to me—after all, I was wife number three. Jade, on the other hand, couldn't understand the concept of daddy not living with Amber anymore.

Knowing the special bond that Jade and I shared, her mother and I decided to let her stay in touch with me.

The first time I went to pick her up for a visit, I found myself traveling down memory lane. I wondered how the other children were doing and how their lives were changing. As I pulled into the parking lot, I saw her, anxiously waiting for my arrival. She said her goodbyes to her mother, and off we went—just the two of us.

Five minutes down the road, she said, "Amber, I thought you weren't coming to get me." Crushed, I asked her why she would think that. As my heart broke, she said that her mommy had told her to hold on to what she treasured—even when it seemed like other people didn't. With tearful eyes, I told her that I would always love her and that her mommy was right.

As we pulled into the driveway of my home, Jade, half-asleep, looked up at me with a smile and said, "I am holding on to you, Amber." After I carried her inside and tucked her into bed, she opened her eyes and said, as if continuing her thought, "Is that okay with you?"

I kissed her forehead and said, "Yes, sweetheart, because I am never letting go of you either."

I went to my room and cried. Even though my marriage was over, my bond with Jade would grow and grow. And for that reason I was grateful for my ex-husband.

~Amber Frazier

88

Isaac's New Family

A new baby is like the beginning of all things —
wonder, hope, a dream of possibilities.
~Eda J. Le Shan

It was Christmas Eve. My two-month-old son was up well past his bedtime and surprisingly happy for such a late hour. The smell of Tortiere, my family's traditional Christmas Eve dinner, still lingered in the air mingling with the pine of the tree and evoking all the memories of a lifetime of family holidays.

The job of entertaining my young son was left largely to my parents, my dad stretching out with him on the floor as he had done so many nights with me as a child. My mind was occupied. I was waiting nervously for my husband's return. Later this Christmas Eve, he was bringing a special visitor to my parents' home. My eleven-year-old stepdaughter, Samantha, had just flown in from her mother's house thousands of miles away.

A lot of thought had gone into this evening. It was the first time Samantha would meet her baby brother. A move across the country when I was pregnant meant she was not there when Isaac was born, and school commitments meant she couldn't visit soon afterwards. Christmas was to be our first chance and, thanks to a late Christmas break and flight schedules, she wasn't to arrive until nearly midnight on Christmas Eve.

This was the moment we had lost sleep over. Being a stepparent leaves you precariously balanced at the best of times, and introducing a baby threatened a shift of tectonic proportions. It was going to be the first time Samantha would have to share her father. At home, her mom had two young boys, but she was used to being the center of attention at our place. We had done everything we could think of to ease the transition. We had picked a special time and way to tell her I was pregnant, we had included her in the plans for the baby's room and discussions about names, and we constantly talked about how lucky little Isaac was to have a great big sister like her. Still, it didn't seem enough.

She arrived. Arriving with a mammoth suitcase, she brushed past me, barely saying hello, and headed straight for her brother. That's when it happened.

It was the moment we really became a family. It wasn't anything my husband or I did. It was two-month-old Isaac. Samantha settled down to play and when she tickled him, Isaac laughed—for the very first time. All that planning, all that worry—and it was a helpless little infant who made it happen. In one moment, that little laugh cancelled out all the complications of divorce, blended families, and stepchildren. We were just us—a family. He made us whole that night, and for that, I will always be grateful. Most would say it was just coincidence, but I choose to believe Isaac was saving that first laugh. Acting on instinct, Isaac's joy came out the moment his new family was complete.

~Megan Venner

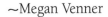

Chapter
9

Divorce *and* Recovery

New Insights
and Ageless Wisdom

A moment's insight is sometimes worth a life's experience.
~Oliver Wendell Holmes

Lessons in Divorce

We cannot learn without pain.
~Aristotle

hey say that with every trial we encounter in life, we learn a lesson. I never really believed this, until I was deciding to end my marriage. In the deep of the night, I would ask myself why my life had turned out this way, and why I had made a choice, as important as marriage, so quickly, and without much thought. Now I realize it was a teaching ground for me, to become a better person, and live a more fulfilling, and happy life.

Through my divorce, I have learned to follow my heart. By listening to every word it whispered, I was able to walk away from a situation that was not healthy for my children, or me.

I have learned to listen to my inner voice and take what it says seriously. I no longer brush the thoughts aside, but instead, stop and listen to hear the answers.

I have learned to express my emotions, whether they are positive or negative. I have learned to accept them as they are, and accept them as part of who I am. I have learned that I am free to feel the way I do, no matter what anyone else may think.

I have rediscovered past loves. I have found the courage to sing, dance and write. I have found the hobbies that I turned away from so long ago to please someone other than myself.

Through my divorce, I was able to look into the hurt in my heart, and finally deal with the turmoil it gave me. I was able to see these hurts, and move forward in my life, finally giving the actions against me closure, through forgiveness.

I have learned that I do not have to be dependent on anyone else.

I have learned to be financially smart. I have learned to take care of myself and my children.

I have learned that I am a great parent, who can display love and discipline. I have learned that I have patience, and that I am teaching my children to be strong and independent. I have taught my children to listen to their hearts, and not to take hurt from anyone.

I have learned how to hammer a nail, shovel the driveway, and cut the grass. I have discovered I can learn to do anything, and be great at it; all I have to do is try.

Through my divorce, I learned to become the person I was meant to be. I went on a journey, deep into my soul and met the me who I had left behind so many years ago. I realized that I am beautiful, capable of love and of giving love in effortless amounts.

I discovered happiness on a newer and higher level. I learned how to get past the rough spots, and remain focused on the happier times ahead.

I learned that I am deserving of a loving, respectful relationship. I discovered true love with another, who loves the individual I have become, and who helps me to flourish in every way.

Through my divorce, I learned that the best lessons in life are learned through the harder times. I've learned that when things seem like they won't get any better, they will. I've learned to hang on, and hold my head up high, looking for a brighter tomorrow.

Most importantly, I learned to live for myself, my goals, my loves, and my life.

Divorce has been my greatest lesson.

~Catherine Graham

Listen to the Woman

Wisdom is before him that hath understanding.
~Proverbs

Deployment homecomings are designed for postcards.

As my ship, carrying me and five thousand other sailors wearing white Crackerjacks, moored for the first time in six months, a sea of friends and family members stood on the pier jumping, crying, waving, and screaming.

Homemade signs inked in rainbow colors bearing a loved one's name swayed. Local vendors lined the street behind the pier, handing out free gifts. The scene was a carnival, made for military families who stayed home and sailors fighting the good fight abroad. It was like one colossal ball of joy.

But I wasn't allowed such joy. Part of me didn't want to come home because I no longer had a wife. She had moved out of our home two weeks before I was due to arrive.

I knew the day would come. Weeks before, she had told me not to expect her. But my heart still sank when I faced the inevitable.

In a marriage, a husband's core responsibilities are typically easy. Three things can keep a wife happy: treating her as an equal, staying on top of her needs, and listening to her. With that blueprint, everything can fall into place. Take one step toward a woman, she'll take two toward you, I always say.

But I was taking steps backward. I hadn't been sticking to the blueprint. Just the opposite—until she couldn't take anymore.

Talk about bad timing. After a huge argument one Friday night, she said she wanted out. It was six weeks before my scheduled deployment. One week before an already-paid-for pleasure cruise. Two weeks before Thanksgiving. One month before Christmas, New Year's, and her birthday.

I didn't give in. Despite pleas for forgiveness, however, I ran into her invisible brick wall. Even the holiday season couldn't ease the storm between us. Once the pleasure cruise ended, the rift between us grew wider. A cold war developed in my own home with no sign of a truce. Finally, I decided to leave her alone.

The living room became my bedroom.

Spoken words between us ceased. She did her thing, I did mine. A married couple of nine years now reduced to hi-and-bye room-mates. And that hurt me, like a dull ache from head to toe. I suffered through some of the worst days of my life, capped off with me pack-ing my bags, off to the ship—alone. No kiss or hug goodbye.

For approximately 180 days, confined to a ship thousands of miles away, I tried to wear a happy mask so I wouldn't alarm co-workers, while I endured flashbacks that nipped at my conscience. Some days, I didn't want to get out of my rack. Few e-mails, no care packages, no letters. And my mind went 100 miles an hour: What is she doing at home? Will I come back to an empty house? Has she already found someone else? My thoughts drained me.

When I did receive e-mails from her, they were businesslike in tone. Bland, dry, heartless, even. Nothing like the daily e-mails I used to get that ended with "Love you." It appeared that love no longer remained—I had killed it by not being the husband she needed.

Somehow, I waddled through the darkness, carried on with the "plan of the day" as sailors say. I kept to myself, working my day-to-day business as a maintenance administrator. Off-hours, books, work-related certifications, and the gym helped nibble away the crawl of time. Hong Kong, Singapore, and Australia put my heartache on hiatus for a while.

But you can't easily shake what hurts deep inside. Flashbacks helped me understand what led to my bankrupt marriage. I finally pulled the wool from my eyes and asked questions that placed a mirror in front of me: How long did I expect my wife to tolerate being a distant second to the Internet and TV? Did I really think I could get away with shallow signs of love, donating hugs and kisses only when her pleas for affection annoyed me? What kind of husband argues 100 percent of the time over purchases for a new house, such as an extra $95 water faucet that would allow washing two cars at the same time? No compromise, no negotiation—just "no"?

One thing I discovered about me stood out: Almost every purchase we argued over and didn't get, I later regretted not getting.

A few times, I even made comments like, "Man, we should've gotten the extra warranty on this thing. How come we didn't?"

She'd say, "Because you said it cost too much. Remember we argued over it?"

Idiotic.

As I would lie in my rack at night, I realized things that made me wish I could kick myself a hundred times. I did love my wife. Very much. Always had. Didn't show it well enough, though. Nowhere near as she'd done for me. I became a living example of the cliché "don't know what ya got 'til it's gone."

Wesley Snipes said it best in *White Men Can't Jump*. In the movie, Rosie Perez grew tired of Woody Harrelson's careless ways and left him for good. Upon witnessing his buddy's misfortune, Wesley uttered simple but powerful words: "Listen to the woman."

Probably my biggest shortcoming. Other issues had seemed more important than what my wife had to say.

As I took inventory of my ways, I concluded that if I were her, suffering in silence for as long as she had, I would divorce me, too. Marriage is a two-way highway. Apparently, I'd made it a "my way" highway. And while I was deployed, she took the nearest exit.

To truly learn from one's mistakes, it takes looking deep into one's self. I've chosen to do that. No bitterness, no hatred, no acts of revenge toward her. She went her way, I went mine. I made my bed, and you know the rest.

Although I'm now a "statistic," I'd marry again. The next time, however, I'll follow the blueprint and always remember what Wesley said.

~Kenneth Williams

91

Divorce Is Like a Cake

One of my second graders, Debbie, had been unusually quiet in my Family Living class. When I asked her if something was wrong, she replied, "I don't feel like talking today. I'm sad. My best friend's parents are going to get divorced. Her father moved out of the house. I told her I would share my dad with her, but I know it isn't the same."

"What does 'revorced' mean?" asked Sandy.

"I know," Steven replied. "'Revorced' is when people get married and walk down the aisle backwards."

"It is not!" declared Susan. "It means when people get unmarried—when they're mean to each other and they split up. And the word isn't 'revorced,'" she added authoritatively. "It's divorced."

"When people get divorced, the wife hates the husband and the husband hates the wife and they scream at each other every day," said Sandy. "They fight about money."

During another discussion about divorce, Kelly said, "My mom and dad are getting divorced for the second time, and my dad gets to keep the dog."

"I feel real sorry for you," said Brian. "Especially about the dog!"

Asked to define the word "father" in a spelling test, Corey wrote: "A father is someone you see on weekends."

"My grandparents got divorced a long time ago," said Debbie. "They took apart their marriage and spread their lives apart. They aren't living anymore, but I loved them both very much."

I was surprised to learn that almost every child in my primary grade Family Living classes seemed to have some personal acquaintance with divorce—be it through friends of the family, neighbors, relatives, or much closer to home—their own parents. For many of them, divorce was just a normal part of life. Like Emily, who said, "I want to be a doctor or nurse when I grow up, so after I get married and divorced, I'll be able to support myself."

Then there was Billy, who stated, "When my mom gets married again next week, we're all going on a honeymoon."

"Oh, I know what a honeymoon is!" said Danny. "It's a vacation a husband and wife go on after the wedding if they can find a babysitter to stay with the kids."

When Brian came to my class the day after winter vacation, and I'd mentioned that I had been in California, he asked me, "Did you see a man named Frank when you were in California? He used to be my father."

"Well, I've got lots of fathers," Mindy said proudly. "I've either got three stepdads or four. I just can't remember anymore."

"I'm never going to get married!" Timmy declared adamantly.

"Yes, you will," Mara disagreed. "You'll get married and then you'll get divorced. Most people do, you know."

"If you don't get married, you'll be so lonely," pointed out Amy.

"No—I won't," said Timmy. "I'll have my teddy bear. At least he won't divorce me."

"I've never even seen my daddy," said Matthew. "Not even a picture. My mom doesn't like to talk about him. I dream about him a lot, though. But he never has a face."

"Sometimes parents fight about the kids," said Kimberly. "My parents are divorced and my mom keeps pulling on one of my arms and my dad pulls the other."

How sad, I thought, that a child would feel like her parents were actually pulling her apart because they each wanted more of her than the other should. Or Matthew, who kept dreaming about a father who had no face.

"I hate that my parents are divorced!" exclaimed Greg. "It's all my fault, too. I bite my nails too much."

Lori tried to look at things from a more positive perspective. "Just because your mother and father got mad at each other, doesn't mean they got mad at you," said Lori.

"And," said Eric, carrying on Lori's thought, "Just because parents don't love each other doesn't mean they don't love their kids."

"Lori and Susan are right," I said. "Sometimes a husband and wife realize that they no longer love each other and decide it will be best for the whole family if they don't live together anymore. But that doesn't mean they stop loving their children, and it certainly doesn't mean that it is the children's fault!"

"Maybe your mom and dad will change their minds and get undivorced," Eric told Greg. "Then you can all be together again."

Greg shook his head. "No, that won't happen." And then, with a thoughtful expression on his face, he said, "You know something? Divorce is like a cake. You cut it in half and it's separated forever."

~Arlene Uslander

92

Me and the Money in the Middle

He pulled out the black case and began to unzip it. My dad is the kind of guy who owns a lot of gadgets and plenty of things to hold them. This black case was no exception. It had pockets galore and I wondered, with a sick feeling in my stomach, what was inside them.

The bright fluorescent lights of the Subway restaurant were startling. I looked across the small, sticky table at my dad, studying his features. We have the same eyes, he and I. Almond shaped, with a bottom lid that creeps slightly higher than those of my mom's. The shape of his eyes, paired with his other features, give him a discerning look that can be jubilant and fun when a smile squishes them together. But sometimes those same almond eyes can be frighteningly serious.

My gaze lifted from his eyes to his forehead and his hair. It was black then, not yet graying, but thinning at the back. From where I was, I couldn't see the spot of skin that had been steadily growing at the crown of his head, but I knew it existed. Much like the problems and the tension that had been plaguing my broken family.

I was seven years old when my parents decided to file for divorce. They called me into the living room of our house and sat on either side of me. Sunlight was streaming in through the windows around our front door and bursting in between the blinds that hung in the living room windows. It was the kind of radiant weekend sunlight I loved to wake up bathed in. It was so beautiful outside. I wasn't nervous at all.

My parents explained to me that they no longer loved each other and that they were going to get a divorce. They stressed that it wasn't because they didn't love me. I can't remember the exact words that were spoken—I was young—but I can remember that sunlight.

I looked at both of them, calm and unsurprised. Then I asked what I thought was the most important question regarding the situation:

"Can I still get a guinea pig?"

I craved the rich, natural light of that sunny day now that I was faced with the terribly unflattering glare of the lights in the Subway. The smell of lunchmeats and toasting mass-produced whole wheat bread wafted around me. The corners of my mouth tugged downwards. It was an effect my father often had on me. Somehow, our conversations generally resulted in a struggle to plug up my tear ducts and swallow my sobs.

He pulled papers from the briefcase.

"These," he started, "are the figures. This is how much I pay your mother in child support." He pointed to some numbers I didn't understand. The papers looked blurry and I felt uneasy. "This is how much I pay for alimony." Another number. More numbers followed. I can't remember any of them. I was fourteen.

"I just wanted you to understand," he said, as he explained. I didn't listen. The lights were so bright, and they were harsh on my dad's features. They made his skin look sallow and blotchy, so I stared at the papers and the crumbs on the table as he kept talking. The papers lying on the table danced in circles as I felt dizzier and dizzier.

My mom was livid when she heard.

"He showed you the numbers? Why would he get you involved?" she yelled at no one in particular. "I can't believe he did that." She was angry and very obviously holding back insults. I just sat in her room on her window seat, making apologies in my head:

"I'm sorry I told her, Dad."

"I'm sorry he doesn't pay you, Mom."

"I'm sorry we cost so much...."

My parents had been fighting over money since 9/11 came and sin-gle-handedly destroyed my father's business. Once he wasn't making money, he decided he could no longer afford to pay my mom alimony. Sometimes, he decided he couldn't afford child support. My mom had decided that it wasn't his decision to make. So had the lawyer she hired, and, eventually, the judge who forced my dad to pay. It was a long, drawn-out process that spanned years. Every phone conversa-tion I overheard was bitter and angry, filled with hushed curse words. My mom would storm around the house and hide her tears and anger after my dad had hung up on her. At twelve, I would tiptoe around her and, if possible, around the situation, packing my little plastic bag with the necessities I needed for Dad's house:

My favorite pea green shirt. Check.

My face wash. Check.

My favorite pair of jeans. Check.

My enormous sense of guilt and failure when I inevitably forgot something I needed and had to apologetically ask my step mom to pick it up. Double check.

It wasn't until my late high school years when my parents resolved their conflicts and became somewhat amicable. They found some-thing they could come together over, a common love: Me and my brother. I think they realized, at some point, that fighting over financ-ing our lives was ruining them instead.

Senior year of high school, I played the lead in the musical. On closing night, I exited the double doors after the show to see my fam-ily standing and chatting. My mom, my dad, my grandparents. They had flowers in their hands and they were — dare I say it? — smiling. At each other. They saw me come out and they both grinned, cameras in hand and pride in their eyes. Pride in my mom's eyes that I had seen tearful so many times, pride in my dad's eyes shaped just like my own. Each of them hugged me and told me how proud they were of me. What I didn't say was that I was proud of them too.

I was standing between them that night, just like I was sitting between them when they told me they were getting a divorce. Sometimes, I cradle in my hands a little white picture frame that I keep in my room at my mom's house. It holds an old Polaroid photo that was taken the morning of June 8th, 1992 — the day my brother was born. We're standing on the front steps of our house, my parents and I, in my last moments as an only child. My mom is on the right and my dad on the left. I, of course, am in the middle. Always have and always will be. And I think, at this point, it's not such a bad thing.

~Madison James

93

Tick Tock

Time dissipates to shining ether the solid angularity of facts.
~Ralph Waldo Emerson

There it stood on the front lawn: tall, stately, mahogany wood and glass. Inside, three brass weights hung from long chains. A brass sun and moon rose and fell across shiny numerals.

My grandfather clock. My prize. My possession. Set out on the green grass like a discarded bath towel.

It was appropriate that this timepiece marked the end of our marriage. We'd sure spent enough years trying to make it work—seventeen to be exact. There are all kinds of reasons for two people to stay together, and all kinds of reasons for them to move apart. It was time for us to move apart. And that was harder than I had expected.

"I'd like to have the grandfather clock," I had said to my ex-husband on the telephone.

"Forget it. It's part of the house and it stays."

He lived in the house now and I was leaving the state. I had wanted to take the clock with me. After all, I had worked hard for it.

I sold Tupperware at home parties for quite some time, and one day they had announced a contest. "You earn points for every sale you make," the owner of the distributorship announced. "Here's a full-color catalog. Find something you want to have. There's everything from microwave ovens to vacuum cleaners and toasters." I opened the glossy brochure and flipped through the pages. My eyes stopped on a photo of a regal clock. I never had anything so beautiful, so elegant. I could hear the three different chimes, the melodies ringing on every quarter, half and full hour. I had to have it.

When I reached my goal, the owner handed me an order form to fill out. My hands shook with joy. I bypassed the blender and the dishwasher and checked the box for the grandfather clock. It was delivered a couple of months later and we set it up in the dining room, where it sat for years.

Now, although just a piece of furniture to my ex, the clock remained a symbol of achievement and success to me.

"Come on," I pleaded. "You don't care about it. Let me have it."

"No," was his clipped reply.

I hung up. He was stubborn. There was no way that clock would be mine.

A few days later, I drove down my old street. There stood the clock on the front lawn where all the neighbors could see it. A glaring symbol of the end of our marriage. The end of our time together. I screeched to a stop and turned into the driveway. I walked up to the door and knocked. He answered from inside. "Take it," he said.

"What?" I didn't think I heard right.

"You can have it."

I swallowed hard. "Thanks," I mumbled, and then turned from the doorway. I wanted to ask why he threw it out on the lawn like a bone for a dog, but I held my tongue. There it stood, and it was mine. I didn't question his second thoughts.

Luckily I had a station wagon. I unhooked the weights and the pendulum and placed them on the front seat. The clock was tall and awkward, but surprisingly light. I'm sure he saw me struggle with it. I gently lowered the top and dragged it across the grass to the rear of the car. I set the top end inside the tailgate and then lifted the bottom. Nudging it forward on the carpeting, I pushed it up to just behind the front seats. I couldn't get the tailgate closed, but it didn't matter—I didn't have far to go.

I jumped into the driver's seat and slowly backed out of the gravel driveway. When I got to my dad's house a few blocks away, I unloaded the clock into the garage. I shimmied it over to the wall and covered it with a large blanket. That's where it sat until a moving truck came to take me to my new home, my new beginning, my new life.

When I look at the clock now in my new living room, chiming those Westminster melodies on the hour, I am reminded of the times of my life. I don't regret my first marriage. I don't regret my divorce. Life is sweeter because of all that I have experienced. I appreciate each movement of the minute hand, each turn of the hour. The days melt one into another, and the clock doesn't stop.

But it did that day when my ex took a step in the right direction. After all, we had spent what felt like a lifetime together. We were two young kids married too soon, but we had many wonderful times together. Not one moment of our marriage was wasted. Each minute was the way it was meant to be. Each hour a blessing. We learned a lot about ourselves, about our loves, about our lives.

Life changes.

Tick tock.

~B.J. Taylor

94

Lessons from the Lake

From a near-death experience at age seven, I acquired the tools to help me overcome life's greatest challenge thirty years later: the end of a marriage to the man I had built my dreams and life around. Starting all over again in a new place with three little children was not easy. Indeed, the lessons learned, wisdom gained, and tools acquired at such a young age have shaped me into who I am and have given me the strength to face many hurdles head-on.

I grew up next to the neighborhood playground, which bordered a thick forest surrounding a lake whose body spanned three towns. "The woods," and "the lake," provided a safe haven to explore nature and enjoy the simple things as we grew through childhood. Wild berries ripened in the spring sun and burst in my hand as I picked them from the bushes. With my fingers stained red, and my face dripping with juice, I took bucketfuls of blackberries and raspberries home, but could not resist eating the bounty that I carried, and rarely had much leftover by the time I got to my mother's kitchen. Never quite learning the art of skipping stones on the smooth surface of the lake, wading in shallow coves, and canoeing and boating drew me there on summer days. There was a dam at the lake, and when the water was not mightily falling over it, I could walk across it like a bridge to the town on the other side to pick apples. On autumn nights I enjoyed campfires in the woods with my friends, and in the winter we skated on the frozen lake.

In the first grade, my best friend was a tiny girl, my age—but half my size—named Bobbi. One winter day after a long snowfall, we thought it would be fun to run and slide on the ice in our boots and snow pants. So we walked through the forest in knee-deep snow, marveling at how different our familiar places looked, now dazzled in white. We approached our favorite cove, now covered by a thick blanket of snow, except where the older kids had shoveled an area big enough to play ice hockey. "Out of our way! Go shovel your own snow if you want to play on the ice," they hollered. So, we trudged off toward the middle of the lake, hoping to find another place to run and slide.

The silence of the surrounding virgin snow enveloped us as we traversed the frozen lake, far away from the sounds of the older children at play near the shore. After walking awhile on the vast expanse of soft white fluff, we could see what appeared to be a patch of snow-cleared ice to run and slide on. I wondered if the ice was too thin there and I feared it would not hold us, but Bobbi had no doubts. Running ahead of me I can still see her, as she excitedly kicked the ice with the heel of her boot, beckoning me to come, and hoping to prove the ice was thick and strong enough to hold us both. But it was not.

The surface was paper-thin, and after kicking it, Bobbi fell through. I thought of nothing else but running to her, and I fell in, too. Out of earshot from anyone else, we struggled for our lives. We were soaked to the skin within seconds, our snow pants and boots heavy, as we treaded violently to keep our heads above the icy water. Attempting to pull ourselves up onto the solid surface of the lake, large pieces of ice broke off and we'd be submerged again. I knew that crying, whining, and succumbing were not options. No one would hear or see us; we were alone. I tried repeatedly to lift myself out of the icy bath. More pieces of ice broke off, and again I pushed past the broken pieces, but each time I tried to transfer my weight from the water to the surface, the thin ice broke and dropped me back into the lake. We'll reach thicker ice, I thought, as I struggled to survive.

"We're almost there Bobbi, don't give up! Keep trying!" I yelled, not sure if she could hear me, immersed in the sounds of breaking ice and splashing water.

Then from nowhere, three young men appeared. We neither saw, nor heard them approach; we just suddenly knew they were with us. They lay spread-eagled on the ice to distribute their weight, and encouraged Bobbi to grab their single hockey stick as a lifeline. She did, and if they had not pulled her frail little body onto the surface, I don't know how this story would have ended. At the same time, I continued pushing past broken pieces, and pulled myself up. The three strangers cautioned us not to stand and walk, but advised us to crawl to avoid breaking the ice beneath us again. We heeded their advice, and parted company on hands and knees. After crawling toward shore awhile, I looked over my shoulder in their direction, hoping for a sign that it was okay to get off our knees and walk upright again. I have one final image of them in the distance indelibly etched in my memory. They were skating three abreast toward the town on the other side of the lake, kicking up snow dust behind them and disappearing like angels.

Shivering cold, soaking wet, and turning blue, Bobbi and I approached the cove again, not from the shore this time but from somewhere beyond the vanishing point in the middle of the lake. The older children were still playing hockey and some stared in disbelief, some didn't even notice, but my older sister laughed hysterically at our blue lips and wet clothes as if we had foolishly played in a puddle. She showed not a shred of sympathy. We tried to tell her what happened to us, but she obviously did not understand that we had almost been swallowed by the same lake she was playing on, had almost disappeared forever under the ice.

We trudged onward, out of the woods, growing colder and shivering more violently with every step. Passing the neighborhood playground seemed to take forever, but the warmth of my home was not far away now. Arriving at my house, my mother didn't laugh. She realized that by God's grace, our little lives had just been saved. She helped us out of our wet and freezing clothes and submerged us in warm baths. After serving us steaming cupfuls of hot cocoa, she tucked us in bed under piles of thick blankets to help keep each other warm. We snuggled together and the shivering eventually stopped.

We recovered. We survived. We bounced back quickly and soon we were looking forward to the wonder and excitement of the next snowfall with childlike anticipation.

What I learned that day at the lake continues to guide me and help me through difficult times.

Sometimes in life, you are on thin ice without even knowing it. Sometimes, the bottom drops out from under you and you fall. It happened to me when my married life suddenly ended. My nineteen-year marriage had not been a perfect one, but I believed we were attempting to patch things up and move forward in love. Instead, it ended abruptly. My little children suffered the emotional carnage of divorce and their dad's remarriage with stepchildren, and they needed me to extricate them from the wreckage. My life as fulltime mom and primary caregiver was over, I became a single mom in a new location, working fulltime and hoping to re-establish a career. I knew that crying, whining, and feeling sorry for myself were not options. The painful loss of my marriage, redefining myself, rebuilding our family life, restoring my children to wholeness, and keeping my head held high was not easy. At times I felt surrounded by the broken pieces of my former life. But I had long before learned how to persevere, and keep trying, no matter how many times it takes, or how hopeless it seems. Just like the little girl treading the icy waters, I knew what I had to do. "Push past the broken pieces and pull yourself up."

If help is offered as a lifeline, don't be too proud to accept it. As humbling as it might be, sometimes you cannot succeed by yourself and if there are people who want to help you through, you should graciously accept their kindness. Don't be too proud to let someone help you, just as Bobbi accepted the hockey-stick lifeline and was saved.

Sometimes you have to crawl before you can walk again. Starting all over again happens one step at a time and cannot be rushed. Like a baby learning to take its first steps, there are lessons to be learned before you stand, walk, and run. Divorce can put you in a situation where it feels as though life has pushed you a few steps backward. It may be tempting to rush things to catch up to where you think you should be. Don't be too quick to re-marry or even re-couple. Although you may not understand the greater forces at work, sometimes it's necessary to take your time and crawl before you walk, so that the bottom doesn't drop out from under you again.

The world can be a cold place, and just like hot cocoa and warm blankets, friends and loved ones warm me up on the inside. As a single mom, and the only adult in my household, it's important to me to keep healthy adult relationships alive and to be in close friendships with kindred souls, so that when life gets cold and the world is unkind, I have a never-ending source of warmth.

These are the lessons of the lake, gleaned from the day a trinity of strangers saved my life. To this day, no one has ever identified themselves as the heroes of Farrington Lake. No one has come forward to claim honor or receive a medal for saving two little seven-year-old girls from an icy death. But the three strangers taught me life's most important lessons and helped me to survive divorce and raise three little children on my own. Many, many times over the course of my life, the lessons of the lake have helped me to carry on and move forward when things seemed frightening, bleak and hopeless.

~Monica Giglio

95

The Little Family That Melted Away

*J*was standing in line at the checkout counter at the grocery store when I overheard a young woman with a small child telling someone how relieved she was that her divorce was finally going through. As soon as it was done, she would be moving to British Columbia. I thought about my ex-wife Mary.

Mary has multiple sclerosis. That's not the most important thing about her, but it's probably the most obvious. I say probably, because I haven't seen her in many years. I know that she depends on our son for quite a lot. Teevan, who is twenty-one, is trying to finish college, hold down a job, and look after his mother all at the same time. It's a heavy burden for one so young, but it's a task that he's performing beautifully, and it is through his efforts that Mary is able to stay in her home. In some ways, the family that was (and might have been) lives on through his dedication.

Mary and I met in the summer of 1974. It was at a place called Diamond Lake in southern Michigan, where my brother and his family were vacationing at the time. Within a couple of days of our meeting, we were attracted to each other and found ourselves deep in conversation. Then nature took its course. One July morning, as the sun was rising, we rowed out through the mist to the center of the lake and I knew that this would be serious. Soon afterwards, I returned to Edmonton where I had been working, and within a couple of months Mary joined me there. One thing led to another and in the summer of 1975 we were married.

It seemed to be a good match from the start. We were both "upbeat" people who shared a lively sense of humor. We came from families that had provided us each with a loving stable environment and parents who had cared for and respected each other. I was seven years older than her but that didn't seem to be an issue. After years of scratching out a living in the music industry, I found a stable job teaching college. Shortly thereafter, our son was born.

A little more than a year after Teevan's birth everything started to fall apart. I won't recount the specifics; suffice it to say that it was all the things many such situations are: sad, angry, confusing, draining, and ultimately, very lonely. When the divorce came, I was glad to be rid of her and I am sure she was equally happy to see the last of me. In our haste to extricate ourselves from an uncomfortable situation, neither of us looked beyond the next few months and tried to imagine what the future would be like, not only for us but, more importantly, for our son.

When we parted, she was a healthy twenty-three-year-old on her way to a new life in California and I was just past thirty and looking forward to some peace.

Mary seemed at first to have the better of the deal; I had assumed all the debts and she had our son. I had a fledgling career and not much else. Anyone who has been divorced knows the dynamics of how friendships change, so in effect, I was a stranger in town once again. I found a girlfriend and Mary was in a relationship with the man who would eventually become her husband. I would like to say that after the divorce we were able to put our bitter feelings behind us, but they persisted and ultimately, interfered with our relations over the next decade.

I had been happily remarried for some time, with two more children, when I began to hear from relatives that all might not be right with Mary's second marriage and with her health. Once, while visiting a mutual friend, I saw a picture of Mary and I was surprised at how thin she was.

Eventually her marriage unraveled and her illness, which turned out to be MS, progressed rapidly. It was around that time, more than fourteen years after our divorce that we began to talk again, on the phone. I'm not sure when we had our first peaceful words but I do remember feeling relieved that we could be civil to each other. As time passed, the infrequent conversations became as friendly as they could get and I was once again reminded of the girl I had known.

I have been remarried for seventeen years and I have a new family in which I have invested my life and my love. I take my younger son to hockey and my daughter to basketball. My wife and I get together with our friends to play cards and share a few laughs. As a family, we take off for Toronto to see the sights, go to a Blue Jays game and swim in the hotel pool. All so very normal. But sometimes, I do think of that other family, my phantom family. I wonder about the struggle that they are going through. This is not what I would have wished for either of them; the girl in the boat or the baby in the crib.

From this vantage point, far down the road, I can look back and see that what I thought was a mountain wasn't that high; what I thought was a problem wasn't that big and what I thought was forever, wasn't that long. Had we hung in there, it probably could have worked out. Some of the things that happened after the split were much worse than what happened to cause the split. There were many times before either one of us finally closed the door that we could have started to fix what was wrong. A word, a gesture or even a little patience could have made the difference. But that didn't happen and our small family melted away.

I watched the young woman leave the store and I understood how she felt. There are probably many young men and women who are feeling like she is; relieved to be out of a bad situation. But something now tells me there are just as many older men and women who had their bad times, but they stayed and worked it out and now, they are just as relieved that they persevered. Yes, there are some marriages that should not continue, but I suspect that number is a small percentage of those who get divorced. The future is a dream and sometimes the promise of the unknown is more attractive than the reality of the present. But each future eventually becomes a present and sooner or later, we all have to persevere.

~Terry McManus

96

An Unmarked Path

Love at first sight is easy to understand;
it's when two people have been looking at each other for a lifetime
that it becomes a miracle.
~Amy Bloom

*I*t took months for my sister, sisters-in-law, and me to plan my parents' fiftieth wedding anniversary. There were invitations to send out, a memory book to assemble and a video of half-a-century of photographs to be produced.

We secretly wrote and recorded a song especially for them. We marked down a hundred RSVPs, arranged place cards, a band, flowers, and blown-up black and white photos of their wedding to be placed in the center of each specially decorated table.

In their fifty-year-old wedding pictures, my mother and father had the glow of youth, the look that says you could run for miles without ever looking down at your feet, just positive they could never stumble in a million years. In one of the photos, my mother is smiling up at my dad like Ginger Rogers at Fred Astaire.

At the end of the party, my folks danced to "As Time Goes By," my mom in a carefully chosen coffee-colored lace dress and my dad, to my mother's familiar irritation, in a comfortable old sweater.

As the guests were leaving, the caterers wrapped up the elegant leftovers. The grandchildren took the balloons home. And I thought about my folks.

Over the years, my parents gave me everything but the one thing they could not.

With their fifty years of work and children, grandchildren and anniversaries, Thanksgivings and camping trips, they just couldn't show me how to be divorced. In their selfish pursuit of stability and commitment, they never broke our hearts—never moved across the country 3,000 miles away from one another.

They never sent support payments or formal e-mails arranging visitation. The poor souls had full-time custody of all four kids—all of the time. They couldn't offer me an example of how to date while having three children or how to have a boyfriend after I had been out of high school for thirty years.

My mother was never a working single mother. My dad was always there to handle the bills and the yard and was in charge of fixing broken things.

Obviously they had no clue.

I'm not saying that all marriages should be saved. Theirs was—mine should not have been. But, as mad as I have been, my heart knows that the bad parts don't erase the good ones. Sometimes the bad parts just make it impossible to stay.

My marriage didn't earn the Medal of Honor, more like a passel of Purple Hearts. But the picture of it has come to me over these past few years, like a composite sketch of an elusive police suspect. I really had to concentrate on the standout details in order to identify what it was and what it was not.

With some help from my loving, oblivious folks and 20/20 hindsight of my own, I have figured it out. Marriage is loads of raggedy photo albums sitting on a shelf in your living room, which you just take for granted. It is DVDs and popcorn, robes and slippers, and bad hair days. It is checkbooks and irritation and passion and taxes and getting to sleep in—or not. It is laundry and taking turns.

Marriage is eating Hamburger Helper by candlelight because that's what the kids are eating. Marriage is gritted teeth and Home Depot and who gets in the shower first. It's coffee and the morning paper.

It is not dating. It is not maybes. It can be yes for fifty years, and it can fly in the face of every reason to say no.

I remember all this now. I just didn't remember divorce. Until my own, I had no past history of it from which to draw wisdom.

Had my parents been a little more concerned about my future and gotten a miserable divorce — instead of applying their hearts and souls to the process of figuring out how to make ends meet with four kids, arranging summer vacations, and deciding which one of them was going to discipline us, they would not have left me with the indelible belief in the possibility of lifetime commitment.

They did what they could. And what most of us couldn't.

I always thought it was dopey when a TV audience would clap for a couple who had been married for decades. Big deal, right? But things change. Now I give them a standing ovation for decades of devotion, passion and arguments, of past, present, and future, and for decades of a daily decision to stay.

~Jolie Kanat

97

Still Loved

You cannot change the circumstances,
the seasons, or the wind, but you can change yourself.
That is something you have charge of.
~Jim Rohn

When I was about ten years old, my parents got in a huge argument that changed my life forever. Every time before, they had made up, but this time I had a feeling it was going to be different. My parents didn't talk to each other for days, and my dad slept on our pullout couch down in the basement.

Then we went to the county fair as a family. My mom and dad started talking and having fun together again, so I thought everything was okay.

I asked my mom, "You and Daddy are getting along a lot better, aren't you?"

"Well, I don't know about that," she answered.

I was so confused. I think my brother was too, but he was just a normal eleven-year-old and wasn't brave enough to admit how he was feeling.

Then the night came when my parents called my brother and me to come into the living room. They asked us to sit on the couch because they had to talk to us about something.

My dad began by saying, "Cameron... Karissa... your mom and I just can't seem to get along together any longer. We have worked on it and worked on it. We decided it would be best for me to move out and see if that helps."

"No, Daddy!" I yelled. "You can't leave us!" My brother began yelling and screaming, saying he was going to move in with my father. My mom was crying. Everything was a disaster. I couldn't take it, so I ran upstairs to my room.

My dad moved out the Friday after he found a house to live in. I was so insecure about whether or not my parents would get back together. I would ask questions like, "Daddy, do you miss Mommy?"

He would always answer, "No, I don't."

Then I would ask, "Daddy, do you have another girlfriend?"

And he would answer, "That's not something that is going to happen for a while."

After my dad moved out, my brother's anger got out of control. I even started to feel unsafe around him. He ended up moving in with my dad, thinking it would be better over there. But after a while, he saw that it was just the same.

I thought my dad moving out would make it so all the arguing would stop between my mom and him, but it didn't. Every time my dad would drop me off after coming home from his house, he and Mom would get into it with each other.

About six months after he moved out, I was surprised to find out that my dad had a girlfriend. She had a three-year-old who sometimes I just couldn't stand.

Then about eight months after my parents split up, Mom started seeing a guy she had been friends with her whole life. He had three boys. One of them was a year older than me, and another one was a year younger than me. I liked that I had someone to play with again. But after a while, they were always at our house, and I ended up not having any time to just spend alone with my mom anymore.

It seemed that nobody understood how I felt. I thought about running away and hoped that it would cure all of my sadness, but in my heart I knew that running away from my troubles wouldn't help anything.

I wanted to take my anger and sadness out on my dad, so I did some strange things to get back at him. For instance, I was offered the opportunity to go with friends on a trip to New York City, and another time they wanted to take me up to the mountains to learn how to ski. I turned them all down because somehow I thought that if I suffered, my dad would suffer too, and I wanted my dad to realize he had ruined my life. The only thing that came of my behavior was that I didn't end up having any fun—and my dad never even noticed.

It's been two years since my dad moved out, and I have finally decided that I shouldn't sob and cry my whole life over something that I can't change. I only have one life, and if I spend it crying and sobbing, I can never get back the chance to just enjoy being a kid.

And since my parents split up, I have come to understand that no matter how much my parents fight—and who they choose to be with—it doesn't affect how much both of them still love me.

~Karissa Porter, 12

98

A Little Cheat Sheet for Grief

uring the period of my life known as My Divorce (also known as the "I am crying into this coffee cup of Jack Daniels now" phase) my friends and family tried to console me the best way they could. Always a Southern Lady, the sort who will apologize for doing you a favor, I felt bad about needing to be consoled. I didn't set out to be a burden on folks, the same way I never set out to be a big old deathly drain on a particular husband's zest for marriage.

Looking back, I wish I'd had a little sheet of paper to hand out to my friends and family with a list of exactly what, and what not, to say. They struggled to find the right things to tell me, to discover the elusive words that would help me feel better and for the love of God please stop crying. But there was no handbook, no user's guide for when someone's husband all-of-a-sudden disappears under cover of misplaced creativity. What people need, and what I'm now going to share, is a Cheat Sheet for Grief.

Here's how it goes: When someone you care about is all puddled up in a corner crying and trying to eat her own arm, you will want to say things to comfort her. You might, for example, make the mistake of trying to assure her everything will work out all right.

And if you are the one who is puddled up vowing never to love again, you will not agree with this fabulous news. Instead, you might want to throw things at the ridiculous, optimistic fool who said it and perhaps start gnawing on her arm. Or leg. Or whatever is closest. (Secretly, you may hope and wonder if things actually will work out fine and get better, but you also desperately want to know when the heck "better" is going to happen.)

Still puddled up, you are then put in the unenviable position of immediately needing to explain in great detail every single way it absolutely, definitely will not work out. You have a list of all the ways life is more awful than words, and if a giant earthquake erupted and the very epicenter was your kitchen floor or if a tornado sprang fully-formed from the pot of your ficus tree, you would not be the least bit surprised because things are not fine and not getting better. You begin believing that at any moment you will probably just up and die of some weird broken-heart related illness that involves visible panty lines and grief and acne.

To the well-meaning friend: The very best thing you can say when your friend is in this position is, "Oh, Lord, I cannot even imagine how you are holding up. Because I don't know what you're doing, but damn! You look fabulous!"

Yeah, it's a lie.

But it's a heartfelt lie.

Or, "You know, I realize this is probably the worst time of your whole life, I just cannot imagine. But not a soul who doesn't know you up close and personal would suspect a single thing because your hair/complexion/appearance is amazing! You must be twelve kinds of strong inside!"

Yes, it will be a fib and maybe even a real stretch of the imagination. But I promise no one is going to list all the ways they don't look great... at least not while they're trying to chew your arm off.

And, of course, there will be the awkward moments when you are expected to offer up a character assessment of the Other Party. This is very dangerous territory. Some little teeny off-the-cuff remark could be the landmine that will send her into tears. If pressed to comment on the man in question, you can safely say things like "He didn't know what a good thing he had," or "One day he's gonna wake up and realize he made the biggest mistake of his life."

Whatever you do, never ever say, "You'll find somebody else, I just know you will."

You may think this gives her hope and happiness, but instead she'll just cry and carry on as if the living room ficus plant were turning into a funnel cloud. The last thing she wants to add to her List of Things to Worry About is finding a new man.

It's hard not to interject, "Come on! Snap out of it! Chin up!" because it's hard to stand by and watch someone you love puddle up in grief and sadness and likely some rather terrible fashion decisions. But I am a firm believer that it's perfectly fine to get messy when messy is what you feel. I think it's best to just sit with it and feel your horrible, nasty, corrupt, vile, and unwelcome grief—feel it all the way through, so purely—that when you are done with it, you are really well and truly done with grief and can move on with great finality. And possibly barbecuing some marriage mementos in the charcoal grill.

But until Moving On occurs, if you are faced with a woman in full grief mode and you really don't know what to say, the very best thing you can do is listen. Your friend will love you for the kindness, and all your arms and legs will survive intact.

~Laurie Perry

99

The First Thing I Did After My Divorce Was Final Was...

✔ count my blessings. The pain of it was excruciating, but even as bad as it was there were many good things to be thankful for.

~Kim

✔ crumble. I had been strong for so many months, that when it finally was over I was overwhelmed with emotion. I finally took time to grieve.

~Adam

✔ spend time alone in prayer and meditation. It was not a celebration or a victory as much as a release of a loved one.

~Bill

✔ think about the dreams that were shattered, and acknowledge to myself what I did wrong to bring down the marriage.

~Peter

✔ set a one-month, a three-month, a six-month and a twelve-month goal to start living the kind of life I really wanted for myself.

~Kathy

✔ pack my bags (again) and leave the state for a new career opportunity.

~Lila

✔ continue my college education which landed me a BA in Criminal Justice.

~Cynthia

✔ get down on my knees in the moonlight... and flatten his tires. The escaping rush of air was a last-gasp sigh of relief.

~June

✔ take off my wedding band and replace it with a ring I had bought to symbolize my commitment to myself.

~Katie

✔ open up my closet and ecstatically tell my clothes that we now have space all of our own!

~Gladys

✔ cry myself to sleep that night. Next day, I left for Las Vegas with a new girlfriend and had a great time!!!

~Jack

✔ introduce myself to the wonderful man that I am married to now! He is my best friend!

~Glenna

✔ tell my ex-husband that NO, I would not pay for our three children's wedding clothes for his marriage to the woman he left me for.

~Andrea

✔ drive to the Grand Canyon with my teenage son to watch the changing landscape during sunrise. We had a new beginning.

~Dawn

✔ snuggle up with my children and ensure them that things will be great again.

~Martin

✔ turn on the stereo and sing, "She's a brick house, She's mighty mighty," and then go out and buy a new bed.

~Brenda

✔ buy a piano. I didn't have a bed to sleep in, but brushing up on my musical talents seemed more important.

~Jennie

✔ buy a washing machine.

~Drew

✔ throw away the bleach because I didn't have to launder white cotton underwear anymore.

~Marilyn

✔ ask my girlfriends if there was such a thing as a "divorce shower!"

~Gail

✔ thank God for getting me through the worst experience of my life.

~Nancy

✔ thank God for all the strangers who reached out to help, for no other reason than that they could. Then I never looked back.

~Jay

✔ find a sober support group of sisters who were going through the same life event that I was.

~Paula

✔ go to a Tupperware party and laugh with my friends. It was over and I needed to move on.

~Jessica

✔ drink the bottle of champagne I'd purchased for our tenth anniversary.

~Sherm

✔ buy a red sports car and get a new hairstyle!

~Sheri

✔ cry, get a tattoo and get rid of all the pictures of my ex mother-in-law.

~Stacy

✔ go out to a movie—a tear jerker that my husband would never go see with me.

~Eva

✔ ask God's forgiveness, change the locks, and take myself out to supper.

~Elsie

✔ buy a portable radio to play at night while I slept. That way I didn't feel so all alone.

~Val

✔ have dinner with my ex as thanks for being understanding and mature during the court proceedings.

~Ana

✔ go over, shake his hand, thank him for the wonderful years we had together, and wish him well.

~Carrie

✔ mourn the loss of the greatest insurance plan I had ever had. :)

~Patty

✔ go to the bank to see if the settlement check was good.

~Harriett

✔ frame that little paper of freedom.

~Lani

✔ look into the mirror and say, "Now I am a free guy!"

~Bryan

✔ ask my ex-wife to marry me again.

~Ronnie

Buying a Ticket to Life

Sadness flies on the wings of the morning
and out of the heart of darkness comes the light.
~Jean Giraudoux

That October morning, I awoke with a very uneasy feeling and I had no idea why. As the day went on, I continued to feel something gnawing at me. I kept checking my calendar to see if there was some place I needed to be or something I needed to do. It's always possible I'd forgotten an appointment, but nothing came to mind. No matter what I did, I couldn't shake the ominous feeling. Finally, as evening approached, it hit me — this was the tenth anniversary of the day my ex-husband and I faced our marital problems and separated. I thought I would never forget the date my life unraveled, but to my amazement, I had.

The memories of when my life consisted of lying in bed and crying tears of rejection and pain came flooding back. I remembered feeling paralyzed by fear, not knowing if my future would involve marriage or divorce.

Little did I know then, that now I would have tears of utter joy and thankfulness rolling down my cheeks for the amazing journey I took to reach the destination that awaited me.

There were some tears of sadness for the death of my marriage. I think it is always heartbreaking when two people love each other but somehow lose each other in the process of living. I am happy to report we remain friends. I'm proud of both of us; we agree that we did a terrific job of destroying our marriage, but we are great at divorce. We kept the wonderful memories of those years, which thankfully are many—and let go of all hurt and pain we inflicted upon each other.

I never want to completely forget that horrendous time because I now cherish every pain-free day, which is an everyday event.

When I was newly divorced, I found life scary and intimidating. At first, I felt I was being punished, but in reality I was given the opportunity to find myself and create a new life. I had no idea where it would take me, but I was ready to take the leap. Although I was frightened to travel in a new direction, it was also exciting to ponder my options. I didn't know exactly what I wanted, but I knew what I didn't want: the old me. I was not the same person I had misplaced all those years ago. Prior to this time, my epitaph could have read, "She died without ever having lived." Thankfully, that would no longer be the case. I was now strong and embraced the courage I never knew I had.

I remembered a very old joke about a man who prays to God every week to win the lottery, to no avail. Then one day when he makes his usual prayer, God answers him and says, "I'd love to help you win the lottery, but you've got to help me out and buy a ticket."

I chose to buy a ticket to life.

I've enjoyed all my adventures, the places I've seen and the people I've met.

Sometimes I feel as though I'm living life backwards. Most people become independent, start their careers and create the life they want in their twenties. I never stood on my own two feet until I was forty-seven. I moved out of my parent's house the day I got married. I also quit working at age thirty-three and enjoyed all the benefits of retirement at an early age.

When my marriage ended, I grew up and became an adult. Buying a house all by myself gave me a feeling of real independence. Starting a writing career at the age of fifty has opened up a whole new world. Most importantly, I have had the courage to unlock my heart, allowed myself to fall in love again and to be happy in a relationship.

Some people never experience giving and receiving love. I've been blessed to have that blissful feeling twice in my life.

If I had it all to do over, I wouldn't change a thing. I would go through that agony again in a second to be where I am today, crying tears of joy.

I'm so glad I bought a ticket to life.

~Tena Beth Thompson

Write Your Relationship in Pencil

To exist is to change,
to change is to mature,
to mature is to go on creating oneself endlessly.
~Henri Louis Bergson

s my eleven-year-old daughter was doing her homework, her pen ran out of ink. That pen was as drained as I felt. As I rummaged in the kitchen drawer looking for a new pen, I realized, my marriage and our family life was as messy as this junk drawer. I grabbed a pencil, sat down beside my daughter and wrote our sentiments: Out of ink. Out of sorts. Out of patience. Out of control. Out of steam. Out of it! We ended up laughing at a very sad but accurate description that fit both of us.

When my daughter entered the fifth grade, the teacher insisted the students use ink instead of pencil. "I hate starting over! I'm so scared when I use ink. It reminds me of all the mistakes I've made and all the mistakes I'll make again. I hate not being able to erase the bad parts. I have these ugly stains where I've messed up. I'd rather use pencil." She complained constantly when she did her homework. "I just know the teacher is going to red-ink my whole essay." Tracey's complaints reflected my own sentiments and concerns about life. Unlike her, I was not learning fifth grade work; I was bordering on the brink of divorce.

"Start off in pencil, weigh your words carefully, and when you have it exactly as you want it, recopy it in ink," I advised her.

I felt just as anxious as my daughter. Repeatedly we both intended to start over, striving to do our best the next time. Inevitably we both left blotches that were sometimes almost identical to the previous ones. Her teacher's red ink corrections were tangible and irritating. My red ink marks were invisible, always an after-thought; no matter how hard I tried to self-correct, old habits were hard to break.

It never seemed to get easier for either of us. Tracey was forever crumpling paper and throwing it forcefully in the trash. My husband and I were forever deflecting one another's remarks. Life was miserable for our son and daughter as we lived a life of turmoil.

After years of marriage, lost in a realm of uncertainty, I sifted through decades of debris, fact and fancy, reasons and whys, truth and lies, as I tried to decide what to do. What I knew for certain was that once I wrote my signature in ink on the legal documents, there would be no erasures. No tossing another sheaf of paper in the trash; no starting over. Tracey was right; ink made it feel so final. I worked part time and I had to decide whether to forsake my comfy lifestyle. Each day became a quest for contentment. I could whole-heartedly relate to my daughter's angst.

I began to realize that today's hurdles represented tomorrow's therapy sessions. Tomorrow held no promise, yesterday was only a memory, and when present and past began to blur, I knew I had to make a decision, no matter how afraid I was. As the sands of time sifted through my mind, I realized that although I had been struggling for a foothold in ever-shifting sands, I was ultimately the architect of my own life. I had to make changes.

My husband and I divorced. We still harbored hostilities, but as the weeks turned into months, it became easier to speak to one another without snipping. I stopped red-inking his every comment and I finally closed the invisible book of real infractions. Before long, it felt like we were relating to one another in "pencil." I learned to pause, weigh my words, and erase hurtful thoughts before I tossed them out.

It took time for us to come to terms with how we were each responsible in some way for our divorce. The reasons, we agreed, were varied and many, from marrying too young and for all the wrong reasons, to incompatibility.

Two years after our divorce, as we gathered for a birthday party, I sat in a rocker in a corner of the living room, off to myself. I thought, If only I could rewrite my life, I'd do things so differently. There would be less chaos, less drama. More fun and frolic, calm and happiness.

I gazed at the gilded edges of our set of outdated encyclopedias and imagined that each volume contained a year of our lives. In my mind I perused Volume One: the print was clear and crisp, the pages new and the events exciting and thrilling. Each child had his or her own imaginary volume filled with milestones and memories that made me smile, wince, and laugh. I paged through the final volumes and imagined the title: *Marriage on the Rocks*. I noticed worn and ripped pages, rude remarks, off-handed one-uppers, ugly ink splotches, scratch-throughs, scribbles, and red ink remarks that did nothing to improve our craft of parenting or partnering. Such a waste, I thought as I closed the last imaginary chapter on our married life.

I can't go back and do it over, but I have learned that I am the editor of my own life. I can choose to use snappy words and impact statements that create ire, or I can listen with the intent to hear instead of be heard. The only one who can fix my life is me.

My ex-husband and I have both remarried and our marriages are happy, sound, and secure. No more snide remarks, sideways glances, or rolling of the eyes. Our children are grown now with young children of their own. Tracey and Jason are busy writing their own life stories.

If they adhere to one piece of motherly advice, I hope it's this: Write your relationship in pencil; erase the mistakes before they grow into huge messy splotches. Don't red-ink everything your spouse says or does. Use the eraser as often as needed. Think before you speak, because words are powerful. There is nothing stronger than indelible marks; written or spoken, they affect future generations. They can bruise the soul... yet they can also heal the heart if they are chosen with love and understanding.

My darlings, write your life with care.

~Linda O'Connell

~Meet the Contributors~
~About the Authors~
~Acknowledgments~
~Share with Us~
~More Chicken Soup~

Meet the Contributors

Christa Allan is a wife, mother, grandmother and a high school English teacher. Christa and her husband Ken live in Louisiana. Visit her blog at www.cballan.wordpress.com.

Zoe Alvarez is a writer, happily married, who lives in New England. When it comes to relationships she remains the eternal optimist.

Arlene Aoki started submitting stories to *Jack N' Jill Magazine* when she was in grade school. Arlene wrote off and on for a small Texas newspaper, and has published a story in *Good Old Days Magazine*.

Catherine Armstrong will soon receive her degree in Sociology from Townson University. Currently she is working as an Administration Assistant for Baltimore County Public Schools. She enjoys running, biking, and lacrosse games and hopes to publish her children's book on blended families.

Air Force brat, Hoosier, small town girl, single mom, **Jenny Austin** received her BA and MA at Indiana University in Bloomington. Jenny works with adults with developmental disabilities and also teaches English Composition at Ivy Tech Community College. Jenny's non-human loves include cats, traveling, and licorice. E-mail at jennyanndiana@yahoo.com.

Beanie Baldwin has one daughter, four grandchildren, a loving fiancé and is enjoying her retirement by pursuing her passion for writing. She has been published in several anthologies, *The Rambler* magazine, and online. She is currently working on a biography that focuses on her trial and present victory over breast cancer.

Deborah Batt is a social worker currently working in the adoption department of the Children's Aid Society. She enjoys traveling and working with children and is aspiring to work overseas in an orphanage. She is also writing her first novel.

Anna Bern is a speaker, writer, and editor. Her writing has appeared in *Reader's Digest, Newsweek* and *Spirituality & Health*.

Lynn Berroteran received her bachelor of science in microbiology, with honors, from New Mexico State University in 2007. She is currently working on her first novel.

Pam Bostwick's articles appear in magazines, newspapers and anthologies, including *Chicken Soup for the Soul: Children with Special Needs*. She is legally blind and hearing impaired. She loves her country home, the beach, playing guitar and is a volunteer counselor. She has seven children and ten grandchildren. She happily remarried 7/7/07. Email her at: pamloves7@verizon.net.

Elizabeth Breau, Ph.D. teaches English at an all-boys Catholic school in Newark, New Jersey. She is a regular contributor to *ForeWord Magazine* and has also published in *Thirdspace, The Women's Review of Books, African American Review, Callaloo, Fibromyalgia Frontiers,* and *The Jewish State*. Please e-mail her at coolgardens77@hotmail.com.

Cynthia Briggs celebrates her love of cooking and writing through her nostalgic cookbook *Pork Chops & Applesauce, A Collection of Recipes and Reflections* and her apple dessert book titled *Sweet Apple Temptations*. She is presently writing a murder mystery titled *Drop Dead Ugly*. Contact Cynthia through her website at www.porkchopsandapplesauce.net.

Christine Bush is a family therapist in private practice in eastern Pennsylvania. She is also a motivational speaker on women's issue and family life. In her spare time, she writes mystery and romance novels for Avalon Books. She can be reached at www.ChristineBush. com or ChristineABush@aol.com.

Emily Capeles is now remarried with three stepchildren and a child of her own. She is a stay at home mom. She plans to enjoy every day with her new husband and family. She can be contacted at Emkate12@aol.com.

Jeannette Cezanne, now stepmother to teenagers (they've grown up since her story was written and they all survived), lives and writes in Manchester, New Hampshire. Visit her on the web at www. JeannetteCezanne.com.

Angela Chiaro is a high school teacher and a freelance writer. She spends her free time reading and writing. Her love of adventure and history guides her from country to country.

Dorothy Megan Clifton, originally from Cheshire, England, loves to write, and in particular loves to tell stories. She is also an accomplished actress and public speaker. Divorced for many years, she has two children and five grandchildren with her first great-grandbaby due to arrive shortly. Life is good.

Brenda Crawford received her bachelor of arts in theology and history along with a secondary education license from Notre Dame College. She teaches high school theology in Cleveland, Ohio. Brenda enjoys reading, writing stories, visiting coffee shops, researching old artifacts, and all things spiritual. Please e-mail her at: blt1022blc@aol.com.

Cinda Crawford writes fiction and non-fiction. She also hosts the *Health Matters Show* at http://www.healthmattersshow.com, and is an ELT (Essential Life Therapy) Practitioner. Cinda offers help and hope for healing from chronic illnesses such as Chronic Fatigue Syndrome and Fibromyalgia. E-mail: info@healthmattersshow.com.

Michele Cushatt is a speaker and writer whose works have appeared in magazines such as *Today's Christian Woman* and *Hearts-At-Home*. Michele is a wife and mother of three boys. Making her home in Colorado, she spends her free time running, skiing, camping, and reading. Please e-mail her at michele@michelecushatt.com.

Samantha Ducloux Waltz's essays can currently be read in the *Chicken Soup for the Soul* series, *Cup of Comfort* series and a number of other anthologies. She has published adult non-fiction under the name Samantha Ducloux and Samellyn Wood. She lives in Portland, Oregon.

HJ Eggers is joyfully married to beloved Shawn in Juneau, Alaska. Her dear son is a Coastie in Michigan. She got super lucky with mother-in-law Maggie. By publishing her first story in *Chicken Soup for the Soul*, she is now searching for yet another outrageous dream to activate. Contact her at hjs01234@aol.com.

Terri Elders, and her son, Steve, frequently reminisce about Bob Elders, who, long ago, and long enough for a camera to catch, convincingly captured all the élan of the fabled James Dean. Terri lives with her husband, Ken Wilson, near Colville, Washington. Write her at telders@hotmail.com.

Victoria Fedden lives in Fort Lauderdale, Florida with her husband. She received her bachelor of arts in English from Florida Atlantic University where she is currently teaching and working on her MFA. She is writing a memoir about her eclectic upbringing. (She had a monkey!) Please e-mail her at victoriafedden@gmail.com.

Linda Fitzjarrell lives in Colorado with her husband and three children. She enjoys hiking, photography, and playing violin in her church orchestra. Linda credits her sister, Kathy Ide, for bringing her story to life. Kathy is a professional freelance author, editor, and speaker. Please visit her web site at www.KathyIde.com.

Amber Frazier has been writing short stories and poems since the day she could pick up a pencil. She works full time at a public school in Virginia. She recently became a first time mom and enjoys reading to her son, James Wyatt. She also enjoys scrapbooking and painting.

After living in the same place for her entire life, **Mia Gardner** has moved 1,600 miles away from the life she knew. Mia is remarried, working in a field she loves, and doesn't rely on her new husband to provide her with the tools she needs around the house.

Kathleen Gerard's writing has been widely-anthologized and featured on National Public Radio. Her fiction has been nominated for Best New American Voices, a national prize in literature, and several of her plays have been staged and performed regionally and off-Broadway in NYC. E-mail her at katgerard@aol.com.

Born in Toronto, Canada, **Debbie Gill** is a community writer for the *Town Crier*, a bi-weekly publication in Brooklin, Ontario where she now resides. She holds an administrative position with the local school board, and enjoys traveling, entertaining, and spending time with her family. She is currently working on her second novel.

T'Mara Goodsell is a single mother who supports her freelance writing habit by juggling several jobs. She won her first paid writing award in high school and has a degree in secondary English and psychology education. She lives with her two teenagers near St. Louis, Missouri and can be e-mailed at t-mara@charter.net.

Catherine Graham is a stay at home mother of three children. Catherine enjoys writing, singing, dancing, being with her loved ones, and reading. She is currently working on having her first inspirational novel for women published. You can visit her website at www.freewebs.com/thejourneytome or e-mail her at ineffabletwo@hotmail.com.

Tracy Gulliver is a freelance writer who has had pieces published in magazines and anthologies. "Father's Day" is an excerpt from her recently completed book, *Unplanned: A Mother's Journey Through Her Daughter's Pregnancy*. She can be contacted at tgulliver@citlink.net.

Linda Hanson writes from her home near cornfields in Iowa but has lived in several states and worked in eight hospitals. Happily married for over thirty years, she is the proud mother of two, and soon to be grandmother and stepgrandmother of four. She is busy on her first novel.

Dawn Smith Heaps has written short stories to entertain her family for years. She lives with her daughter in North Florida and enjoys family time, volunteering, beachcombing, and taking creative writing classes. This is the first story she has submitted for publication. Please e-mail her at heapsd@bellsouth.net.

Karen Hessen is a mail carrier who has worked previously as a nurse, innkeeper, and health educator. She and her husband, Douglas, live in Oregon. She has two adult adopted children. Her avocations are writing and public speaking. Karen can be reached at 503-357-4908 or HESSEN26HR@netscape.net.

Pat Holdsworth resides in South Folorida enjoying life with her husband, Gary, her daughter Brett, her stepdaughter, Christine, son-in-law Michael, and grancdchildren, Katie and Sean. She can be reached at path2happiness@yahoo.com.

Sachiko Iwanaga is originally from Hawaii and has two children. She spends most of her spare time enjoying anything that has to do with the ocean—swimming or paddleboarding. Her dream is to be a member of the women's interisland outrigger canoe race team.

Vera Jacobs is remarried and lives with her husband, three sons, and a stepdaughter. She writes in a largely futile attempt to make sense of her life.

Jolie Kanat is a professional writer in every medium, including a full-length non-fiction book, *Bittersweet Baby*, a columnist for the *San Francisco Chronicle*, recording Perspectives essays for NPR, songwriting for Time Warner and Universal Studios productions, producing two CDs for children with special needs, and greetings cards for Schurmann Fine Papers. Please contact her at: jolieokay@gmail.com or on her website, www.joliekanat.com.

Maggie Kelly is a freelance writer and published author. In addition to homeschooling two teenagers, she spends her time nudging her husband toward retirement, and dreams of palm trees and seashells in Florida.

Betty King is a lifestyle and devotion newspaper columnist, speaker and author of *It Takes Two Mountains to Make a Valley, But It Was in the Valleys I Grew, The Fragrance of Life, Safe and Secure in the Palm of His Hand*. She lives with the disease Multiple Sclerosis. She may be reached at Baking2@charter.net or www.bettyking.net.

Lynn Kinnaman has been writing all her life. She's published two books and over a hundred magazine and newspaper articles. She's currently completing a novel and working on nonfiction projects that celebrate resiliency and the power of positive change. Please visit her website: www.worksbydesign.com for more information and a free newsletter.

Andrea Langworthy is a staff columnist for the *Rosemount Town Pages* newspaper. You may read her columns on her website, www.andrealangworthy.com.

G. M. Lee works as a counselor for disability support services. Her writing has appeared in *Prayers and Promises for the Armed Forces*, *Brio*, and other publications. She is an active member of American Christian Fiction Writers.

Linda Lou is a technical writer/corporate trainer as well as a humor writer and occasional stand-up comic. Her memoir, *Bastard Husband: A Love Story*, is an autobiographical account of her first year alone in Las Vegas after a mid-life divorce. Linda Lou is also a monthly columnist for www.Living-Las-Vegas.com.

Amber Lutz hopes to continue her passion for writing while carrying out her dream of becoming a veterinary technician. She plans on graduating from college before the summer of 2010 and then settling down in South Carolina. Contact her at Lutz.Amber@yahoo.com.

Evie Mack does lay counseling part-time. She enjoys walks with her dog, reading, and gardening. Evie loves to write short stories from real life, history and the Bible. She is currently working on a collection of inspirational parables.

Nancy Madsen-Ostinato is a Children's Ministry Program Assistant and is currently working toward publishing *Like a Little Child: A Book of Simple Truths* which won second place in the non-fiction book category at the 2006 Blue Ridge Mountains Christian Writer's Conference. Nancy can be reached at ostinato@iglide.net.

Bettye Martin-McRae began writing ads and proofreading in 1955. Published in newspapers, *Guideposts*, *Charisma and Christian Life*, *Focus on the Family*, *Christian Reader*, *Mukes and More Magazine* and *Chicken*

Soup for the Soul, she writes through her Writers' Ongoing Workshops. You may reach her via e-mail at Bunkhouse@wtconnect.com.

Mary Mason lives in Dallas, Texas. She remarried in 2004, and now lives with her childhood sweetheart, Mike, and his teenage son, John. She is an accountant working for the state as an audit training specialist, where she writes technical materials for her job. In her spare time, she loves to scrapbook, quilt, garden, and listen to music. You can contact her at mmason51@tx.rr.com.

Laurie Max is a new grandmother preparing to turn the big "6-0" in 2008! After teaching grade school, she is now a studio potter creating and selling whimsical, hand-crafted pottery. Expressing herself through her writing is another passion that has been a part of her creative journey. E-mail her at lgmaxg@aol.com.

Virginia McCormack, MSED, helps single moms create joyful lives in her coaching practice, Moms For Joy. She enjoys running on the beach, decorating her new home, and being with her three children. Her mother is in heaven and continues to be a source of Virginia's inspiration. You may reach Virginia at www.momsforjoy.com.

T. McCracken, like all good cartoonists, has drawn for the *New Yorker*, although they've never had the good sense to buy her work. Hundreds of others, though, from the *Saturday Evening Post* to the *Oregonian*, have. Her cartoons for everyone from anemic agriculturists to Zen zoologists are at www.mchumor.com.

Heather McGee received her BBA in Finance from the University of North Texas in 1995. She currently works from home while raising her two children, Justin and Shelby. She enjoys spending time playing with and reading to her children, playing the piano, and making and eating various desserts.

Terry McManus is a college professor in London, Ontario who has written extensively about men and their relationships. He is also involved in the music business as a songwriter and as a manager. He can be reached through his website, www.terrymcmanus.com.

Laurence Mitchell is a professional mediator, a public presenter on peacemaking and domestic violence. She has had several articles published in local magazines. Topics include empowerment, accountability, bullies, and youth sports. Laurence writes children stories and is always looking for a publisher. She likes to challenge the imagination and the heart. Please contact her at coach@anathlete.com.

Rick Moore has worked as a newspaper columnist, a radio announcer, and a professional musician. An award-winning business writer, his writing has been published in numerous newspapers and magazines and on the Internet. He currently is pursuing a songwriting career in Nashville, Tennessee. Contact him at rmwrites@comcast.net.

Shirley Neal is a freelance writer and photographer who lives in Ontario, Canada. She teaches travel, writing, and photography. Shirley is an accomplished playwright and screenwriter, and recently sold her screenplay to a film production company. Introducing people to the world beyond their doorstep through words and pictures is a dream realized. Contact her at sneal@interhop.net.

Welby O'Brien has a teaching degree from Biola University and a master's degree in counseling. Through conference speaking and her books *Formerly A Wife*, and *Good-bye for Now* (WingSpread Publishers), Welby bares her soul while sharing a practical message of comfort, help and hope. Her web site is www.welbyo.com.

Linda O'Connell, an early childhood educator in St. Louis, is an accomplished multi-genre freelance writer. She has been published in several *Chicken Soup for the Soul* books, literary and mainstream magazines and newspapers. Her husband, Bill, and her children and grandchildren fill her life with happiness and her heart with love. Contact her at billin7@juno.com.

Joanne Palmer writes about the humor in being human from more personal experience than she'd care to admit.

Laurie Perry is a Southerner of mixed pedigree, from Texas, Louisiana, Mississippi and every small town in between. She currently lives and writes in Los Angeles where she chronicles her life in an online diary, www.crazyauntpurl.com. Her first book, *Drunk, Divorced & Covered in Cat Hair* is available in bookstores nationwide.

Joel Pett, winner of the 2000 Pulitzer Prize for editorial cartoons, has been the editorial cartoonist at the *Lexington Herald-Leader* since 1984. His cartoons have appeared in hundreds of newspapers and magazines nationwide, including *The New York Times*, *The Washington Post, Los Angeles Times, The Philadelphia Daily News, The Boston Globe, The Atlanta Journal-Constitution* and *USA Today*.

Karissa Porter is fifteen years old. She enjoys hanging out with her friends and playing outdoors. She started writing when she was six and is hopeful that she will continue writing for the rest of her life.

Becky Povich began her writing career in her late forties. Her stories have been published in *Chicken Soup for the Soul* books, and in a new St. Louis magazine, *Divine Whine*. She also has taken a recent interest in photography and art. She may be contacted at WriterGal53@aol.com.

Mary Pritchard has a BSN in nursing and is a published author and writes paranormal romance and romantic suspense. She enjoys reading, writing, gardening, and spending time with her feline and canine muses. Please e-mail her at meow63@yahoo.com.

Carol Randolph is founder and executive director of New Beginnings, a nonprofit support organization for separated and divorced men and women, serving the Washington, D.C. metro area since 1979 (www. newbeginningsusa.org). She has been married to her second husband for twenty-two years and has two children.

Jenna Romano's articles, essays and stories have appeared in anthologies, magazines, and newspapers over the years. Jenna is a former teacher, has traveled extensively, and lived in Europe. She currently works as a singer/storyteller.

Cartoonist **Dan Rosanndich** offers over 3,000 cartoons which are categorized by subject matter and available for licensing. Visit WWW. DANSCARTOONS.COM to learn more and Dan also specializes in "custom" cartoons for any specific types of projects.

John E. Schlimm II is an author, educator, and artist. He has served in the White House, as a publicist in Nashville, and as a professor of communications. He is the author of several books, including *The Pennsylvania Celebrities Cookbook, Straub Brewery*, and *Corresponding with History*. Contact him at johnschlimm@yahoo.com.

Eloise Elaine Ernst Schneider is a teacher, artist, and freelance writer who has published articles, books, and songs. She signs her canvases "Eloise" and sells her art on her web site www.1artist4hire. com. Her devotional children's book, *52 Children's Moments*, is carried by Amazon. Elaine is the managing editor of Lesson Tutor, a lesson plan site found at www.lessontutor.com.

Father to a nine-year-old boy and twin six-year-old girls, **Joel Schwartzberg** is an award-winning writer and screenwriter whose work has appeared in *The New York Times Magazine, New Jersey Monthly, The Huffington Post* and *The New York Daily News*. A collection of Joel's essays, *The 40 Year-Old Version: Humoirs of a Divorced Dad*, will be published in June, 2009 (Wyatt-MacKenzie). Joel lives in Montclair, New Jersey and can be e-mailed at joelscorp@gmail.com.

JP Shaw lives in Abbotsford, British Columbia with her husband and two boys. She has a love for romance stories, and is currently working on publishing her first novel. She enjoys scrapbooking, web design, and spending time with her family. You can contact her at http://jpshaw.wordpress.com.

Dayle Shockley's articles and essays have appeared in dozens of publications. She is a special contributor to *The Dallas Morning News*, the author of three books, and a contributing writer to many other works. Dayle considers God as the source of her strength. To contact her visit her web site at www.dayleshockley.com, or feel free to e-mail her at dayle@dayleshockley.com.

Christine Smith is the mother of three, grandmother of thirteen, and foster mother to many others. She has been married to her husband, James, for thirty-nine years, and loves reading and writing, church activities, and spending time with her family. Please e-mail her at iluvmyfamilyxxx000@yahoo.com.

Melinda Stiles taught English in Wisconsin and Michigan for twenty-seven years. She retired and moved to Idaho to write. Her stories have appeared in the *Kalamazoo Gazette, Woven on the Wind, Reminisce, Pass/Fail, Chicken Soup for the Teacher's Soul* and *Chicken Soup for the Sister's Soul*. She can be reached at thel@salmoninternet.com.

Born in England in 1962, **Joy Summers** particularly enjoys writing fictional short stories about unconventional or unusual people and situations. Joy finds the motivation to write from immersing herself in nature, and derives inspiration from meeting and observing eccentric characters.

B.J. Taylor admits that divorce was the hardest thing she has ever had to go through. But for her, life has been so much sweeter on the other side. They say life is what you make it, and now every day is filled with sunshine, every evening with shining stars. You can't turn back the clock and make things different, but you can make them better from this moment forward. And that's what B.J. is doing now.

Tena Beth Thompson writes about life and shares her experiences with a touch of humor. Her first book, *Separation: More Than Just Surviving* for women was published in 2007. Tena Beth also contributed to *Chicken Soup for the Shopper's Soul* and *Chicken Soup for the Soul in Menopause*. Tena Beth resides in Las Vegas.

Mike Twohy, the creator of "That's Life," has been drawing cartoons as far back as he can remember. In addition to "That's Life," Twohy has had cartoons published in magazines including *The New Yorker, Saturday Review, TV Guide, Audubon* and *Esquire*.

Arlene Uslander is the author of fourteen non-fiction books, and has won several media awards for excellence in journalism. She lives in Sonora, California, is a retired teacher, a professional writer and free lance editor. Arlene enjoys reading, music, traveling with her husband, Ira, and enjoying their grandchildren, Eric, Ryan, Carly and Levi.

Katherine Van Hook has been writing prose and poetry since childhood. She resides in Lexington, Kentucky with her husband, Eric, and sons, Collin and Ryan. She and her sons are members of the "Lexington Poetry Meet Up" group in Lexington Kentucky.

Megan Venner is a writer and journalist based in Nova Scotia, Canada. While she has spent years working in newsrooms across Canada, she now makes her living writing from home. She is consistantly inspired by her stepdaughter and two sons.

Annemarie Wagner is the mother of three children. After her second divorce she re-enrolled in college and will proudly graduate at the age of fifty with a major in English Communications. She is now in a partnership in which she has finally found the peace and joy of a healthy relationship.

Melinda L. Wentzel, aka Planet Mom, is a freelance writer and slice-of-life newspaper columnist whose primary aim is to unearth the humor contained in everyday life experiences—especially those related to parenting. She and her husband reside in Williamsport, Pennsylvania with their three daughters (ages nineteen, six and six). Log on to www.notesfromplanetmom.com for more information.

Kenneth William is an author living in California. He's published stories in several books, including *Chicken Soup for the Mother and Son Soul*. Kenneth hopes to publish his own book one day and become a fitness trainer.

Marie Williams is a forty-something divorced mom of two teenagers. Ironically, she works in the singles industry as an event coordinator and host for a speed dating company and is still looking for her perfect match! She has not given up on the idea of Internet dating.

Rob Williams received his MFA from Columbia University. His writing has been published in journals and magazines including *Maisonneuve, San Diego Citybeat*, and *Pindeldyboz*, and various anthologies. He lives and teaches in San Diego, California, and is writing a novel about Hollywood invading a small town in the mid-1950s.

Joyce Zymeck is a writer, teacher, mediator, and mental health clinician in Tucson, Arizona. She earned a graduate degree in counseling psychology in 2006. She has also toured as a singer-songwriter, with two self-released CDs recorded with her former duo.

Chicken Soup for the Soul®

Who Is
Jack Canfield?

*J*ack Canfield is the co-creator and editor of the *Chicken Soup for the Soul* series, which *Time* magazine has called "the publishing phenomenon of the decade." Jack is also the co-author of eight other bestselling books including *The Success Principles™: How to Get from Where You Are to Where You Want to Be, Dare to Win, The Aladdin Factor, You've Got to Read This Book,* and *The Power of Focus: How to Hit Your Business and Personal and Financial Targets with Absolute Certainty.*

Jack has recently developed a telephone coaching program and an online coaching program based on his most recent book *The Success Principles.* He also offers a seven-day *Breakthrough to Success* seminar every summer, which attracts 400 people from fifteen countries around the world.

Jack is the CEO of the Canfield Training Group in Santa Barbara, California, and founder of the Foundation for Self-Esteem in Culver City, California. He has conducted intensive personal and professional development seminars on the principles of success for over a million people in twenty-three countries. Jack is a dynamic keynote speaker and he has spoken to hundreds of thousands of others at more than 1,000 corporations, universities, professional conferences and conventions, and has been seen by millions more on national television shows such as *The Today Show, Fox and Friends, Inside Edition, Hard Copy, CNN's Talk Back Live, 20/20, Eye to Eye,* and the *NBC Nightly News* and the *CBS Evening News.*

Jack is the recipient of many awards and honors, including three honorary doctorates and a *Guinness World Records Certificate* for having seven books from the *Chicken Soup for the Soul* series appearing on the *New York Times* bestseller list on May 24, 1998.

To write to Jack or for inquiries about Jack as a speaker, his coaching programs, trainings or seminars, use the following contact information:

Jack Canfield
The Canfield Companies
P.O. Box 30880 • Santa Barbara, CA 93130
phone: 805-563-2935 • fax: 805-563-2945
E-mail: info@jackcanfield.com
www.jackcanfield.com

Who Is
Mark Victor Hansen?

*M*ark Victor Hansen is the co-founder of *Chicken Soup for the Soul*, along with Jack Canfield. He is also a sought-after keynote speaker, bestselling author, and marketing maven. For more than thirty years, Mark has focused solely on helping people from all walks of life reshape their personal vision of what's possible. His powerful messages of possibility, opportunity, and action have created powerful change in thousands of organizations and millions of individuals worldwide.

Mark's credentials include a lifetime of entrepreneurial success. He is a prolific writer with many bestselling books, such as *The One Minute Millionaire*, *Cracking the Millionaire Code*, *How to Make the Rest of Your Life the Best of Your Life*, *The Power of Focus*, *The Aladdin Factor*, and *Dare to Win*, in addition to the *Chicken Soup for the Soul* series. Mark has had a profound influence in the field of human potential through his library of audios, videos, and articles in the areas of big thinking, sales achievement, wealth building, publishing success, and personal and professional development.

Mark is the founder of the *MEGA Seminar Series. MEGA Book Marketing University* and *Building Your MEGA Speaking Empire* are annual conferences where Mark coaches and teaches new and aspiring authors, speakers, and experts on building lucrative publishing and speaking careers. Other MEGA events include *MEGA Info-Marketing* and *My MEGA Life*.

He has appeared on *Oprah*, *CNN*, and *The Today Show*. He has been quoted in *Time, U.S. News & World Report, USA Today, New York Times,* and *Entrepreneur* and has had countless radio interviews, assuring our planet's people that "You can easily create the life you deserve."

As a philanthropist and humanitarian, Mark works tirelessly for organizations such as Habitat for Humanity, American Red Cross, March of Dimes, Childhelp USA, and many others. He is the recipient of numerous awards that honor his entrepreneurial spirit, philanthropic heart, and business acumen. He is a lifetime member of the Horatio Alger Association of Distinguished Americans, an organization that honored Mark with the prestigious Horatio Alger Award for his extraordinary life achievements.

Mark Victor Hansen is an enthusiastic crusader of what's possible and is driven to make the world a better place.

Mark Victor Hansen & Associates, Inc.
P.O. Box 7665 • Newport Beach, CA 92658
phone: 949-764-2640 • fax: 949-722-6912
www.markvictorhansen.com

Who Is
Patty Hansen?

*P*atty Hansen, with her writing partner Irene Dunlap, coauthored *Chicken Soup for the Kid's Soul, Chicken Soup for the Kid's Soul 2, Chicken Soup for the Preteen Soul, Chicken Soup for the Preteen Soul 2, Chicken Soup Christmas Treasury for Kids, Chicken Soup for the Child's Soul* and *Chicken Soup for the Girl's Soul* — all books that kids love to read and use as guides for everyday life. Patty is also the coauthor of *Condensed Chicken Soup for the Soul* and *Out of the Blue: Delight Comes into Our Lives.* She has written some of the most loved stories in many of the books in the *Chicken Soup for the Soul* series.

Prior to her career as an author, Patty worked for United Airlines as a flight attendant for thirteen years. During those years in the air she received two commendations for bravery -- the first when (as the only flight attendant on board) she prepared forty-four passengers for a successful planned emergency landing, and the second for single-handedly extinguishing a fire on board a mid-Pacific flight, which averted an emergency situation and saved hundreds of lives.

Until April of 2008, Patty was the president of legal and licensing for Chicken Soup for the Soul Enterprises, Inc., and helped to create an entire line of Chicken Soup for the Soul products and licenses. She remains an active part of Chicken Soup for the Soul Publishing, LLC.

Patty shares her home life with her daughter Elisabeth, twenty-three, Elisabeth's husband, Chris, and their son, Seth, age three-almost-four, and newborn daughter, Kira; daughter Melanie, twenty-one; mother, Shirley, ninety; housekeeper and friend, Dora; two rabbits, five horses, four dogs, three cats, four birds, thirty-two fish, eight pigeons, thirty-six chickens (yes, they all have names), a haven for hummingbirds, and a butterfly farm.

If you would like to contact Patty:

Patty Hansen
P.O. Box 10879
Costa Mesa, CA 92627
e-mail: pattyh@PJHenterprises.com

Chicken Soup for the Soul

Thank You!

*W*e wish to express our heartfelt gratitude to the following people who helped make this book possible:

- Our families, who have been chicken soup for our souls!

- Jack's family: Inga, Travis, Riley, Christopher, Oran and Kyle for all their love and support.

- Mark and Patty's daughters: Melanie Hansen and Elisabeth Del Gesso; Elisabeth's son Seth and new little daughter, Kira (our grandchildren!) for lovingly supporting us through our divorce and encouraging Patty while this very special book was being created.

- To Shirley Shaw, Patty's mother: Thanks Mom, for living the example of a great marriage and for all your gentle advice and shared wisdom that sustained and nourished me along my path of rocky relationships. You always make me feel better.

- Patty Aubery for being there on every step of the journey. Russ Kamalski for all of his love, support, endless late working hours and making Patty laugh in spite of it all.

- Barbara LoMonaco, Chicken Soup's Webmaster and Editor, for nourishing us with truly wonderful stories and cartoons.

- D'ette Corona, our Assistant Publisher… what can we say other than that without you, this project would never have been completed. Your dedication and ability to juggle multitudes of projects is amazing. You are a bright and shining star in our universe!

- To Elisabeth Rinaldi for working side-by-side with Patty all the way from Russia with love!

- Amy Newmark, our Publisher, and a divorced and happily remarried woman herself, for wholeheartedly embracing this book concept, and for her creative vision and expert editing.

- Book producer, Brian Taylor, of Pneuma Books, for his creative direction and the fabulous design for the cover and interior.

- Veronica Romero, Lisa Williams, Teresa Collett, Robin Yerian, Jesse Ianniello, Lauren Edelstein, Lauren Bray, Patti Clement, Michelle Statti, Karen Schoenfeld, Debbie Lefever, Patti Coffey, Connie Simoni, Catalie Chen, Lauren Mastrodonato, GinaRose Kimball and Lindsay Schoenfeld who support Jack's and Mark's businesses with skill and love.

- To everyone who submitted a story, we deeply appreciate your letting us into your lives and sharing your experiences with us. For those whose stories were not chosen for publication, we hope the stories you are about to enjoy convey what was in your heart.

- Because of the size of this project, we may have left out the names of some people who contributed along the way. If so, we are sorry, but please know that we really do appreciate you very much.

We are truly grateful and love you all!

~Chicken Soup for the Soul

Chicken Soup for the Soul
for the Soul
Empty Nesters

101 Stories about Surviving and Thriving When the Kids Leave Home

Jack Canfield,
Mark Victor Hansen,
Carol McAdoo Rehme,
Patricia Cena Evans

This book provides support during a very emotional but exciting time for parents — sending their children off to college, new homes, or careers. It's a must-read for empty nesters or soon-to-be empty nesters grappling with their own bittersweet new freedom. These heartfelt stories about gazing at surprisingly clean bedrooms, starting new careers, rediscovering spouses, and handling the continuing, and often humorous, needs of children, will inspire, support, and amuse parents.

978-1-935096-22-1

Check out our great books about

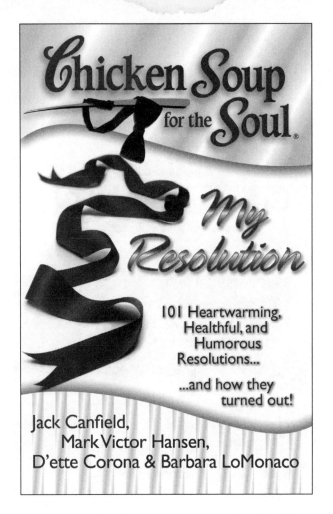

Everyone makes resolutions — for New Year's, for big birthdays, for new school years. In fact, most of us are so good at resolutions that we make the same ones year after year. This book is an uplifting look at those resolutions. Why did we make them? How did they turn out? What did we learn? Stories talk about readers who learned to be proud of who they are, what they achieved, and what they know they can achieve going forward.

978-1-935096-28-3

Life Changes

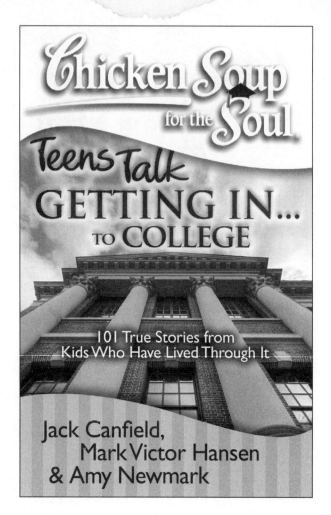

Chicken Soup for the Soul

Teens Talk
GETTING IN...
TO COLLEGE

101 True Stories from Kids Who Have Lived Through It

Jack Canfield,
Mark Victor Hansen
& Amy Newmark

This book isn't about how to get into college — it's about providing emotional, support. The stories in this book are written by kids who have been there and want to pass on their words of support to the kids about to go through the whole ordeal. Story topics include parental and peer pressure, the stress of grades and standardized tests, applications and interviews, recruiting, disappointments, and successes. Parents and students alike will find it a great source of inspiration.

978-1-935096-27-6

College-bound kids?
Teens Talk Getting In...

On Being a Parent

Inspirational, Humorous, and Heartwarming Stories about Parenthood
978-1-935096-20-7

Parenting is the hardest and most rewarding job in the world. This upbeat and compelling new book includes the best selections on parenting from Chicken Soup's rich history, with 101 stories carefully selected to appeal to both mothers and fathers. This is a great book for couples to share, whether they are just embarking on their new adventure as parents or reflecting on their lifetime experience.

Grand and Great

Grandparents and Grandchildren Share Their Stories of Love and Wisdom
978-1-935096-09-2

A parent becomes a new person the day the first grandchild is born. Formerly serious and responsible adults go on shopping sprees for toys and baby clothing, smile incessantly, pull out photo albums that they "just happen to have" with them, and proudly display baby seats in their cars. Grandparents dote on their grandchildren, and grandchildren love them back with all their hearts. This new book includes the best stories on being a grandparent from 33 past Chicken Soup books, representing a new reading experience for even the most devoted Chicken Soup fan.

Books
for Families

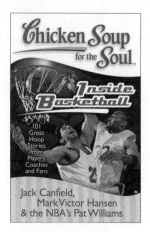

Inside Basketball

Chicken Soup has a slam dunk with its first sports book in years, and its first on basketball, with the Orlando Magic's very own Pat Williams, well-known author and motivational speaker. Pat has drawn on his basketball industry connections to compile great stories from on and off the court. Fans will be inspired, surprised, and amused by inside stories from well-known coaches and players, fascinating looks behind the scenes, and anecdotes from the fans.

Tales of Golf & Sport

Golfers are a special breed. They endure bad weather, early wake up calls, great expense, and "interesting" clothing to engage in their favorite sport. This book contains Chicken Soup's 101 best stories about golfers, golfing, and other sports. Chicken Soup's approach to sports books has always been unique — professional and amateur athletes contribute stories from the heart, yielding a book about the human side of golf and other sports, not a how-to book.

The Golf Book

Chicken Soup and Golf Digest magazine's Max Adler and team have put together a great collection of personal stories that will inspire, amuse, and surprise golfers. Celebrity golfers, weekend golfers, beginners, and pros all share the best stories they've told at the 19th hole about good times on and off the course. Chicken Soup's golf books have always been very successful — with the addition of Golf Digest's industry connections, this book should hit a hole in one.

Books for Men!

Moms Know Best

"Mom will know where it is…what to say…how to fix it." This Chicken Soup book focuses on the pervasive wisdom of mothers everywhere, and includes the best 101 stories from Chicken Soup's library on our perceptive, understanding, and insightful mothers. These stories celebrate the special bond between mothers and children, our mothers' unerring wisdom about everything from the mundane to the life-changing, and the hard work that goes into being a mother every day.

Like Mother, Like Daughter

Fathers, brothers, and friends sometimes shake their head in wonder as girls "turn into their mothers." This new collection from Chicken Soup represents the best 101 stories from Chicken Soup's library on the special bond between mothers and daughters, and the magical, mysterious similarities between them. Mothers and daughters of all ages will laugh, cry, and find inspiration in these stories that remind them how much they appreciate each other.

Moms & Sons

There is a special bond between mothers and their sons and it never goes away. This new book contains the 101 best stories and poems from Chicken Soup's library honoring that lifelong relationship between mothers and their male offspring. These heartfelt and loving stories written by mothers, grandmothers, and sons, about each other, span generations and show how the mother-son bond transcends time.

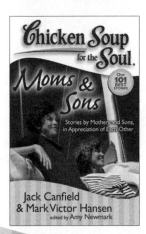

Books for Mom!

Chicken Soup for the Soul
Share with Us

*W*e would like to know how these stories affected you and which ones were your favorites. Please e-mail us and let us know.

We also would like to share your stories with future readers. You may be able to help another reader, and become a published author at the same time. Please send us your own stories and poems for our future books. Some of our past contributors have launched writing and speaking careers from the publication of their stories in our books!

Your stories have the best chance of being used if you submit them through our web site, at:

www.chickensoup.com

If you do not have access to the Internet, you may submit your stories by mail or by facsimile. Please do not send us any book manuscripts, unless through a literary agent, as these will be automatically discarded.

Chicken Soup for the Soul
P.O. Box 700
Cos Cob, CT 06807-0700
Fax 203-861-7194